"H.G. Wells once wrote *An Experiment in Autobiography*, and this title is a good description of *Swamp Gas Times* by Patrick Huyghe. There are very few books about UFOs that put the phenomenon in a setting of the character and atmosphere of a workaday journalistic world...

"[Huyghe's] vision raises the sheer thrill of our dawning realization that we are indeed living within domains of high strangeness... What makes this remarkable book special is that it relates all these matters to American journalism as it evolved over two decades. Both journalism and the UFO inhabit unstable worlds; magazines, newspapers and staff are shown as being in an almost constant state of change. Editors, private financiers, policies, all can change within a matter of months... Thus his UFO reporting is against a professional background of varying levels of ever-changing technology, the whims of rich proprietors, and a rapidly changing print and media culture, changing again in turn as regards content and style, taste, fashion, and evolving social history.

"We see in *Swamp Gas Times* the UFO as a live cryptozoological animal, grazing on information flow as it moves through many different dimensions and interpretations of media, opinion, and changing forms of fashionable taste and expression... These stories are of a world full of hairline cracks and fissures, a world constantly crumbling at the edges of the discursive investigational eye like an M.C. Escher drawing of possible impossibilities... In the face of such things, [Huyghe] manages to combine a vigorous analytic logic with a brave ability to face the utterly absurd elements in many of the experiences he describes...

"Here is great insight, as well as the irresistible thrill of UFOlogy..."

Colin Bennett, *Phenomena Magazine*

Swamp Gas Times

My Two Decades on the UFO Beat

PATRICK HUYGHE

Anomalist Books
San Antonio * New York

Contents

To Pamela Weintraub,
whose invaluable hard-boiled editorship
came with nary a shout,
nor a puff of cigar smoke in the face

Introduction

A fine mess I got myself into. Little did I know how a passion I had as a teenager would lead, some 35 years later, to this—a book about my journalistic pursuit of that most elusive of subjects, the UFO. The truth is that I have spent a good part of my career in journalism writing on the subject. Not many people realize it, of course. I didn't shout it from the rooftops: *Hey, I'm a UFO writer.* For many people, the subject reeks of tabloid journalism, but I see it differently. Would it have been better to spend my time chasing ambulances for the *Daily Press,* or Monica Lewinskies for *Newsweek,* or the medical miracle of the day for the *CBS Evening News?* I think not. I just happened to chase UFOs—or at least the people who do.

Frankly, I feared my work on the UFO beat would hinder my journalistic career, so I never brought it up in front of editors and colleagues, unless I was asked about it. Which was not often. Chances are if someone was aware of my UFO writing, they were interested in the subject themselves. In which case it was okay to admit that, yes, I did write about UFOs. Not mentioning my UFO writing was simply a matter of protecting the respectability I needed for my public career as a science journalist.

How did I come to write about science? Directly as a result of my interest in UFOs, as it turns out. (So much for those who think the subject rots the minds of the young.) I'll explain just how this happened. In fact, I will reveal everything I know about that big gray area at the intersection of journalism and UFOlogy.

For me it all began back in 1966, the month of March in particular. I was an impressionable 13-year-old at the time. No one who read the papers, or listened to the news on the radio, or watched any television could have missed the story. Something very strange was happening over Michigan.

At 8:30 on the night of the 20th, the sheriff's office in Dexter received a call from Bob Wagner that a UFO was in the swamp. Two deputies answered the call and trekked through the woods with Wagner trying to locate what they could see in the distance—a brilliant light that faded, reappeared, and disappeared again. Before the deputies' arrival, Frank Manor, Wagner's father-in-law, and his son had seen, about 500 yards away from them, a brown object with a quilted texture that had a flat bottom and cone-shaped top. The lights at each end of the object glowed a bluish-green, and intensified to a brilliant red. Several minutes later, the lights brightened then blinked out with the sound of a rifle ricochet.

Later that night, just before 10:00, a Dexter patrolman spotted an airborne object with red and green flashing lights. At that point the Washtenaw County sheriff dispatched all available deputies to the scene. Six patrol cars, two men in each, and three detectives surrounded the area around Quigley and Brand Roads. They later chased a flying object along Island Lake Road without catching it.

The following night 87 coeds at a Hillsdale College dormitory watched blue, red, and white lights visible to the east near the ground. An assistant dean and civil defense director also witnessed the strange lights.

News of the these sightings spread nationwide and the Air Force's Project Blue Book, which was charged with investigating UFO reports, was deluged with calls from the media. In response, Blue Book sent their UFO expert, astronomer J. Allen Hynek, to look into the matter. Hynek's whirlwind investigation lasted just 2 hours and 45 minutes and took place in an atmosphere of "general bedlam" with press interest and excitement running at "fever pitch." When Hynek held a press conference on the 26th, he dismissed the sightings as "swamp gas."

Those two words created quite a ruckus. The press and public were outraged and their reaction was immediate and hostile. The *South Bend Tribune* called Hynek's findings an "insult" while the *Richmond News Leader* demanded that the Air Force stop its policy of attempting "to discredit the testimony of witnesses." Even the high brow *New Yorker* chimed in: "We read the official explanation with sheer delight, marveling at their stupendous inadequacy. Marsh gas, indeed!"

Of course, I did not read the *New Yorker,* the *South Bend Tribune,* or the *Richmond Times Dispatch* as a teenager. But I did read the stories that appeared in my local paper, the *Daily Press* of Newport News, Virginia; and though I recall nothing of what they said, the message was essentially the same. The swamp gas explanation was ridiculous. While some people had their faith in government shattered with Watergate in 1974, my own was shattered with the Air Force's response to the Michigan sighting. I learned right then and there that you can't always trust authorities.

When you add that revelation to the not-so-thinly veiled, widely held assumption that the underlying event, the UFO sighting, might actually represent vehicles from outer space—well, quite honestly, I was hooked. Who wouldn't be? It was ideal fodder for the brain of a young boy. In fact, I would venture to speculate than any reasonably aware 13 year old in 1966 would have been bitten by the UFO bug.

And not just 13-year-olds. I was in good company. UFOs were attracting congressional interest. The swamp gas tactic backfired on the Air Force. People were not prepared to just swallow that explanation and forget the whole thing. Michigan Congressman and future President Gerald R. Ford requested that the House Armed Services Committee hold hearings. "The American public deserves a better explanation than that thus far given by the Air Force," he said. The hearings were approved and held on April 5, 1966.

During the day-long session Hynek, still smarting from accusations that he was merely a puppet of the Air Force, publicly broke ranks with his employer. He read a statement saying that there were aspects of UFO reports that were worthy of scientific investigation. And so it was that the members of the House Armed Services Committee came to endorse the idea that someone other than the Air Force should conduct a study of UFOs. As soon as the hearing was over, Air Force Secretary Harold D. Brown, who had received the same advice from his Ad Hoc Committee to Review Project Blue

Book, ordered the Air Force Chief of Staff to carry out the recommendation. Just five months after the Michigan sightings, the Air Force approached the University of Colorado at Boulder to conduct a scientific study of UFOs. And Edward U. Condon, a physicist with an international reputation, was offered the job of project director.

Those were heady days. The UFO story became my number one extracurricular pursuit during high school. I wanted to know everything about the UFO subject. I bought paperback after paperback on the subject, including the 50-cent Ace book, *The Report on Unidentified Flying Objects,* authored by Edward J. Ruppelt, the former head of Blue Book, who seemed to say there was more to the UFO story than we had been told. I became a member of Washington, D.C.-based NICAP, the National Investigations Committee on Aerial Phenomena, directed by a retired Marine, Major Donald Keyhoe. NICAP was going head-to-head with the Air Force on UFOs, demanding that the Air Force tell us the truth.

At the same time, I began publishing a small newsletter on the subject. I called it the *UFO Analysis and Research Bulletin* and made copies on the duplicating machine in my father's office that printed everything with an odd purplish tint. Despite its name, the newsletter contained little research and next to no analysis, but it immediately achieved its goal. While I never could afford to subscribe to all the small UFO publications available at the time, most of them were willing to exchange publications; mine for theirs and theirs for mine. Suddenly I was receiving UFO news from throughout the United States, as well as from Canada, Brazil, France, Italy, Sweden, and other places around the world.

This influx drove home the point that UFOs were an ongoing worldwide phenomenon. So in 1967 I began keeping track of all the sightings that came across my desk and in 1969 published a special issue of my bulletin devoted to one year: "A Report of Over 1,000 Worldwide 1968 UFO Sightings." A little more than half of the reports for that year came from North America, and half of these came from five states: Ohio, Florida, Connecticut, Pennsylvania, and New

York. Most of the sightings took place in August, followed by November and March. The peak days of the week were Mondays, Wednesdays, and Saturdays. One in ten sightings involved a landed UFO, and in half of these cases the witnesses reported seeing "occupants." These were the days when most investigators would dismiss cases in which "aliens" were seen; the term alien abductions was not even in our vocabulary at the time. How things have changed.

Though my report exceeded what anyone else had attempted at the time, it did have its flaws. I had tried to encode so much information into so little space that it was rather hard to decipher. Each case was listed by date and location only, and into the letters of the location I encoded whether it involved an occupant or a landing, and whether I judged it to be a "good," "average," or "poor" report. Its chief flaw was the omission of a direct source for each report, merely listing in the acknowledgments all the publications from which my sighting "index" for the year had been compiled.

Despite its obvious faults, that report may well be my greatest contribution to UFO research. Its publication was duly recognized by the members of the Seventh Annual Congress of Scientific UFOlogists (which was anything but), hosted by the American Flying Saucer Investigating Committee and held in Columbus, Ohio in June of 1970. Even author John A. Keel, who had written a number of seminal UFO works, including *UFOs: Operation Trojan Horse,* called it "really superb." I was a very happy 16-year-old.

By 1969, however, UFOs were again *non grata.* The University of Colorado's Condon Committee had essentially concluded that the study of UFOs was a waste of time, though a close reading of its nearly 1,000-page report clearly suggests otherwise. But then everyone had expected a whitewash. The previous year a near-mutiny had erupted when the project's anti-UFO roots were publicly revealed. Two of its scientists were dismissed and the project's administrative assistant resigned. One of the dismissed was the project's number two scientist, David R. Saunders, a psychologist and statistician at the University of Colorado.

In 1967 Saunders had begun a computerized UFO catalog called UFOCAT. He continued to add cases to the catalog after he left the project in 1968. By 1970 it contained 15,278 entries, including 13,000 from the files of Project Blue Book—and the thousand or so reports I had gathered for the year 1968 and published in my report. (UFOCAT today contains over 111,500 entries.) I felt as if I had made a real contribution to UFO research, and so did Saunders. We corresponded regularly, and two articles by Saunders appeared in my periodical, which in the spring of 1970 I had renamed *UFO Commentary*. Saunders' "UFO Activity in Relation to Day-Of-The-Week" appeared in the Winter, 1970 issue, and his "UFOCAT: A Computerized Catalog for Sightings and Related Data" appeared in the Spring, 1971 issue.

In the summer of 1970, when Saunders heard that I was going to France to visit my father's family, he asked if I could deliver a copy of the huge computer printout of UFOCAT to Aimé Michel, who lived in the French Alps. Michel had published two books in the 1950s—*The Truth About Flying Saucers* and *Flying Saucers and the Straight-Line Mystery*, which had cemented his reputation as one of the world's best-known UFOlogists. And so it was that I came to visit French UFOlogist Pierre Delval of *Phénomènes Inconnus* in Grenoble that summer. I remember very little of the day except how sick I felt as Delval drove his little car up the windy mountain roads. When we reached the top, there was the famous French UFOlogist like the king of the mountain. I handed him the copy of UFOCAT and then proceeded to get carsick again as we drove back down the mountain.

In the fall of 1970 I became a freshman at the University of Virginia, and my days of editing a UFO newsletter were numbered. I no longer had the time to publish a 20-page quarterly. I did, however, manage to put out three issues during my first year of college before calling it quits in the summer of 1971. Actually, I remained the publisher of *UFO Commentary*, while the editing chores fell on the shoulders of my then assistant editor in Idaho, Allen Benz. This arrangement limped along for five issues, until the Spring of 1973, when the subscription list, which never amounted to more than a hundred names anyway, was taken over by Gene Steinberg, publisher and editor of *Caveat Emptor.*

I disliked letting go of my publication. I had become quite attached to it, but it had enjoyed a five year run, which is not shabby as amateur zines go. The publication was a joy for me, and sometimes I think that my real enthusiasm was linked more to the passion of publishing than to my interest in UFOs. And for this, I owe one person a debt of gratitude. Back in 1967 I had seen in my local newspaper a letter-to-the-editor about UFOs from a man in Hampton, Virginia, named Larry W. Bryant. I had looked up his address in the phonebook and immediately sent him a copy of my UFO newsletter. He responded immediately with a subscription check for $2 and his whole-hearted support of my efforts. Later he gave me a real mimeograph machine he had found abandoned by the roadside.

This little donation immeasurably improved the look of my newsletter—black ink! I still remember that intoxicating smell of printer's ink. All I needed now was an artist to illustrate the cover. Though her specialty was flowers and other still lifes, my very talented mother volunteered to draw the saucers I wanted. Suddenly, the newsletter had a professional look, and before long I was getting requests for copies from as far as Brentano's bookstore in Paris.

That publishing experience had a profound effect on me and though I graduated from the University of Virginia with a degree in psychology, I would go on to obtain a graduate degree in magazine journalism from Syracuse University in 1977. By that time, my UFO interest had receded far into the background. But it would soon be reawakened by circumstance.

With my degree in journalism in hand, I moved to New York City, the magazine capital of the Unites States, in January of 1978, to find a job. Before long, I discovered that the studio apartment I had moved into on the upper East side of Manhattan was just less than a block away from one of the legends of the early days of UFO research, Ted Bloecher.

Bloecher had founded Civilian Saucer Intelligence of New York back in 1952 with Isabel Davis, worked for a time at NICAP headquarters, produced the *Report on the UFO Wave of 1947,* and had begun compiling the "Humanoid Catalog" with David Webb. Hearing Bloecher talk about the cases from this catalog rekindled my interest in the subject. Bloecher and I quickly became friends and he soon introduced me to a New York artist of some renown who had developed a passion for the UFO subject. His name was Budd Hopkins. But that's getting ahead of my story.

Getting a journalism job in New York was no easy task. I applied for numerous positions and submitted to the "typing tests" required by job agencies. I tried out for a job at *Candy Marketing Monthly* (or was it *Weekly?*), Fairchild Publications, *Iron Age,* and dozens more. I even applied for a mystery editing job, which, when I was given a sample to edit, turned out to be pornography. The months rolled by and the money saved up in the bank dwindled. Then early one morning, my neighbor across the hall knocked on my door. She recently had landed a job as a senior editor at *Us,* a new magazine that the *New York Times* was about to publish as a competitor to Time-Life's *People.* She told me they were desperately in need of help and could I come in to work for the day?

And so it was that I started working for the magazine division of the *New York Times,* a fate that turns out to be quite relevant to this story. It's the beginning of the answer to a question that many people have asked me over the years: just how did you get that piece on UFOs into the *New York Times?*

It was a great first job, but *Us* was a celebrity magazine and I had absolutely no interest in the stars of the entertainment industry. During my 15 month stint at *Us* I rose through the ranks—starting out as an assistant copy editor and ending up as a senior editor—as people higher up the ladder either quit or got fired, a typical experience at magazine start-ups. These former *Us* staffers ended up getting jobs at other magazines eventually, which meant that I now had contacts throughout the publishing community, and contacts, it turns out, is the name of the game in publishing.

In any case, after seeing the manuscripts that writers were turning in to *Us* magazine, I said to myself, "I can do that," and decided to go freelance in 1979. One of the first stories I worked on concerned the hundreds of former servicemen who had been forced to attend, and in some cases, walk through, ground zero at nuclear weapons tests that had taken place in Nevada during the 1950s and early 1960s. I had asked someone on the staff of *Us* for a contact at the *New York Times Magazine* and was given the name of an editor there who was quite interested in this story. The article, which I researched and wrote with friend and fellow journalist, David Konigsberg, was published as "Grim Legacy of Nuclear Testing" in April of 1979.

After this story appeared, I proposed another—a UFO story—to my editor at the *New York Times Magazine*. It was a long shot, as the *Times* rarely touched the subject, but I had my ducks all in a row. Back in December of 1978, the CIA, under pressure of an FOIA lawsuit, had finally released nearly 1,000 pages of its UFO documents. The *Times* had run this news in the daily newspaper without going into much detail and I had just the ticket to an in-depth story. It just so happened that I had met the attorney who had filed the suit on behalf of an Arizona-based UFO organization called Ground Saucer Watch (GSW). Ted Bloecher had taken me to a wine and cheese get-together at the home of Budd Hopkins, who, as I said, enjoyed discussing the UFO situation. At one of these meetings, Peter Gersten, a likable criminal lawyer from the Bronx and the volunteer attorney for GSW, showed up. We got along immediately.

That is how I came to write a major UFO story for the *New York Times*. (I'll have more to say about the experience of writing for the *Times* in the preface to that story later in this book.) Many editors in the industry saw this story and as a result they all wanted me to write a UFO story for them. I even received a letter from Scott DeGarmo, who was then editor of the new, large-size, glossy reincarnation of *Science Digest*. He was impressed by the article and invited me to write about science for his magazine. I loved science, so I took him up on his offer. And that, in short, is how I came to be a science journalist.

Some of my science journalist colleagues might wonder if my interest in UFOs should perhaps have disqualified me from writing about the subject for the *New York Times* and other publications. I certainly don't think so. Should an interest in football disqualify you from being a sports writer, or a love of celebrity disqualify you from being an entertainment journalist, or a passion for politics prevent you from being assigned to the news desk? On the contrary, having a personal interest in a subject is often what makes that person a better journalist on that beat. Besides, I had no secret agenda. I simply wanted a fair treatment of the subject. I deplored articles that summarily dismissed the subject or routinely heaped it with ridicule. My interest was in the truth, as cliché as that may sound, and I knew the truth was not "out there" but "in here." I am convinced that the truth can be found only by dropping our all-knowing attitudes about the subject and looking at the evidence dispassionately. Everyone who has done so honestly ends up admitting that *there is something there,* though no one knows what that is exactly. I'll have more to say about my personal beliefs on the subject in the afterword.

I can't imagine many journalists actually aspiring to the UFO beat. In fact, it has barely existed as a beat at all, and when it has, the publications that have covered the subject on a regular basis often did not have the best of reputations. I know of only a few people who actually have worked the UFO beat as journalists on a regular basis in the seventies. One is Bob Pratt, who for many years did an excellent job writing UFO stories for that disreputable tabloid so loved by millions, the *National Enquirer.* Another is Antonio Huneeus, who covered the UFO beat for the *New York City Tribune,* a defunct daily paper that was owned and operated by the Reverend Moon; he now writes the bimonthly UFO column for *Fate.* And then there was the late Harry Lebelson, who wrote the UFO column for *Omni* magazine during its early years.

I never was officially assigned the UFO beat, of course. I took it upon myself, writing as a freelancer for one magazine or another on the subject until about 1988, when I began covering UFOs on a regular basis for *Omni* magazine. Of course, *Omni*, which was as respectable as you could get for a magazine that combined science fiction and science fact, did suffer from its naked association with *Penthouse*, which like *Omni* was published by Bob Guccione. But all in all, the UFO beat has been a rather civilized one, especially when compared to the media hordes that mob big-time sports, politics, and celebrity bashes.

Apart from a few sterling exceptions, the national news media have done a pretty bad job of covering the UFO subject. While conspiracy mongers believe this has been by design, to keep us in the dark, I think it's not been at all deliberate. There is certainly no media conspiracy with regard to UFOs. If there had been, it would have been obvious to me at the time I did these stories over the past two decades. UFO sightings get covered by the media like fires, as one-shot events, usually by junior reporters who know not much about anything, including UFOs. The media have little or no desire to get at the bottom of the UFO story, and rightfully so perhaps. Hardly any tangible evidence offers itself for analysis, and so much ridicule surrounds its pursuit.

Granted, UFOs are a long shot. But in terms of potential, I doubt there could be a greater journalistic payoff, if indeed we are talking about extraterrestrial visitation here. Ultimately, we are weighing the possibility of contact with another intelligence, a non-human intelligence. I've always thought the UFO story was a grand one. I still do.

The following UFO stories, which I wrote, appeared in a variety of publications between 1977 and 2000. Actually, four of them never did, though they were supposed to, and one was written especially for this volume. For each story I have prepared a brief preface (and an occasional postscript), which I hope provides some insight into the editorial process involved, my own journalist career, or a further commentary on the UFO personalities and events described. The stories themselves are, for the most part, reprinted as they appeared, unless otherwise noted, the only changes being largely cosmetic: the addition of a comma here or there, a paragraph broken up, or the deletion of the magazine subheads, which in most cases are inappropriate for a book such as this one. In a few instances I have corrected an error that crept into the editorial process, but these too were minor, unless otherwise noted.

It's easy to read UFO stories and believe. It's just as easy to read UFO stories and dismiss the subject as a load of bunk. What is hard to do is confront the subject head-on and grapple with it with honesty and integrity. That's what I've tried to do. That's the scoop, the saucer scoop, and nothing but the truth.

CHAPTER 1

The "Raid" Over Washington D.C.

One of the things I found odd right from the beginning is how UFO stories often lack an historical context. Since nothing happens in a vacuum, I suspected that we might be able to find some clue to the identity of any particular UFO incident by looking at contemporaneous events. So it was that I came to review the local and world events that surrounded one of the largest UFO flaps in history, the UFO sightings over Washington, D.C. in 1952. It turns out we had quite a good reason to be nervous of aerial invaders at the time.

I wrote this particular story for two reasons. First, the 25th anniversary of that incident was approaching, and anniversary stories are saleable quantities for freelance writers. Second, these events took place just a month before I was born; that's personal context.

The story appeared in SAGA UFO REPORT, August 1977, under the title "The 1952 UFO 'Raid' That Panicked Washington D.C."

✳

It must have been one hell of a week. Nine days so full of headline news that *The New York Times* probably gave second thoughts to putting out two front pages on every edition.

It was all there: an exiled king, a flood, several strikes, the leap year presidential candidates, an earthquake in California, a number of excommunications, at least two wars, and an invasion of some sort over Washington, D.C. And garlic enough for a whopping case of indigestion.

It began on Saturday, July 19, 1952. The President of Finland opened the XV Olympic Games before a crowd of 70,000, and our own president, Harry S. Truman, returned to the White House in good health after a three day stay at the hospital fighting a virus infection.

On the same day, Dwight D. Eisenhower, the Republican nominee for president, announced that he planned to stump the South. The occasion marked the first time ever that a Republican presidential nominee would conduct a full-scale campaign below the Mason-Dixon line.

Washington, D.C., unruffled by the political season, displayed its lush summer greenery. Though the temperatures hovered just under 80 degrees that Saturday night, an unmistakable freshness hung in the air. At home, Washingtonians and others around the country leafed through Montgomery Ward's new fall-winter catalogue. They noticed that, except on the cover and in the millinery section, there were no pictures of live models in it. People were disappointed. Dresses, coats, and sweaters were hung on headless, armless, and legless dummies, and stockings were draped over disembodied hands. Spokesmen for the company said that Montgomery Ward didn't want a customer's attention diverted by a pretty girl.

Meanwhile, at the Washington National Airport, about three miles south of the heart of the city, an invasion of some kind was about to take place. The radar scopes in the darkened room of the control center emitted a faint lavender glow. A fresh eight-man shift had just taken over, but only one man was watching the scope at 11:40 p.m. as the antenna outside swept the sky with its beam. When the revolving beam struck a plane, a violent spot of light, a blip, would appear on the scope. It was a clear evening, the air traffic light.

Suddenly seven round spots appeared on the scope. It looked like a formation of slow planes, but none were scheduled to appear in the area. Then in a burst of speed, two of the objects streaked out of radar range at an estimated speed close to 7,000 miles per hour. These were no airplanes, the controller thought, and yelled for his superior. The senior controller came in, witnessed the same phenomenon on the screen, and yelled for the technician, who made sure the scope was in proper working order. It was.

The senior controller called National's control tower and the tower at nearby Andrews Air Force base and both confirmed the blips on their scopes. The targets moved into every sector of the scope and flew through the prohibited air corridors over the White House and the Capitol. Harry Truman had just turned off his nightlight.

Capt. Casey Pierman, piloting Capital Airlines Flight 807, which had taken off from Washington National, was alerted to be on the lookout for unusual lights. Shortly after midnight, the controller heard the captain shout, "There's one—off to the right…and there it goes." During the next few minutes the captain reported six more such objects "like falling stars without tails," which rapidly moved up, down, and sideways. Sometimes the objects would just hover, motionless. All the movements were confirmed on radar.

Two hours later Capt. Howard Dermott on incoming Capital Flight 610 reported that a light was tagging along behind and to the left of the airliner. Within minutes of touchdown on the runway, the object pulled away. But the fun had just begun. The objects were on radar off and on till daybreak. When an Air Force F-94 was sent up to investigate, the objects disappeared.

At the Democratic National Convention that day, Adlai Stevenson requested that the Illinois delegation not put his name in nomination or vote for him, but the delegation ignored his request.

In Heroldbach, Germany, 19 Roman Catholics were excommunicated for exploiting claims that the Virgin Mary had been seen there. Thousands of people had flocked to the village in the two years since the claims that the Virgin Mary, clad in white and wearing a white veil, had appeared in a local chapel. The wooden stalls erected in the church to sell food and refreshments to the pilgrims were also ordered removed.

Decisions of another kind were taking place in Washington. On the fourth floor of the Pentagon, intelligence officers were holding conferences. Talk of "temperature inversions" seeped to the press corps clamoring for an official statement. The explanation, however, was thinner than the air over the city, as any good radar operator could spot inversion-caused blips. Besides, two veteran airline pilots had seen the lights where the three radar sets had pinpointed them.

There were no *Virgin Marys* in Germany, the Vatican said. There were no *flying saucers* over Washington, the Air Force announced. Everything came apart the next day. That's what happens when you tell a lie, your mother would remind you—the sky caves in.

A dozen people were killed in an earthquake in Tehachapi, Calif. And in Mexico City it started raining. It was no ordinary rain: it would pour for four days and four nights. And although Mexico City is located 7,300 feet above sea level, people in the city were waist high in water. Boys and unemployed men earned extra pesos transporting pedestrians across river-like streets using U.S. Navy life rafts and primitive boats made of packing cases. Some, wearing hip boots or swim trunks, carried their customers piggyback.

Later in the week, on a southbound flight to Montevideo, Uruguay, Mrs. Marie Westbrook Capellaro, wife of an Italian banker, would press her camera against the window of the Stratocruiser to take pictures from 12,000 feet. Suddenly the cabin door popped open and the plane yawed. When her husband turned toward her, he found an empty seat. She had already dropped without a trace into the ocean.

The Korean peace talks were dead-locked, and the French were fighting in Vietnam. It was thoughtful of New York's Governor Dewey to send a gift of 600 small-mouth bass fingerlings to Emperor Bao Dai of Vietnam. The fish were one-and-a-half inches long and six weeks old. In Saigon the fish would be dumped into a lake at 5,000 feet elevation where they would swim and frolic in peace until they were three years old and mature.

The ways of politicians were no more baffling, however, than the strange objects that were reported over Dallas, Texas, Peoria, Illinois, and Burlington, Vermont, that day. They appeared without authority.

On Wednesday, Egypt's King Farouk said, "Soon there'll be only five kings: the king of England and the four kings in this deck of cards." As Gen. Mohammed Naguib seized power there, the monarch, down to his last yacht, sailed from Alexandria with 204 pieces of luggage and an equal number of millions of dollars.

The next day, U.S. Steel President Ben Fairless, Presidential Advisor John Steelman, and United Steelworkers of America President Philip Murray reached an agreement on the steel strike, and the trio went into Harry Truman's office for all the necessary signatures. Murray was on the cover of *Time* magazine that week. He always kept on hand Pope Leo XIII's encyclical *Rerum Novarum,* the Catholic outline for industrial justice. Murray had survived among a pack of wolves by having a heart too big for them to eat.

There were wolves everywhere that week. In East Germany the Communist government dissolved five historic German provinces into thin air. They were replaced by 14 administrative districts. In reprisal, Harry Truman abolished the garlic quota, which had severely reduced garlic importation from Italy, the chief foreign supplier, because Italy had done a good job in combating communism. More than six million pounds of dried garlic cloves would find their way into the U.S. the following year.

In a daily stroll in Moscow, U.S. Ambassador George F. Kennan stopped short in front of a number of posters announcing the Soviet Union's annual Red Air Force Day celebrations. One depicted a U.S. Navy plane being shot down in the Baltic in 1950; another, the Neptune bomber downed off the coast of Korea the year before; and in the third, Red fighters forcing down a U.S. cargo plane in Hungary the previous winter. The Russians were good artists, but they had never publicly admitted the downing of the planes, and still wouldn't. The Soviets sent the ambassador an invitation to the air show. Kerman, infuriated, refused, and sent his air attaché instead.

The power, real and imagined, of the Big Red Bear had us holding the seat of our pants and looking up at the sky. A skywatch program was initiated along the northern and coastal regions of the United States. But because of a lack of volunteers, New York City's 10-day-old skywatch would soon have to operate on a part-time basis despite a warning by the U.S. Air Force that Russian bombers might bore in under the 5,600-foot floor of effective radar screening for a sneak attack.

The chemistry was there: anything could happen. You couldn't help taking a peek up there every time you stepped outside. The urge was irresistible. Reports of unidentified flying objects were coming in from every part of the country. There was an invasion of some kind taking place.

On Friday the sun finally came out in Mexico City, and Oscar Collazo himself was relieved. Not because of the rain or Mexico City, but because his sentence of death by electrocution for the attempted assassination of President Truman in November 1950 had been commuted to life imprisonment. Though Collazo had lived in this country for 14 of his 38 years, he burned with unquenchable conviction that the United States had enslaved his native Puerto Rico, which, on the next day, would in fact celebrate its independence as a free commonwealth, autonomous in internal affairs under its own constitution.

On Saturday, FBI Director Hoover celebrated his 35th year in command, Bob Mathias paced an American sweep of the grueling Olympic decathlon, and Adlai Stevenson—five feet six inches tall, 180 pounds, eyes inclined to bulge, quick smile—won the Democratic presidential nomination. It was also the day Air Force jet fighters made an effort to intercept some unknown flying objects above Washington, D.C.

At about 10:30 p.m. on July 26th the same radar operators who had seen the mysterious objects the week before picked up a spread of objects in an arch around Washington from Herndon, Va., to Andrews Air Force Base. A call to the other two radar sites confirmed the electronic observations. Outside, witnesses to the aerial show added their sightings to the record. Commercial pilots reported a number of objects ranging in description from "a cigarette-like glow" to "a white light."

By 11:30 p.m., when four or five of the targets were continuously being tracked, a call went out for two jet fighters to intercept. But the squadron usually charged with protecting the capital from air attack was no longer stationed at Bolling Air Force Base just across the Potomac River. Because of runway repairs there, the Air Force had secretly moved the squadron 100 miles away to New Castle County Airport in Wilmington, Del. So it took longer than normal for the scrambled jets to arrive over the capital.

All reporters and photographers were ushered out of the radar rooms on the pretext that classified radio frequencies and procedures were in effect to vector the interceptors in on the glowing objects. As the jets moved in, all civilian air traffic was ordered away from the area. Later, the Air Force refused to admit that it had scrambled jets to intercept the UFO targets.

When the two F-94s arrived on the scene the blips simultaneously disappeared from the radar scopes. After a thorough but fruitless search of the area, the planes returned to base. A few minutes after the interceptors' departure, the unidentifieds were back on the radarscopes. The Air Force was playing cat and mouse with what might have been visitors from another planet.

In the meantime people living near Langley Air Force Base near Newport News, Va., began to call the Langley tower to report they were looking at bright, rotating, multicolored lights. The tower operators spotted the lights themselves and called for an interceptor.

The F-94 pilot saw the light, but as he headed toward it, the light suddenly went out "like somebody had turned off a light bulb." The crew continued their run, and after a while got a radar lock-on on another object, only to have it broken again as the object gained speed.

Now the targets reappeared on the scopes at Washington National. The traffic controllers again called Air Defense Command and two more F-94s headed toward Washington. But this time the objects stayed on the scopes when the planes reached the area.

Time and again the controllers would direct the interceptors toward a group of objects, but before the jets could do no more than spot the lights, the targets would speed away. Except once.

Lt. William Patterson, piloting one of the F-94s, spotted a light exactly where the radars had located the target. He cut in the plane's afterburners and went after it. But even at maximum speed, he couldn't close in on the object, and this one also disappeared.

With the jets now low on fuel, the pilots decided to return to their base. Minutes later Brigadier General Landry called intelligence authorities in Dayton, Ohio, where the Air Force investigation of UFOs was taking place, to find out what was happening in the skies over Washington.

Dwight Eisenhower was at his cabin in Fraser, Colorado, showing his running mate, Sen. Richard M. Nixon, the proper way to cast for trout.

Truman was taking it easy at his home in Independence, Mo. He had been told about a flight of B-36 bombers on a simulated run over Chicago that had alarmed many residents. As the big planes roared over the city at 15,000 feet, engine noise synchronization had caused what seemed to those below to be a cosmic racket.

The president was worried about that other cosmic racket—over Washington—but his thoughts came back to the B-36. He was struggling with his decision over the replacement of the B-36 with a new intercontinental jet bomber, Boeing's eight-engined B-52.

But it was hot that day, 102 degrees, so all Truman did was send a message of condolence to Pres. Juan D. Peron of Argentina on the death of his wife, Eva.

Dr. lsley Boone, ex-president of the American Sunbathing Association, had a remedy to the heat suffered by the nation that week: nudism.

On July 29th, the Air Force held the longest and largest press conference since World War II. Maj. Gen. John A. Samford, director of Air Force intelligence, headed the conference. He stated that the Air Force was reasonably well convinced that the radarscope sightings of the past two weekends were the result of temperature inversions, and that flying saucers constituted no menace to the United States. No Reds. No craft from outer space. No alien beings. And weather did not constitute a menace to this country.

Some people had a word for the Air Force handling of the situation. Peculiarly British and essentially Eighth Army-ish, the word was snafu—situation normal, all "fouled" up. There are differing degrees of snafus, however. There is the "self-adjusting snafu" and the "non-self-adjusting snafu." And then there's the climatic "cummfu"—which appropriately describes the events of that week, and which, roughly translated, means "complete, utter, monumental military foul-up."

These sightings, which took place 25 years ago, remain today one of the most publicized and discussed cases on record. Interestingly enough, later research conducted by Dr. James E. McDonald, at one time senior atmospheric physicist at the University of Arizona's Department of Atmospheric Sciences, concluded that the Air Force's temperature inversion theory was untenable. So weather, that permanent topic of conversation, became the fall guy for some unexplained event that continues to haunt us. And even today some are still groping for such explanations.

But the fact remains that the center of this country's power had been left wide open to attack from who-knows-what during those two weeks in 1952. We won't buy the temperature inversion story, and the word "UFO" is simply not a sufficient explanation. So the question remains: *Who and what were they?*

CHAPTER 2

A Close Encounter with J. Allen Hynek

To a teenager with an interest in UFOs, astronomer J. Allen Hynek, the Air Force scientific consultant on UFOs, posed an awesome figure. The man who had called the 1966 Michigan sightings "swamp gas" would part company with the Air Force—or vice versa—a few years later and establish the independent Center for UFO Studies (CUFOS).

But, as it turns out, the swamp gas explanation that so many ridiculed was not so outrageous; it was certainly less outrageous to most people than the notion of extraterrestrial visitors. Hynek may well have been correct about some of the Michigan sightings after all. At the press conference, he quoted a description of marsh gases by Dutch astronomer Minnaert: "The lights resemble tiny flames, sometimes seen right on the ground, sometimes merely floating above it. The flames go out in one place and suddenly appear in another, giving the illusion of motion. The colors are sometimes yellow, sometimes red and blue-green."

"Marsh gas," Hynek said at the press conference, "usually has no smell, but sounds like the small popping explosions similar to a gas burner igniting. The gas forms from decomposition of vegetation. It seems likely that as the present spring thaws came, the gases methane, hydrogen sulfide and phosphine, resulting from decomposition of organic materials, were released."

And, in fact, Hynek never claimed that swamp gas could account for all the Michigan sightings. In the introduction to his press conference, Hynek clearly said that this was his solution for the Dexter-Hillsdale sightings only. He also thought that kids playing "pranks with flares" had added to the excitement, and he dismissed a "UFO photo" taken on March 17 as a time exposure of the moon and Venus. Of course, the press latched on to Hynek's swamp gas explanation and made hay of it. That's journalism for you.

Over the years, I would meet Hynek several times: at lectures he gave in the Hampton Roads area of Virginia; at the screening for CLOSE ENCOUNTERS: SPECIAL EDITION in New York City; and at a UFO conference in Brewster, New York, in 1984. Hynek was not the angel I had made him out to be in this profile of him, and CUFOS remains small, impoverished, and inefficacious; though as far as UFO organizations go, you can't get any better. The same can be said for Hynek, who died in 1986. This profile, based largely on a lengthy telephone interview, appeared in the April 1978 issue of NEW AGE, under the title "UFOlogy Lives!"

✳

To unbelievers, Dr. J. Allen Hynek's thirty-year pursuit of the UFO phenomenon qualifies him as a first-class crackpot: they consider his constant chatter about lights-in-the-sky, occupants scurrying from saucer-shaped objects, abductions by visitors from elsewhere, and landing sites scorched and otherwise marked by the descent of UFOs nothing more than chaff for the consumption of a gullible public. To a number of scientists, Hynek's interest in UFOs is a kind of heresy. To the "enlightened" fanatic, he is a prophet of the New Age that will be inaugurated by contact with extraterrestrials who will exponentially raise human consciousness.

Hynek's extensive knowledge of UFOs is recognized worldwide, and many believe he has managed to bring to the investigation of the phenomenon an aura of scientific respectability long sought. Regardless of the phenomenon's ultimate resolution, the name Hynek is destined to be associated with UFOs just as Darwin's name is linked to evolution, Freud's to dreams, and Nixon's to Watergate.

A persistent yet soft-spoken sixty-seven-year-old man with white hair, moustache, and goatee, Hynek, who for twenty years investigated UFOs for the Air Force, established the Center for UFO Studies in 1973 because of apparent lack of scientific interest in the subject. But the publicity that Steven Spielberg's *Close Encounters of the Third Kind* generated for Hynek, who had acted as the film's technical advisor, means that he is no longer simply dealing with the raw material of UFO sighting reports: he has taken on a new role, that of intermediary between the phenomenon—whatever it may be—and the earthside public. But as a promoter for UFOs, Hynek is merely pointing, not selling, and avoiding exaggeration at all costs.

For shouldering the task of public relations for such an unacceptable subject, Hynek may eventually, if proved correct, be recognized as a modern-day Galileo. Currently a professor of astronomy at Northwestern University, Hynek is typical of scholars whose careful probing into the chemistry of the unknown has led to questions concerning their own credibility. His image as the grand old man of UFOlogy necessarily attracts ridicule by the barrel. And, not surprisingly, the widespread community fascinated with UFOana has hailed him as a guru.

Yet Hynek has managed, through all the talk of little green people and swamp gas, to retain an edge of objectivity and a glint of humor, which in themselves reveal a sanity not often so evident in his hardbitten, skeptical colleagues.

"A lot of people think that UFO reports are products of people's imagination," says Hynek, "but that doesn't really wash, because if it were just imagination, it seems to me we should get all sorts of weird reports: pink elephants, flying cubes, rotating church steeples—God knows what."

Underlying his devotion to the study of UFOs is his insistence on the reality of the phenomenon—and not on any particular interpretation. "One thing is for sure," says Hynek: "UFO reports exist—nobody can deny that. And I, for one, can no longer deny the stories that these people tell. To them, they've had a real experience." According to a Gallup Poll estimate, 15 million people have seen what they believe to be a UFO.

Hynek works out of an upstairs office on Chicago Avenue in Evanston, Illinois, where he pores over stacks of papers—UFO reports, speaker requests, and administrative paperwork—scattered about the room. He puffs on an ever-present pipe, as he did in his brief appearance in *Close Encounters,* and behind a pair of professorial glasses one notices a squint in one eye that perhaps indicates a critical perspective alien to the open friendliness of the other.

"Sometimes it strikes me that we are dealing with a different form, a different aspect of reality," says Hynek, momentarily expressing a personal belief rather than a working hypothesis. This attitude reflects a drastic change of thought for the once skeptical professor.

Hynek's first encounter with the subject occurred in 1948, while he was teaching astronomy at Ohio State. One day two men from the Air Technical Intelligence Center, located at nearby Wright-Patterson Air Force Base, showed up at Hynek's little office at the McMillian Observatory. "It was quite a surprise," recalls Hynek. "They introduced themselves, talked about the weather, hemmed and hawed, and finally got around to what did I think about flying saucers.

"Well, I said, I thought that it was a case of post-war nerves, that people are always seeing strange things. We got to talking about how many things could be misidentified, and I said, 'Oh hell, we get lots of reports of strange lights that turn out to be meteors and so forth.' "

The words worked like magic, and the officers immediately signed him on as consultant to the Air Force on UFOs. For the next twenty years Hynek mulled through thousands of UFO reports and acted as the Air Force's official debunker on UFOs for Project Blue Book, the government's UFO investigatory branch at that time. "I was imbued with what I call the Air Force Theorem: 'It can't be, therefore it isn't,'" says Hynek. "And I adapted quite easily to that role, because I was quite skeptical. I thought UFOs just had to have natural explanations."

On occasion, in the rush of energy expended searching for these required natural explanations, Hynek would pull a boner. The most notorious, the swamp gas explanation of the 1966 Michigan UFO sightings, also marked the turning point in his beliefs about UFOs. "The swamp gas episode boomeranged like hell on me and the Air Force," remembers Hynek. "I began to feel guilty about my skeptical attitude. And once you open the gates to the possibility that all these people can't possibly be mistaken, then you see a lot of those other cases in a totally different light."

Because of increasing public mistrust of the Air Force's handling of the UFO situation, another investigation of the phenomenon was begun after the Michigan sightings. Its findings, detailed in the Condon Committee Report released in 1969, were as negative and as flawed as the Air Force's effort had been. Put simply, the conclusions didn't match the available evidence. But the Air Force was satisfied with the negative "independent" evaluation, and Project Blue Book closed its doors.

"They sent me a nice little letter saying that my services were no longer required," says Hynek. "But I was hardly talking to the officers at Blue Book by then, because we were so much on opposite sides of the fence that it was almost pointless to continue." Hynek continued to receive UFO reports but felt at the time that further investigations could only be carried out underground.

Then in 1973 a tremendous wave of UFO reports swept the southeast United States. "I was in Samoa at the time," recalls Hynek, "and I remember seeing the news on the hotel's teletype machine that a UFO had been sighted in Athens, Georgia. And I thought, well, that's strange—getting a UFO report way out here in Samoa. When I got back a few days later, things were pretty wild. There were all kinds of UFO reports in the Unites States at the time, and since there was nobody minding the store, I got a little mad.

"People would call in their sightings to the police, and chances are, the police would laugh at them and say, 'What have you been drinking?' And then they'd call the Air Force, who would say, 'We are no longer concerned with this problem.' People didn't have any place to turn to, and I felt that a great many potentially scientific data were being lost."

Buttressed by his scientific background, which includes a stint as associate director of the Smithsonian Astrophysical Laboratory at Harvard in 1956 (during which time he was in charge of the first U.S. optical-satellite tracking system), Hynek took it upon himself to create a Center for UFO Studies. "I felt a certain obligation," says Hynek, "since there are damned few people in this country who have both the scientific background and as much experience as I've had in the subject. I found myself, willy-nilly, in a unique position. And I felt responsible. I thought that somebody who had their head screwed on straight—although some people may doubt that I do—ought to monitor this thing. Just because you can't explain it, doesn't mean you can't study it. It's not the subject matter that determines whether something is scientific, it's the method of approach."

Hynek enlisted the aid of numerous scientists—from Oak Ridge National Laboratories, the Jet Propulsion Laboratory, the French Center for Space Studies, the Johnson Space Center, and several universities—who offered to help in their spare time.

The Center for UFO Studies attempts to investigate all worthwhile cases through a system of both amateur and professional investigators scattered throughout the country. In addition, the Center also operates a computerized data bank that contains about fifty thousand UFO cases, of which 80 percent—the standard Hynek gleaned from his Air Force days—could probably be explained. Of course, that leaves over ten-thousand UFO reports that cannot.

"What are they?" says Hynek. "People always want the answers. I have to tell them, 'I'm sorry, I don't have any answers. All I have are questions—questions that could be answered by research, if we had the people and the funds to do it. Without funds, even a scientist can't do much.'

"I scrape my memory but I don't know of any subject in the past thirty years that has sparked so much conversation, so many differing opinions, so many midnight discussions, so many frayed tempers, than the UFO subject, and yet on which virtually no money has been spent. That, to me, is quite paradoxical."

At present, without adequate funds, the Center can do little more than provide reliable information on UFOs, mainly through the *International UFO Reporter* and a number of special reports edited by Hynek and his wife, Mimi. Hynek considers this a considerable accomplishment in itself.

"For information about UFOs," Hynek explains, "people have been turning to the tabloid press and adventure magazines. Well, that's a hell of a way to acquire a knowledge of UFOs. Young people today have to get their information about flying saucers the way I had to get information about sex."

The subject of Hynek's lifetime devotion also fascinates his five children, who range in age from fifteen to thirty-four. "They see the subject from the inside," says Hynek, "and they see me as an otherwise rational human being."

It is precisely this rational being who, in helping Spielberg with *Close Encounters,* raised eyebrows outside the impassioned UFO community and endangered his own credibility. Hynek admits that his enjoyment of the film was somewhat dampened by the "Hollywood overdramatization." He emphasizes that the film is a fictional composite of non-fictional UFO encounters, such as were reported in his book *The UFO Experience.* In fact, the film *Close Encounters of the Third Kind* took its name from a term coined by Hynek in that book.

"A close encounter," Hynek repeats, hoping to clarify the confusions and inaccuracies that have accompanied the release of the film, "is a sighting in which the witness was within 500 feet and details of the UFO could be made out. In the first kind of close encounter, there is no interaction between the object and the environment or witness. The second kind are those in which animals may be frightened, burn marks may be left on the ground, tree branches or foliage may be curled or burnt, cars stopped, electronic equipment interfered with, and people can have burns, nausea, eye trouble, or be temporarily paralyzed. Close encounters of the third kind are those in which the beings or occupants are reported."

According to Hynek, "The scene in a typical scenario of a close encounter of the third kind is always isolated, and it's usually late at night. Then, as the person driving usually says, 'As I rounded a bend in the road, I saw ahead of me this strange craft, and there were some creatures working around it or on it, and as soon as they noticed I'd discovered them, they clambered back and the thing took off.' "

As technical advisor for the film, Hynek insured that all the details would ring true, and he believes that Spielberg has not violated the sense and spirit of the subject, or damaged its image. Indeed, a team of sociologists now plans to study the impact of this and other UFO movies which are expected to follow *Close Encounters*.

Members of the UFO community have also taken advantage of the subject's newfound notoriety to remind President Carter—who himself sighted a UFO in 1969—of his campaign promise to open the government's files on UFOs. The White House recently requested that NASA resume the government's inquiry into reports of UFOs, but NASA, already facing a lack of public confidence in its own projects, rejected the offer in December 1977, saying that such an inquiry would be "wasteful and probably unproductive."

Such "foresight" has added considerably to Hynek's frustration. Moreover, as much as he might like to be nominated to spearhead a new objective investigation of the phenomenon, his present position— ironically enough—disqualifies him. From exactly such a paradox springs the Platonic subtlety: "Neither they who know are to inquire, for as much as they know; nor they who do not know, for as much as to inquire they must know what they inquire of." The double bind present in any objective scientific investigation of the UFO phenomenon indicates that the course that Hynek has charted for himself may turn out to be the best in the long run—the very long run.

CHAPTER 3

The Great UFO Paper Chase

Getting the NEW YORK TIMES interested in a UFO story, as I explained in my introduction, was no problem. Basically, the story was timely and surprising (formerly classified government documents indicating a surprising interest in UFOs); and the newspaper had been quite pleased with my previous story on the legacy of nuclear testing in the 50s and 60s, which quite by chance I turned in a couple of weeks before the Three Mile Island incident.

But writing for the NEW YORK TIMES, or at least its Sunday magazine back in the late 1970s, was an experience like no other. The fact checkers and copy editors questioned every word. "What do you have to back this up? Is this really what you mean? Is that the proper adjective?" They went through the article word by word, as they had my previous story. They wanted me to be sure I was saying exactly what I meant. It was a demanding process, but it was standard operating procedure. An article on coffee would have been subjected to the same scrutiny.

My article in the NEW YORK TIMES MAGAZINE bore the title "UFO Files: The Untold Story," and appeared at the rear of the October 14, 1979, issue, with the following subhead: "Though officials have long denied that they take 'flying saucers' seriously, declassified documents now reveal extensive Government concern over the phenomenon."

✳

The Defense Department message bears the classification CON-
FIDENTIAL. "Subject: Suspicious Unknown Air Activity."
Dated Nov. 11, 1975, it reads:

"Since 28 Oct 75 numerous reports of suspicious objects have
been received at the NORAD COC [North American Air Defense
Combat Operations Center]. Reliable military personnel at Loring
AFB [Air Force Base], Maine, Wurtsmith AFB, Michigan,
Malmstrom AFB, [Montana], Minot AFB, [North Dakota], and
Canadian Forces Station, Falconbridge, Ontario, Canada, have visually
sighted suspicious objects.

"Objects at Loring and Wurtsmith were characterized to be helicopters. Missile site personnel, security alert teams, and Air Defense
personnel at Malmstrom Montana reported object which sounded like
a jet aircraft. FAA advised 'There were no jet aircraft in the vicinity.'
Malmstrom search and height finder radars carried the object between
9,000 ft and 15,600 ft at a speed of seven knots...F-106s scrambled
from Malmstrom could not make contact due to darkness and low altitude. Site personnel reported the objects as low as 200 ft and said that
as the interceptors approached the lights went out. After the interceptors had passed the lights came on again. One hour after the F-
106s returned to base, missile site personnel reported the object
increased to a high speed, raised in altitude and could not be discerned
from the stars...

"I have expressed my concern to SAFOI [Air Force Information
Office] that we come up with a proposed answer to queries from the
press to prevent overreaction by the public to reports by the media that
may be blown out of proportion. To date efforts by Air Guard helicopters, SAC [Strategic Air Command] helicopters and NORAD F-
106s have failed to produce positive ID."

Numerous daily updates kept the Joint Chiefs of Staff informed of
these incursions by UFOs. Representatives of the Defense Intelligence
Agency and the National Security Agency as well as a handful of
other Government desks received copies of the National Military
Command Center's reports on the incidents. One report said that an

unidentified object "demonstrated a clear intent in the weapons storage area." Though Air Force records show that the CIA was notified several times of these penetrations over nuclear missile and bomber bases, the agency has acknowledged only one such notification. Subsequent investigations by the Air Force into the sightings at Loring Air Force Base, Maine, where the remarkable series of events began, did not reveal a cause for the sightings.

Despite official pronouncements for decades that UFOs were nothing more than misidentified aerial objects and as such were no cause for alarm, declassified Government records now indicate that, ever since UFOs made their appearance in our skies in the 1940s, the phenomenon has aroused much serious behind-the-scenes concern in official circles. Details of the intelligence community's protracted obsession with the subject of UFOs have now emerged with the release of long-withheld Government documents obtained through the Freedom of Information Act (FOIA). Though these papers fail to resolve the UFO enigma, they do dispel many popular notions about the UFO controversy, as well as give substance to a number of others.

Official records now available appear to put to rest doubts that the Government knew more about UFOs than it has claimed over the past four decades. From the start, it has been convinced that most UFO sightings could be explained in terms of misidentified balloons, cloud formations, airplanes, ball lightning, meteors, and other natural phenomenon.

But the papers also show that the Government remains perplexed about the nagging residue of unexplained UFO sightings, which amount to approximately 10 percent of all UFO sightings reported. Do they pose a threat to national security? Are they just a funny-looking cover for an airborne Soviet presence? Even the possibility that these unknowns could be evidence of extraterrestrial visitations has been given serious attention in Government circles.

While official interest in UFOs has long been thought to be strictly the concern of the Air Force, the bulk of whose records have been open to public view for more than a decade, the documents on

UFOs that have been released under the FOIA indicate otherwise. The Departments of the Army, Navy, State, and Defense, and the Defense Intelligence Agency, the National Security Agency, the Joint Chiefs of Staff, the FBI, the CIA, and even the Atomic Energy Commission produced UFO records over the years. Many of these agencies still do, and many of their documents remain classified. But it is the CIA that appears to have played the key role in the controversy, and may even be responsible for the Government's conduct in UFO investigations throughout the years.

UFOs have been the province of the nation's intelligence community ever since the beginning of the cold war, when the notion took hold that some flying saucers might actually represent a secret, technologically advanced, foreign weapons system. "Every time we were concerned," recalls Herbert Scoville Jr., a former chief of the CIA's Office of Scientific Intelligence, "it was because we wanted to know: Did the Russians do it?"

As the cold war gave rise to the fears of the McCarthy era, official concern over UFOs even led to the surveillance of several private UFO organizations (as many of their members have long insisted) and to the scrutiny of dozens of individuals suspected of subversive UFO activities.

Perhaps most telling of all, the Government's documents on UFOs reveal that despite official denials to the contrary, Federal agencies continue to monitor the phenomenon to this day.

The monumental task of unearthing the newest batch of records on UFOs from a bureaucracy that has denied their existence for years can be traced to the efforts of a handful of inquisitive individuals who, armed with the FOIA, set off in the mid-1970s on a paper chase of U.S. Government documents on UFOs. They include Bruce Maccabee, a physicist working for the Navy, who obtained the release of more than a thousand pages of FBI documents on UFOs; W. Todd Zechel of Prairie du Sac, Wis.; Robert Todd of Ardmore, Pa.; Larry Bryant of Arlington, Va.; and Brad Sparks, a student in astrophysics at Berkeley whose five-year pursuit of the CIA's UFO file eventually provided the foundation for the ground-breaking Freedom of Information Act lawsuit filed by Ground Saucer Watch (GSW), an Arizona-based UFO organization.

At the request of GSW director William H. Spaulding, Peter Gersten, an attorney in the New York law firm of Rothblatt, Rothblatt & Seijas, filed a civil action against the CIA in December of 1977 demanding all UFO records in the agency's possession. The suit seemed to have achieved its goal when late in 1978 the agency released about 400 documents—nearly 900 pages of memos, reports and correspondence that attest to the agency's long involvement in UFO matters. But the civil action has not seen its final day in court.

By Gersten's account, the agency has arbitrarily withheld documents, made deletions without merit, and failed to conduct a proper search for UFO materials. The agency's current actions, he says, perpetuate its 30-year policy of deliberate deception and dishonestly about UFOs. "What has been released to us seems to have been rather carefully selected," says Gersten. "We suspect that the agency is withholding at least 200 more documents than the 57 they have admitted they are keeping from us to protect intelligence sources." Victor Marchetti, a former executive assistant to the agency's deputy director, agrees with Gersten. The entire exercise, Marchetti wrote recently in a magazine article, "has the same aroma of the agency's previous messy efforts to hide its involvement in drugs and mind-control operations, both prime examples of a successful intelligence cover-up."

The first sighting to be labeled a "flying saucer" by the press occurred on June 24, 1947, when an Idaho businessman flying his plane near Mt. Rainier observed nine disc-shaped objects making undulating motions "like a saucer skipping over water." As early as World War II, Allied bomber pilots had told of "balls of light" that followed their flights over Japan and Germany. A U.S. Eighth Army investigation concluded that they were the product of "mass hallucination."

These and other incidents were reported in a 1973 book by David

Michael Jacobs, *The UFO Controversy in America,* which until the recent release of Government documents was the most comprehensive reconstruction of the Government's UFO involvement.

When Scandinavians reported cigar-shaped objects in 1946, U.S. Army intelligence suspected that the Russians had developed a secret weapon with the help of German scientists from Peenemunde. The CIA, then known as the Central Intelligence Group, secretly began keeping tabs on the subject.

When the unknown objects returned to the skies, this time over the United States in the summer of 1947, the Army Air Force set out to determine what the objects were. Within weeks, Brig. Gen. George Schulgen of Army Air Corps Intelligence requested the FBI's assistance "in locating and questioning the individuals who first sighted the so-called flying discs…" Undoubtedly swayed by flaring cold war tensions, Schulgen feared that "the first reported sightings might have been by individuals of Communist sympathies with the view to causing hysteria and fear of a secret Russian weapon." J. Edgar Hoover agreed to cooperate but insisted that the bureau have "full access to discs recovered."

The Air Force's behind-the-scenes interest contrasted sharply with its public stance that the objects were products of misidentifications and an imaginative populace. A security lid was imposed on the subject in July 1947, hiding a potentially "embarrassing situation" the following month, when both the Air Force and the FBI began suspecting they might actually be investigating our own secret weapons. High-level reassurances were obtained that this was not so.

By the end of the summer, the FBI had "failed to reveal any indication of subversive individuals being involved in any of the reported sightings." A RESTRICTED Army letter that found its way to Hoover's desk said that the bureau's services actually had been enlisted to relieve the Air Force "of the task of tracking down all the many instances which turned out to be ashcan covers, toilet seats and whatnot." FBI personnel had begun to suspect that the bureau was "merely playing bird-dog for the Army." Incensed, Hoover moved quickly to discontinue the bureau's UFO investigations.

In September of that year, the Commanding General of the Army Air Force received a letter from Army Chief of Staff Lieut. Gen. Nathan Twining, saying that "the phenomenon reported is of something real and not visionary or fictitious," that the objects appeared to be disc-shaped, "as large as man-made aircraft," and "controlled either manually, automatically or remotely." At Twining's request, a permanent project, code named Sign and classified RESTRICTED, was established in December of 1947.

Sign failed to find any evidence that the objects were Soviet secret weapons and before long submitted an unofficial "Estimate of the Situation," classified TOP SECRET, which indicated that UFOs were of interplanetary origin. The estimate eventually reached Air Force Chief of Staff Gen. Hoyt Vandenberg, who rejected it for lack of proof. Sign's inconclusive final report remained classified for the next twelve years.

After Sign, the Air Force continued to collect UFO data under the code name Grudge. This six-month project found no evidence of foreign scientific development and therefore no direct threat to national security. It did, however, stress that the reported sightings could be dangerous. "There are indications that the planned release of related psychological propaganda would cause a form of mass hysteria," the report stated. "Employment of these methods by or against an enemy would yield similar results...governmental agencies interested in psychological warfare should be informed of the results of this study."

A press release following the termination of Grudge allowed the public to believe that the Air Force was no longer interested in UFOs. But the Air Force continued to collect reports through normal intelligence channels until the dramatic sighting of a UFO at the Army Signal Corps radar center in Fort Monmouth, N.J., in 1951 led to the reactivation of Grudge. The Air Force project was renamed Blue Book in 1952, a year that saw a record number of UFO reports.

The situation got out of hand during the summer of 1952. On the morning of July 28th, the *Washington Post* revealed that UFOs had been tracked on radar at Washington National Airport, the second such incident in a week. Reporters stormed Air Force headquarters in the Pentagon, where switchboards were jammed for days with UFO inquiries. Military installations across the country handled such a volume of reports that "regular intelligence work had been affected," reported the *New York Times*.

These events prompted action at CIA headquarters, apparently at a request "from the Hill." From the start, the agency's involvement was to be kept secret. An August 1st CIA memo recommended that "no indication of CIA interest or concern reach the press or public, in view of their probable alarmist tendencies to accept such interest as 'confirmatory' of the soundness of 'unpublished facts' in the hands of the U.S. Government."

The CIA's Office of Scientific Intelligence (OSI) found that the Air Force's investigation of the UFO phenomenon was not sufficiently rigorous to determine the exact nature of the objects in the sky. Neither did the Air Force deal adequately with the potential danger of UFO-induced mass hysteria, or the fact that our air vulnerability was being seriously affected by the UFO problem. OSI chief H. Marshall Chadwell thought that our nation's defenses were running the increasing risk of false alert and, worse yet, "of falsely identifying the real as phantom." He suggested that a national policy be established "as to what should be told the public" and, furthermore, that immediate steps be taken to improve our current visual and electronic identification techniques so that "instant positive identification of enemy planes or missiles can be made." Ever vigilant, the CIA was keeping an eye on the possibility that UFOs could be of Soviet origin.

By the winter of 1952, Chadwell had drafted a National Security Council proposal calling for a program to solve the problem of instant positive identification of UFOs. In a memo that accompanied the proposal, Chadwell urged that the reports be given "immediate attention." He thought that "sightings of unexplained objects at great altitudes and traveling at high speeds in the vicinity of major U.S. defense installations are of such nature that they are not attributable to natural phenomena or known types of aerial vehicles." He said that OSI was proceeding with the establishment of a consulting group "of sufficient competence and stature to...convince the responsible authorities in the community that immediate research and development on this subject must be undertaken."

But CIA Director Gen. Walter B. Smith's interest apparently lay elsewhere. In a letter to the Director of the Psychological Strategy Board, he expressed a desire to discuss "the possible offensive and defensive utilization of these phenomena for psychological warfare purposes." Only later, after an order from the Intelligence Advisory Committee, did Director Smith authorize recruiting an advisory committee of outside consultants.

The scientific panel met for four days beginning January 14, 1953. Chaired by Dr. H. P. Robertson, an expert in physics and weapons systems, the panel essentially bestowed the scientific seal of approval on previously established official policy regarding UFOs. The distinguished panelists felt that all the sightings could be identified once all the data were available for a proper evaluation—in other words, the phenomena, according to the panel's report, were not "beyond the domain of present knowledge of physical sciences." Neither did the panelists find UFOs to be a direct threat to national security, though they believed that the volume of UFO reports could clog military intelligence channels, precipitate panic and lead defense personnel to ignore real indications of hostile action. The panel worried about Soviet manipulation of the phenomenon; that the reports could make the public vulnerable to "possible enemy psychological warfare." The real danger, they concluded, was the reports themselves.

Fearing that the myth of UFOs might lead to inappropriate actions by the American public, the panelists decided that a "broad educational program integrating efforts of all concerned agencies" must be undertaken. They sought to strip UFOs of their "aura of mystery" through this program of "training and 'debunking.'" The program would result in the "proper recognition of unusually illuminated objects" and in a "reduction in public interest in flying saucers." The panelists recommended that their mass-media program have as its advisers psychologists familiar with mass psychology and advertising experts, while Walt Disney Inc. animated cartoons and such personalities as Arthur Godfrey would help in the educational drive. To insure complete control over the situation, the panel members suggested that flying saucer groups be "watched because of their potentially great influence on mass thinking if widespread sightings should occur. The apparent irresponsibility and the possible use of such groups for subversive purposes should be kept in mind."

The panel's recommendations called for nothing less than the domestic manipulation of public attitudes. Whether these proposals were acted upon, the CIA will not say. But the report was circulated among the top brass at the Air Technical Intelligence Center, the CIA's Board of National Estimates, the CIA's bureau chiefs, the Secretary of Defense, the chairman of the National Security Resources Board, and the director of the Federal Civil Defense Administration, who eventually sent a representative to meet with CIA officials in order to "implement the appropriate aspects of the Panel's Report as applicable to Civil Defense."

The Government's efforts in the 1950s and 1960s to squelch public apprehension over UFOs went beyond debunking and even touched the fiber of constitutionally protected free speech. According to historian David Michael Jacobs, in 1953 the Air Force pressured *Look* magazine into publishing disclaimers throughout an article by retired Maj. Donald E. Keyhoe titled "Flying Saucers From Outer Space." Then again, in 1965, the Army—in a prepublication review—denied clearance for a UFO-related article by one of its employees, Larry Bryant, a technical writer, until he took the issue to court.

Meanwhile, the CIA and the FBI proceeded routinely in the surveillance of UFO organizations and UFO enthusiasts. People with UFO interests were checked out by the FBI at the request of the CIA, the Air Force, or private citizens inquiring about possible subversive activities. But none caused as much consternation as the case of Major Keyhoe and the organization he directed, the National Investigations Committee on Aerial Phenomena (NICAP).

The CIA appears to have had a protracted interest in NICAP, which was founded in 1956 and utilized by Keyhoe as an organizational tool for challenging the alleged Air Force cover-up on UFOs. Both the CIA and the Air Force were upset by NICAP's wide-ranging influence. Its prestigious board of directors included, among others, Vice Adm. Roscoe Hillenkoetter, the first CIA director (1947-1950). "The Air Force representatives believe that much of the trouble…with Major Keyhoe…could be alleviated," states a CIA memo dated May 16, 1958, "if the Major did not have such important personages as Vice Admiral R. H. Hillenkoetter, U.S.N. (Ret.)…on the board…." The Air Force suggested that if the Admiral were shown the SECRET panel report he might understand and take "appropriate actions." Whether or not the Air Force got through to the admiral, Hillenkoetter resigned from NICAP in 1961.

The sixties saw further CIA interest in NICAP. After a flurry of Washington-area sightings in 1965, the agency contacted NICAP about seeing some of its case files on the matter. Richard H. Hall, then NICAP assistant director, chatted with a CIA agent in the NICAP office about the sightings, NICAP's methodology, and Hall's background. The agent's memo on the visit suggests that the CIA had some role in mind for Hall, predicated upon his being granted a security clearance. Nothing apparently came of the suggestion. A later set of CIA papers reveals an interest in NICAP's organizational structure and notes that "this group included some ex-CIA and Defense Intelligence types who advise on investigative techniques and NICAP-Government relations." There are presently three former CIA employees on the NICAP board of directors, including Charles Lombard, a congressional aide to Senator Barry Goldwater, who is himself a NICAP board member; and retired U.S. Air Force Col. Joseph Bryan III. Bryan feels, as he did back in 1959 when he joined the board, that UFOs are interplanetary. NICAP's current president is Alan Hall, a former CIA covert employee for 30 years. [NICAP is no longer in existence.]

In 1966, mounting discontent from members of the press, Congress and the scientific community compelled the Air Force in 1966 to commission an eighteen-month scientific study of UFOs under the direction of Edward Condon, professor of physics at the University of Colorado. The politically expedient study, in which one-third of the ninety-one cases examined remained unidentified, reiterated official policy with one novel twist: UFOs "educationally harmed" schoolchildren who were allowed to use science study time to read books and magazine articles about UFOs. Condon wanted teachers to withhold credit from any student UFO project. The Air Force took the cue and disbanded Project Blue Book in 1969.

Less than a decade later, the White House, perhaps in an attempt to make good Jimmy Carter's campaign promise to tell all about UFOs, suggested via science advisor Frank Press that possibly NASA cold undertake a review of any significant new findings since Condon's study. NASA examined the offer, but saw no way to attack the problem on a scientific basis without physical evidence. They envisioned a public-relations nightmare if they were to accept such a project, and so rejected it. A frank, in-house evaluation of NASA's options, however, noted that a hands-off attitude only begged the question. So in good spirit, the space agency offered to examine any piece of physical evidence brought to its attention. That position led one Federal aviation official to comment: "If you get a piece of the thing, fine. But don't bother me with anything else."

These days, the Air Force admits to nothing more than a "transitory interest" in the phenomenon, although military directives still exist for reporting UFOs.

The CIA is still wary of the possibility that UFOs may be of Soviet origin. "The agency's interest," says Katherine Pherson, a public-affairs officer for the CIA, "lies in its responsibility to forewarn principally of the possibility that a foreign power might develop a new weapons system that might exhibit phenomena that some might categorize as a UFO. But there is no program to actively collect information on UFOs." The agency's interest cannot be denied, however, as two 1976 memos reveal.

The first, dated April 26th, states: "It does not seem that the Government has any formal program in progress for the identification/solution of the UFO phenomenon. Dr. [name deleted] feels that the efforts of independent researchers, [phrase deleted], are vital for further progress in this area. At the present time, there are offices and personnel within the agency who are monitoring the UFO phenomenon, but again, this is not currently on an official basis."

Another memo, dated July 14th, and routed to the deputy chief in the Office of Development and Engineering, reads: "As you may recall, I mentioned my own interest in the subject as well as the fact that DCD [Domestic Collection Division] has been receiving material from many of our S&T [Science and Technology] sources who are presently conducting related research. These scientists include some who have been associated with the Agency for years and whose credentials remove them from the 'nut' variety."

If nothing else, the success of the UFO paper chase may have lent UFOs a measure of respectability that has eluded the subject for the past third of a century. Though it appears that no UFO sighting has ever represented an airborne Soviet or foreign threat, the possibility that such an event could occur remains foremost in the cold-war conscious Government mind. Should that threat come to pass, military officials believe, our nation's sophisticated defense system would know about it before someone getting a glass of milk in the middle of the night sees the threat hovering outside the kitchen window. Or so we are made to understand the Air Force's seemingly nonchalant advice to the public: "If you see a UFO and you feel the situation warrants it, call your local police."

✳

Postscript

In response to my UFO story, the NEW YORK TIMES published two letters to the editor in the November 11, 1979, issue. Linda S. Davies of Rockville, Maryland, obviously a UFO community insider, wrote in part: "Once public pressure compels the UFO-secrecy bureaucracy to cough up the remainder of its Pandora's box of data (including any crashed-saucer documentation), perhaps we can write finis to what lately has been called the Cosmic Watergate."

The other letter, written by Philip J. Klass, the field's arch skeptic, was predictably indignant. Klass accused me of not thoroughly studying the government documents I cited, though I had, in fact, spent several weeks studying and discussing them with Peter Gersten among others. Klass also insisted that the government had shown no serious concern about UFO reports since 1969 and that the CIA's only active interest had lasted less than a year— a quarter of a century previously. Obviously Klass had written his letter before he even had finished reading my article, which quotes two 1976 CIA documents that clearly state otherwise.

Over the years many people have asked me questions about my NEW YORK TIMES UFO story. Just a year ago I received a query about it from a writer named Terry Hansen, who was preparing a book on the sociology of the media's role in the UFO controversy. His questions about how my NEW YORK TIMES story came about has led, indirectly, to this book. He wanted to know whose decision it had been to lead off the story with the 1975 UFO flap over military bases. Hanson contends that this news, while covered locally, was suspiciously absent from the national media. It turns out that the decision to start with this series of incidents was entirely my own. I picked the most dramatic, most recent, most "official" incident I could find. My answer engendered an interesting exchange:

HANSEN: What are your general impressions of how the national news media cover the UFO story?

HUYGHE: Mostly they do a pretty bad job of it. But I don't think it's deliberate. There is certainly no media conspiracy with regard to UFOs. If there had been, it would have been obvious to me at the time I did these stories...

HANSEN: I'm not sure if you know it, but the NEW YORK TIMES has a history of suppressing coverage of certain events upon request of the Central Intelligence Agency. Even the NEW YORK TIMES has admitted this. (See, for example, "Role of CIA In Guatemala Told in Files of Publisher," NYT, June 7, 1997, p. 9.) For many years it was publisher Arthur Hays Sulzberger's policy to help the CIA whenever possible. Would you classify this type of government-media collusion as a "media conspiracy"? If not, why not?

HUYGHE: No. I do not see this sort of thing as a "media conspiracy," because the media are not conspiring on their own. In other words, the media are not deciding to do this: it comes at the request of the government. I am familiar with the history of the NEW YORK TIMES in this regard, the CIA requesting a delay of a story, or to "kill" a story entirely. I would call this a form of media collusion with the government, not conspiracy.

HANSEN: I appreciate that you would have no reason to believe, based on your experience, that there is any media conspiracy regarding UFOs. But given the fact that the NEW YORK TIMES (and other major media organizations) have cooperated with the CIA to suppress coverage of certain sensitive issues on national-security grounds, how can you be sure that such things don't happen in the case of UFOs, particularly since UFOs have often been a national-security concern according to the government's own documents?

HUYGHE: I'm not saying I'm sure that such things never happen in the case of UFOs. But based on my experience with the media in the late 1970s, early 1980s, I can say that I perceived no apparent conspiracy or collusion by the media with regard to UFOs at that time. I disagree with your comment: "UFOs have often been a national-security concern according to the government's own documents." First, of all, I would not say "often," but perhaps "occasionally." Second, we don't know if the "national security" classification of those documents pertains specifically to the UFO itself—rather than to the agents' identities or intelligence gathering techniques involved—or even whether the UFO involved was a true unknown.

HANSEN: The term "conspiracy" means different things to different people, of course, so this is largely a semantic issue. I'm fairly certain, though, that the American public would define secret collusion between the news media and the government as a conspiracy of some sort! News organizations promote themselves as sources of objective coverage. When covert spin control or outright news suppression is undertaken on behalf of the intelligence community, it can be damaging to the public's assessment of news credibility, no matter what you call it.

By the way, I don't take the view that most journalists and writers are trying to suppress this story. On the other hand, there is some good social science research that suggests their coverage tends to be significantly biased toward the government's position on the UFO controversy in some cases. I think this results mostly from a generally deferential attitude toward government-supplied information, some of which is either completely untrue or slightly deceptive. The extent to which top-level collusion has taken place is much harder to assess for the obvious reasons that neither the intelligence community nor the media corporations are anxious for such information to reach the public. When this disclosure happens at all, it is usually many years after the fact. The government-media interaction is a sociologically complex dance with lots of subtle aspects.

My email exchange with Hansen ended at this point, but I would like to add a few words on the subject. Hansen errs in concluding that the coverage of the UFO subject by journalists is "significantly biased toward the government's position." Hansen might just as well have said that it is "biased toward the scientific position" or "biased toward the skeptical position." Do scientists take part in this conspiracy? Do skeptics? Though some of the more paranoid members of our society might think so, I would argue otherwise. Government agencies are not alone in holding this "UFOs-are-worthless" position.

You can follow Hansen's argument in his now published book, THE MISSING TIMES. In it he suggests that government agencies have "fed" the media what information it wants on UFOs. No doubt it has. Sometimes the media is aware of it; sometimes it's not. But the bottom line is that the CIA and other government agencies are sources of information for reporters, and like all sources of information, government agencies have an agenda and the information they provide is not always reliable.

Hansen believes that the government has had a profound and controlling influence on the media's UFO stories. As I said earlier, I doubt it, but even if it has, that says nothing about the reality of UFOs. UFOs don't have to be real for you to be able to manipulate information about them. Indeed, that's what the 1953 Robertson Report was all about. There is no doubt that UFOs are sometimes a pawn in a political game, but that does not necessarily make UFOs alien vehicles from outer space.

CHAPTER 4

UFOs and the CIA's Photo Analysis Unit

Writing for the NEW YORK TIMES certainly boosted my writing career. And the responses I received from that article—both from inside the UFO-research community and from those having no previous interest in the subject— encouraged me, for better or for worse, to continue writing about the controversy. My first spin-off of the story was a "Q&A," a published interview in other words.

One of the most interesting interviews I did in the course of preparing the NEW YORK TIMES story centered on the work of Arthur C. Lundall, former director of the CIA's National Photographic Interpretation Center. I felt that Lundahl's views would carry weight with the UFO-research community, especially since he had been involved with the subject as far back as 1953. My story appeared in the February 1980 issue of THE MUFON UFO JOURNAL, under the title "Interview with Arthur C. Lundahl." The journal's editor, Richard Hall, appended his comments on the sections marked with an asterisk at the end of the interview.

✳

In December 1978, the U.S. Central Intelligence Agency released more than 900 pages of UFO-related documents that attest to the Agency's interest and involvement in UFOs over the past 30 years. Among the CIA's UFO papers were documents written by, concerned with, or addressed to Arthur C. Lundahl, the former director of the CIA's National Photographic Interpretation Center (NPIC). Lundahl joined the CIA in 1953 and served as NPIC director from 1963 to

1973, the year he retired. In the course of doing an extensive article on the government's scrutiny of the UFO phenomenon for *The New York Times Sunday Magazine* (published on Oct. 14, 1979), I interviewed Lundahl at length about the CIA's 1953 Robertson Panel Report, Edward Condon's Colorado UFO project in 1967, the CIA's involvement in UFOs, as well as his own interest in the phenomenon.

What kind of help did the CIA provide the Condon UFO project? Didn't the Air Force contact you in February 1967 to help Condon?

Arthur Lundahl: Yes, that's correct. But I really couldn't provide any real help in the substantive sense because I don't know anything about UFOs at all. You see, Dr. Condon had been away from Washington for some time, and he was unwitting perhaps of the status of technology in the photogrammetry field. You know, there are all kinds of esoteric hardware, new kinds of photographic techniques for enhancing images and things like that. Since at the time I was director of NPIC, the Air Force asked me if I would have Dr. Condon and two of his assistants over to talk about the state of the art in the photogrammetry field. He was a very nice man and a brilliant, well-known scientist. We had a nice visit, and I think he came back another time. But as far as any substance, any additions, or suggestions going into the report, I claim none of those whatsoever.

In a CIA memo dated February 7, 1967, you state that you wanted to "preserve a CIA window" on the Condon UFO project. What did you mean by that?

Lundahl: That, in the parlance of the trade, means just a seat like a mouse in the corner to hear what's going on. It involves no responsibilities, only curiosity. I, the little mouse in the corner, was interested because I was responsible for interpreting any kind of picture that the United States might have at its disposal, whether it be Cuban missiles or anything else, so I sure wanted to know a little bit about the phenomenon involved. If there was something worthwhile coming out of the Condon project that would aid in the interpretation of subsequent pictures, I thought it would be good for the national welfare to know what those characteristics were—what they found.

Other CIA memos in 1967 mention such things as "the second UFO project assigned" and "UFO Mensuration Support project." What do they refer to?

Lundahl: Well, mensuration is frequently used alternately with photogrammetry. But I didn't have any UFO project. I think it may be a vagary of the text. I don't know the answer but I'll offer a guess that Condon may have said "I've got this thing here in my briefcase" and passed some pictures over and asked us to give him a dimension on the object. You probably know, but I should mention, that photogrammetry is the science of extracting quantitative information on the real world from measurements off of pictures. As I dig back in my memory, it seems that instead of being called a project the better word would have been "task."*

The CIA memos also show that you advised Condon not to make any reference to the Agency's help in his UFO project. Why?

Lundahl: The phenomenon is a fulminating subject, you see. There are lots of wild-eyed nuts in this field who sit on mountaintops doing drugs and waiting for the sunrise. There are guys with psychic phenomena pouring out of their ears. There are weird people all over. And of course, the CIA is a kind of exciting enough name in itself. And if you mix fire and kerosene together, you get the whole place excited. I wanted to be careful and not imply that we were substantially involved. I was hoping he wouldn't make a big case about the fact that the CIA was in the project.

Were you satisfied with the conclusions of the Condon project?

Lundahl: I really don't think they did a very good job as scientists. Speaking as a geologist, I really don't think of the Condon project as a detached, cold-blooded view of the subject. Some of the staffers realized that they were part of a big sham; that it wasn't going to be an even-handed treatment of the matter. They found that Condon would just produce a great big kind of document that was going to sweep it all under the rug. The biggest whitewash of all was when the National Academy of Sciences put some kind of foreword on the book. I don't think they even read the damn thing.

Did you join the CIA before or after the CIA produced the Robertson Panel Report in 1953?

Lundahl: I joined the CIA just afterwards. But I knew a little bit about the Robertson Panel because at that time I had been working for the U.S. Navy Photo Interpretation Laboratory (in Anacostia, D.C.), where I was assistant chief engineer. Some naval officer named Newhouse had taken some pictures out in Utah in a place called Tremonton. He had turned them over to the Air Force, and they had scanned them and did whatever they were going to do with them. Then the Air Force passed them over to us. I was in the front office handling budget and finance at the time, so I didn't do any analysis of the film. But I had a couple of men who worked on it. They spent quite a few hours looking at the images. While we were studying the photos somebody called up from the CIA, I think it was General Phil Strong. He was the executive secretary of the arranging committee for the Robertson Panel, I think. He explained that they had these note-worthy scientists coming together and could someone from our organization bring this film over and have it projected and stand by to answer whatever questions they could.

Robert Neasham and Harry Woo showed the film to the panel many times and told them what analysis they had done on it. The problem was that they didn't have a single number to go on: they didn't know how big the things were or how far away they were. As Archimedes said: "Give me a place to stand, and I will move the earth." Well, we needed one number to get the other. So they had blocked out a hypothetical matrix of possibilities and presented them to the panel. The panel was polite, interested, and respectful and thanked the men for coming over. My men were dismissed, and that was all there was to it. But I found out years later when I was reading paperbacks on the episode that the Robertson Panel pretty much thought the images were high-flying birds.*

Did that upset your men, who had spent 1,000 hours analyzing the film?

Lundahl: No, I don't think it upset them. We didn't know what it was we were looking at. The images were not sharply resolved; there was no clear cut geometry that anybody could see. There were objects up there, but none of us knew anything about migratory birds. Although it had seemed to us that migratory birds at that height, whatever height it was, would not have been able to make a good target on the film.

Was the CIA officially interested in UFOs?

Lundahl: I don't know what the CIA's interest was. I never found an official version or opinion of any CIA position on the matter. In fact, I found a gross lack of interest as far as any of the people I talked to were concerned. The people that I talked to didn't seem to have any interest. Now, there may have been other people in large numbers working on this that I knew nothing about. Maybe I shouldn't say a gross lack of interest; it's simply an exciting subject. But there was no official pushing attitude on UFOs. Gen. Strong followed it. He was in the Office of Scientific Intelligence (OSI), and we were just friends.

What was Gen. Strong's interest in UFOs?

Lundahl: What I remember best of Strong and the Robertson Panel in the 1950's was the concern over the welter of UFO reports coming in on various channels that might clog the North American defense pattern. Had there been some kind of real attack or threat of some kind, it might have gotten lost in the shuffle of confusing information. I think Phil Strong's main interest was to make sure that communications would not be done in by this thing, illusory or real or whatever it was. That's the main thing that got the CIA and the Robertson people together in the first place.

Was anyone else in the CIA interested in UFOs while you were there?

Lundahl: I remember another CIA man named Al Moore in OSI who was very interested in this subject in 1953-54. We were both Naval reserve officers. Moore was just wrapped around the axle full of interest in the UFO phenomenon. As I looked at his face and listened to his words I formed a feeling that this guy was more enthusiastic about the subject than Phil Strong ever was. He eventually left the CIA and opened up a patent law office in Mississippi. He was of the opinion that UFOs were something very real and that the extraterrestrial hypothesis was probably the least unacceptable one. That was his personal belief. Nothing official.

Did the CIA have an active UFO project while you were there?

Lundahl: I had a job which got me involved with everybody's business. A picture can be made of anything, and ipso facto I was involved with everybody and everything. It seems to me that had there been some real ongoing UFO project I would have known something about it. If they had any pictorial evidence they would have had to bring it to my place for analysis. They knew I was trustworthy and not a crackpot. It seems to me that I would have had a fair chance of knowing. But I never heard of a single project, a single funded endeavor of any kind dedicated to finding out some kind of answer to the UFO enigma.* Whatever I knew about it was entirely coincidental. I read paperbacks on the subject. But some outside observer might look at my job, which was very important, and notice my Tremonton background and my meetings with Condon, and they'd believe that I had a huge bunch of projects going on, analyzing pictures, reporting them to the President just like Cuban missiles, and keeping all this from the public. Well, I can assure you that nothing is further from the truth. The interest in UFOs may well have randomized among its employees, as it did with me. But I used to go to budget review functions, I used to listen to mission summations; and no where along the line did I ever gather the impression that this was a real ongoing effort with the CIA.

Within the past year or so the National Investigations Committee on Aerial Phenomena (NICAP) in Washington, D.C., has undergone a reorganization. Were you not offered the position of NICAP director?

Lundahl: I really wasn't offered the position. Somebody called me up about a year or two ago but I had no idea if he was calling from the Defense Department or NICAP. He sounded off his name as if he were familiar to me, but I never did figure out who had called me. Anyway he started telling me about NICAP's financial problems and change of command. At one point he said there would be someone new to take over at NICAP. Then as an aside he said: "Hey, Art, that might be a good job for you in retirement. You're not doing anything now." I said: "Are you crazy? If I were starving I wouldn't take a job like that." And he asked me why not. I said: "Do you realize with the background I have in CIA, if I suddenly showed up at NICAP, I couldn't even hold the front portals until the 4:30 whistles blew. There'd be more crazy people in there than you could shake a stick at with allegations I could never cope with—wild!" He said: "Yeah, I didn't think of it that way. I guess it would be a fiery mixture." You bet your boots, I said. If you call that a job offer, that's what happened.

How do you feel about your employment with the CIA?

Lundahl: I don't have any slings and arrows to throw at the CIA. I found them to be an excellent employer. I thought they were wonderful, dedicated people. I've had tremendous experiences there, meeting people, and dealing with big issues. I don't know of any job I could have had that I would have enjoyed more. I guess the only way to top it would have been to have a great big fat UFO land out there on the monument grounds and we'd covered it from three sides with metric cameras with all kinds of things, including magnetic spin recorders, and then we got it all measured up and we went on NBC live at 8 o'clock Sunday night and told the world what was there. I guess that would have been a topper, but we never had a shot at that.

Remarks by Richard Hall:

These notes correspond to sections of the interview marked with an asterisk.

The question of whether Art Lundahl and the CIA are or were "officially" involved with UFO investigations is an important one. Lundahl has always denied it, and has often professed great ignorance of the subject. However, it is known from private sources that during the early 1960's the Air Force routinely referred movie films of UFOs (from gun cameras and other sources) to NPIC for analysis, while Lundahl was NPIC Director. Also, Lundahl had another "window" on the Colorado Project through a friend at Raytheon Corporation who did some photo-analysis for the Condon Committee.

The Navy photo-analysis lab did have "numbers" to go on in analyzing the Newhouse film, and Lundahl must have known that. They had lens resolution data and someone in government had frames of the film showing one of the UFOs disappearing over the horizon (frames that were missing when the Air Force returned the film to Newhouse). Ex-Major Dewey Fournet, Project Blue Book Monitor in the Pentagon, told NICAP that the Navy analysis specifically ruled out birds. "…it would be necessary to conclude that Newhouse was lying in many of his statements in order to conclude that the Tremonton objects were birds," Fournet said, and the intelligence officers considered him to be "completely sincere and somewhat reserved." (See *The UFO Evidence*, p. 112.)

The evidence indicates that both the CIA Office of Scientific Intelligence and NPIC, under Art Lundahl, have had a long-standing and official interest in UFOs and that Lundahl probably knows more about the nature and performance of UFOs, as determined by photo-analysis, than anyone in the world. He is also part of an informal Washington UFO "underground" that includes Robert C. Durant (writer of the 1953 CIA panel report) and Dr. Charles Sheldon, expert on Russian missiles and rockets at the Library of Congress, among others. By making disarming public statements and professions of ignorance, Lundahl has served as a CIA "cover" to conceal from the public the extent of the CIA's scientific data and top-level awareness of UFOs.—*Richard Hall*

※

Postscript

I should point out my total disagreement with Hall's statement that Lundahl served as a "'cover' to conceal from the public the extent of the CIA's scientific data and top-level awareness of UFOs." Just because some people within an organization choose to pursue a particular field of inquiry doesn't necessarily mean that the organization as a whole follows suit. This sort of misunderstanding, which runs rampant through UFOlogy, fuels much of the field's paranoia.

CHAPTER 5

Who Cares About Unexplained Cases?

Shortly after leaving US magazine and going freelance, I was drawn back into a full time position, lured by what I thought would be a dream job as a writer at NEWSWEEK. Actually, I was a staff writer for a test issue of a new Newsweek publication called NEWSWEEK FOCUS. This first issue targeted the "Mysteries of the Cosmos," and subsequent issues would be devoted to other single topics. Apparently this "space" issue I worked on did not test well, as Newsweek never went ahead with the publication. Though afterwards I was offered a full time position at NEWSWEEK itself, I turned down the offer.

My dream job was a nightmare. I felt like a cog in a giant wheel, having to process reporters' interviews and a file produced by the research department into a story that then would be edited beyond recognition by a staff of upper level editors. It was not my idea of writing. But enough of journalism.

Since I had written the UFO story for the NEW YORK TIMES, the NEWSWEEK FOCUS editor had me write the UFO piece for this issue. It was the standard news magazine treatment of the subject. The story was titled "UFO Watching" and appeared in NEWSWEEK FOCUS: MYSTERIES OF THE COSMOS, June/July 1980.

＊

If official studies could exorcise phantoms, UFOs would have vanished from the sky more than a decade ago. It was back in 1969 that an Air Force-sponsored study found that most flying saucers were either natural phenomena or hoaxes, and the unexplained remainder weren't worth worrying about. The investigation's director, University of Colorado Physics Prof. Edward U. Condon, said he was "sorry I ever got involved" in such "a bunch of damned nonsense." With that, the Air Force happily closed down Project Blue Book, its UFO-investigations unit. The National Academy of Sciences gravely endorsed the Condon report. Even the public seemed impressed: for awhile, the reported sightings dropped off.

But people have been seeing strange things in the sky at least since the Prophet Ezekiel, and whatever was responsible wasn't about to go away. New reports of UFOs triggered others. Accounts flourished in the less inhibited journals of bizarre confrontations with beings from other worlds and, in 1977, the hugely popular movie "Close Encounters of the Third Kind" brought that notion to the screen in deadpan verisimilitude.

And if UFOlogy needed any bolstering, it got an unexpected boost in credibility from the government's own files as an offshoot of the 1974 Freedom of Information Act. Since the act's passage, requests by UFO investigators (and one lawsuit, against the CIA) have produced nearly 3,000 pages of UFO documents from the FBI, the CIA, the State Department, the Defense Intelligence Agency (DIA), the National Security Agency, the three armed forces, and the Joint Chiefs of Staff.

The government's papers should keep conspiracy theorists in business for years. True, they contain no hard evidence proving that saucers exist. And taken together, the FOI documents show clearly that U.S. officials are far more interested in the chance that the Russians might have developed exotic aircraft than they are in visitors from space. But some of the documents that have been released were heavily censored, and some agencies—notably the CIA—are still withholding files. Moreover, the FOI papers show an uneasy official interest in some highly intriguing sightings as recently as 1978. And there is considerable proof that the government has been less than candid about UFOs.

As CIA spokeswoman Katherine Pherson tells it, from the beginning Washington has had no interest in UFOs except national security—"the possibility that a foreign power may be developing a new weapons system." The censorship and continuing secrecy, officials say, are merely to protect intelligence sources—and the Pentagon may also want to avoid betraying such secrets as the power and range of radar units. Government sources unanimously assert that they are pushing no active investigation of UFOs, but merely collecting reports when sightings might have military significance.

Logical enough. But UFO buffs would find that stance more credible if the government hadn't insisted for years that Project Blue Book was its only UFO file, and that no data were collected after the Blue Book was closed. To make credibility even more tenuous, there is evidence dating back to the Condon report itself of orchestrated efforts to downplay UFO data. In a memo that was leaked from the Condon files, the University of Colorado's assistant dean warned that the institution risked disrepute merely for studying UFOs. "The trick," the memo said, "would be, I think, to describe the project so that to the public it would appear a totally objective study but, to the scientific community, [it] would present the image of a group of nonbelievers trying their best to be objective but having an almost zero expectation of finding a saucer."

Such tortuous dissembling, of course, doesn't prove that there was a conspiracy to cover up—let alone that saucers full of extraterrestrial visitors are hovering overhead. But it does feed suspicion that Washington's UFO policy is less casual than it seems, and official disingenuousness continues to pop up in the FOI files.

In 1975, for instance, classified Air Force cables nervously recorded a series of UFO sightings over five defense installations across the northern United States and Canada. Messages were issued by the Department of Defense and circulated to the Joint Chiefs, the CIA and the Secretary of Defense, reporting reliable sightings of objects variously described as helicopters, "bright starlike objects" and "a 100-foot diameter sphere that appeared to have craters around the outside." In one case, at Loring Air Force Base in Maine, a mysterious object was reported to have "demonstrated a clear intent in the weapons storage area." Some of the visitors were tracked on radar. The Air Force took the whole episode seriously enough to invoke new security measures against "unidentified aircraft/helicopters." Yet at the same time, the documents now show, the Secretary of the Air Force warned base spokesmen: "Responses [to the press] should emphasize that the action was taken in response to an isolated or specific incident," not to a wave of UFOs.

Some of the most intriguing reports merely document sightings and leave them unexplained, with no evidence of any follow-up investigations. Perhaps the strangest encounter came in the skies over Iran in September 1976, when pilots of two U.S.-built F-4 jets reported UFOs. The larger of the two objects appeared on radar screens, and both jets suffered a sudden paralysis of their electronic systems.

If UFOs did turn out to be Soviet weapons, what might they be? On the face of it, it's highly unlikely that any nation could keep such a total secret for more than 30 years. Moreover, notes UFO skeptic and aviation expert Philip Klass of *Aviation Week & Space Technology* magazine, if the Russians could build an aircraft that could disappear, evade most radar, make right-angle turns and accelerate straight up at dizzying speed, why would they keep producing conventional planes?

To UFO buffs, however, Washington's concentration on terrestrial security seems myopic. Sightings are automatically discounted, says New York attorney Peter Gersten, the prime document chaser among UFOlogists, simply because "the reports often involve unusual objects with performance characteristics too extraordinary to be Russian. Clearly, if it's not Soviet, we don't seem to care. But the question we should be asking is, 'If they are not Russian, then what are they?' "

By one disputed count, there have been some 75,000 UFO sightings around the world since 1947, including no fewer than 2,000 from citizens reporting they have had encounters with humanoids in UFOs. Somehow, conclusive evidence of the saucers and their inhabitants is always lacking. The strongest suggestion of the physical reality of UFOs remains the fact that some sightings—a little less than 10 per cent of the total—are what the Condon report called "indeed strange and mysterious, impossible by all current knowledge to explain."

By scientific lights, however, that mystery is no more significant than a good ghost story. In an article published in *New Scientist* magazine last October, former NASA engineer and UFO skeptic James Oberg cited an earlier remark by physiologist Hudson Hoagland, a debunker of psychic phenomena: "Unexplained cases are simply unexplained. They can never constitute evidence for any hypothesis." Oberg's piece was written as an entry in a UFO essay competition sponsored by Cutty Sark Ltd. of London, and it won a prize of 1,000 pounds sterling. The whisky distiller had also offered a grand prize of 1 million pounds to anyone who could produce an authenticated fragment of a UFO. There were no claimants.

CHAPTER 6

Scientists Who Have Seen UFOs

While the media abhor "copy cat" crimes, and rightfully so, their own copy cat behavior is well...nearly criminal. All editors want to get a piece of the action on a good story, as they know that readers can't get enough of a hot topic. The revelations about secret government interest in UFOs spawned a variety of other UFO stories. One of them I wrote for editor Scott DeGarmo who wanted a piece on the subject for his magazine, SCIENCE DIGEST. He asked me to write about scientists who have seen UFOs. It was an appropriate story for a popular science magazine, I suppose. What I did not do, but could have done, is mine this idea across professions: "Plumbers who have seen UFOs." "Librarians who have seen UFOs." Etc., etc. My story ran in the November 1981 issue of SCIENCE DIGEST under the title "Scientists Who Have Seen UFOs."

✳

Strange objects have flitted about the sky throughout history, but since 1947 sightings of unidentified flying objects, or UFOs, have become increasingly numerous in the United States and in other parts of the world. Sixty-thousand reports of sightings (some new, some drawn from ancient records) from 140 countries are now recorded in the computerized catalog at the Center for UFO Studies, in Evanston, Illinois, and the number grows larger every day. They include more than 2,000 cases in which UFOs reportedly left behind physical traces of their appearance; more than 1,500 cases in which people said they encountered humanoid entities; 400 cases in which automobiles were said to have been brought to a halt or otherwise affected by nearby UFOs; and dozens of cases in which the visual sightings were confirmed by radar. In the majority of reports, two or more witnesses were involved in the sightings, and many of the observers were of high caliber-scientists, military personnel, pilots, air-traffic controllers, law-enforcement officers, and other responsible people.

The first quarter of 1981 brought more than 300 UFO reports, with high concentrations of sightings in California, Oregon, Texas, and North Carolina. That number is about average, according to astronomer Dr. J. Allen Hynek, director of the Center for UFO Studies, which receives over 1,000 new reports yearly.

Of course, the majority of UFOs turn out to be IFOs—identified flying objects. After rigorous checking by technically trained investigators, about 90 percent of UFO sightings prove to be misidentifications of natural phenomena or man-made objects-stars, planets, meteors, planes, balloons, or satellites. The rest of the reports elude explanation. They differ in many details, but there are also similarities: the shapes, colors, sounds and maneuverability of the objects.

The strongest suggestion of the reality of the phenomena rests in the approximately 10 percent of sightings that remain unidentified. The late University of Colorado physics professor Edward U. Condon, a hard-nosed UFO skeptic, conceded that these sightings were "indeed strange and mysterious, impossible by all current knowledge to explain." But to most who doubt that UFOs are real, the small percentage of unexplained sightings is negligible. The average detective doesn't have as good a track record in solving murders, says UFO debunker Philip Klass, an editor at *Aviation Week & Space Technology.*

Whether or not the unexplained cases imply a larger mystery hinges on the reliability of eyewitness testimony. In the investigation of a UFO sighting, the observer is usually the only data-gathering instrument. But the reliability of eyewitness testimony is itself a subject of great controversy in both law and science. Skeptics maintain that human observers are notoriously unreliable and that all UFO cases can be explained in mundane terms. "Details of specific reports are, by the very nature of the processes of human sensation, perception, cognition and reporting, likely to be untrustworthy," concluded psychology professor Michael Wertheimer in the Condon Report, a 1969 study made for the Air Force. It dismissed the phenomena as not worthy of scientific attention. "Any reports, even those of observers generally regarded as credible, must be viewed cautiously."

But other scientists insist that humans possess quite reliable and useful observational powers. Roger Shepard, a perceptual psychologist at Stanford University, argued, during hearings before the House Committee on Science and Astronautics in 1968, that human powers of recognition "surpass anything that we have yet been able to accomplish by physical instrument or machine." He went on to say: "When an event occurs without warning, leaves little time for careful observation and, indeed, occasions extreme fear or anxiety, the average witness often retains an accurate, almost photographic record of the event—a record, moreover, that can be largely recovered from him even though he lacks the words to describe it himself."

The skeptics claim that UFOs are merely carelessly observed objects or sometimes outright hoaxes. What, then, are we to make of the testimony of dozens—even hundreds—of disinterested observers who have reported UFOs over the years? Though many a science professional will shy away from reporting a UFO, fearing damage to reputation and career, a number of UFO reports by scientific observers are on record.

One such sighting was made by Clyde Tombaugh, the American astronomer who in 1930 discovered the planet Pluto. On August 20, 1949, Tombaugh, who was then working at the White Sands Missile Range in New Mexico, observed "two rows of faint rectangular lights, parallel to each other, that maintained their geometric relationship as they passed silently across the sky. The lights were yellow-green in color." His wife, who was with him at the time, thought she saw a faint connecting glow between the two rows. "I was so unprepared for such a strange sight that I was really petrified with astonishment," wrote Tombaugh. "I doubt that the phenomenon was any terrestrial reflection."

Tombaugh is one of many astronomers who have reported seeing UFOs. One of the first such reports was made nearly 100 years ago by a Mexican astronomer named José Bonilla, who was then the director of the Zacatecas Astronomical Observatory. On August 12 and 13, 1883, he and his assistant observed and photographed more than 400 apparently solid objects of various shapes and sizes as they moved in groups across the face of the sun.

Mysterious "green fireballs" observed over sensitive military installations in Los Alamos, New Mexico, during 1949 and 1950 were a matter of great concern to the Air Force and the FBI. The objects resembled meteors, but they were bright green and traveled horizontally at a low speed. Sightings were made by airline and military pilots, by security personnel and by scientists such as Dr. Lincoln LaPaz, an astronomer, who was put in charge of the investigations. LaPaz, then director of the Institute of Meteoritics and head of the department of mathematics and astronomy at the University of New Mexico, concluded that the fireballs were not natural phenomena. However, astronomer Donald Menzel of Harvard, who also witnessed the objects, was convinced they were no more than unusual meteors.

The British lunar astronomer Dr. H. Percy Wilkins noticed two silvery objects "like polished metal plates" moving against the wind and a third gray oval object in the sky over Atlanta, Georgia, on June 11, 1954. Dr. Wilkins calculated the UFOs to be nearly 50 feet in diameter.

Frank Halstead, then of the Darling Observatory at the University of Minnesota, Duluth, saw on November 1, 1955, a disk-shaped object trailing a cigar-shaped one over the Mojave Desert. The observation lasted about eight minutes, until the objects rose first slowly, then much faster until they could no longer be seen.

A French astronomer, Jacques Chapuis, observed a yellow starlike object for about five minutes from the observatory at Toulouse on November 10, 1957. The object ascended straight up until it was out of sight.

The staff of the observatory at Majorca reported seeing a triangular UFO that was spinning on its axis while on a steady course on May 22, 1960. The report was cabled to NASA.

In 1975, when Stanford University astrophysicist Peter Sturrock conducted a UFO survey of the 2,611 members of the American Astronomical Society, more than half of them responded, and 62 gave reports of events that they could not identify and that they thought might be related to the UFO phenomenon. More than half of the respondents believed that UFOs "certainly" or "probably" deserved scientific study.

Scientists from other disciplines have also reported UFOs. John Zimmerman, a geologist, watched as silvery disks looped around an aircraft and disrupted its vapor trail over California on June 12, 1950.

A formation of 15 rocket-like objects leaving odd, unvapor-like trails was seen over Ann Arbor, Michigan, on July 27, 1952, by Dr. Charles Otis, then professor of biology at Bowling Green State University. He heard no sound coming from the objects.

During the summer of 1948, Carl A. Mitchell, a physicist, observed three green disks as they passed over Easton, Pennsylvania, one second apart.

A Brazilian meteorologist, Rubens J. Villela, and five other witnesses observed a luminous tear-shaped UFO while aboard the icebreaker U.S.S. Glacier during the U.S. Navy's Operation Deep Freeze in March 1961. At one point, Villela reports, the multicolored object divided in two and then disappeared very suddenly. Its appearance, he said, was "out of this world."

A fairly recent UFO sighting by a reputable scientist and a well-respected journalist first came to public attention in an unlikely source: *The New Yorker.* In the October 27, 1980, issue, writer John McPhee tells of a "white sphere" that suddenly materialized outside the right-hand window of the truck in which he and Princeton geologist Kenneth Deffeyes were riding.

"It expanded some, like a cloud," writes McPhee of the incident, which took place north of Winnemucca, Nevada, on November 27,

1978. "Its light became so bright that we stopped finally and got out and looked up in awe. A smaller object, also spherical, moved out from within the large one, possibly from behind it. There was a Saturn-like ring around the smaller sphere. It moved here and there beside the large one for a few minutes and then went back inside.... After the small sphere disappeared, the large one rapidly faded and also disappeared." People within 100 miles of Winnemucca also reported seeing "that damn strange-looking thing in the sky," as McPhee calls it.

Another well-known sighting, by a former nuclear engineer who less than a decade later would become president of the United States, occurred in January 1969, in Leary, Georgia. There were about a dozen witnesses to this UFO, one of whom was Jimmy Carter. Over a 10-minute period, a sharply outlined light in the sky gradually approached the observers, then receded slightly, returned and finally moved away until it disappeared. Carter said the object grew to a size slightly smaller than the moon and changed color from blue to red. He estimated the light's distance to be perhaps 300 to 1,000 yards away.

The computer-systems analyst and author of the skeptical *The UFO Verdict,* Robert Sheaffer, is convinced that Carter's object was actually the planet Venus, which shone brightly in the western sky that night at the same angle above the horizon at which Carter thinks he saw a UFO.

The most likely sources of error in UFO observations are probably perception and memory. In perception, the brain analyzes the visual stimulus and interprets it on the basis of past experience. As a result, "one's visual perception is highly personal and variable," says Dr. Richard Haines, a NASA scientist who specializes in the problems of human perception and studies UFOs as a hobby. It is here, then, during the process of perception, that observers can misjudge sizes, distances, speeds and shapes. Another limitation of normal vision is autokinesis, an illusion in which a bright light in a field of view with no reference points will appear to move when stared at, even though it is stationary. Many observers looking at a bright star will mistakenly believe it to be moving rapidly, usually in an erratic way.

The other major problem with eyewitness UFO testimony is memory. Memory functions are complex, and the actual mechanisms involved are still unknown. What is known is that memory is sometimes subject to distortions, usually involuntary. Frank Drake, a professor of astronomy at Cornell University, reports that nearly half the details provided by meteor witnesses are inaccurate after the first day and that memory further deteriorates until, after five days, "people report more imagination than truth."

Most UFO data do not meet the strict guidelines of quality that most scientists feel are necessary to support a scientific inquiry. That UFOs are of fleeting appearance and not subject to laboratory analysis has long been considered a fatal drawback to a scientific investigation of the phenomenon. But neither reproducibility nor objectively recorded data are entirely justifiable demands. "No one wants to be asked to reproduce an eclipse or an aurora or very many other natural phenomena," says Philip Morrison, an MIT professor of physics. "Nor does it mean that scientific information, scientific evidence, must be quite 'hard,' in the sense that it must be recorded objectively without the specific intervention of a witness. Where would Darwin have been were this canon accepted altogether?"

That the case for the UFO must rest entirely on the large quantity of observational data is not such an unscientific proposition. "A witness is simply an extraordinarily subtle and complex instrument of observation," says Morrison. "I think a witness's statement should be regarded in much the same light as the reading of a barometer or the printout of a computer: a large number of judgments, influences, assumptions and hypotheses are necessary to interpret it. The analysis of that chain is the essential feature of scientific evidence."

Other than the observational data, there also exists a smaller quantity of physical data to sustain a scientific investigation of UFOs. Occasionally, UFOs will leave an ostensible "fingerprint" at the site of their appearance, physical traces such as broken branches, burned spots or depressions in the ground.

The "landing" at Delphos, Kansas, on November 2, 1971, is regarded by UFO proponents as a classic physical-trace case. That evening, 16-year-old Ronald Johnson observed a brightly illuminated object, about 10 feet in diameter with a bulge in the center, hovering about 2 feet above the ground. The rumbling noise that had alerted him to the presence of the object changed to a high-pitched sound like that of a jet as the object receded in the southern sky. His parents observed its departure and found in the area where Ronald first spotted the object a phosphorescent ring-shaped area on the ground. The glowing effect was later explained as moonlight reflecting from the ring's white surface. A large limb hanging over the edge of the ring was marked by what appeared to be heat blisters.

Dr. J. Allen Hynek has noted a growing interest among scientists in the UFO mystery over the years, largely because, he says, "the phenomenon simply refuses to go away." Perhaps scientists may be tempted as well by the realization that the data on UFOs do not fall altogether short of yielding solid evidence. "But the data do fall short in one grave respect," says Hynek. "The subject has never been treated professionally. We get people saying: Well, there's no hard data. My answer to that is that no real attempt has been made to get hard data."

The three investigations that most people point to as legitimate scientific studies were simply not professional, says Hynek. The Air Force's 17-year UFO investigation, known as Project Blue Book, had a tendency toward ridicule, and ridicule, he insists, is not part of the scientific method. In the Central Intelligence Agency's 1953 Robertson Panel report, little was said about the scientific investigation of UFOs, insists Hynek, who was a participant. And what about the Condon Report? Well, in a review of it, the American Institute of Aeronautics and Astronautics found a "paucity of thorough scientific and technological analysis."

"We always fall short of pushing through to the hard data because it takes funds to do it, and the funds are not available," Hynek says. "And I always like to point out that we would never have gotten to the moon if we had merely given the project to volunteers to work on during weekends."

Hynek is not alone in deploring the sad state of scientific UFO research. In 1979, the National Security Agency (NSA) released a 1968 draft document titled, "UFO Hypothesis and Survival Questions," which calls for a rigorous examination of the UFO problem by the scientific community. In the draft memorandum, the NSA analyst briefly considers some of the "human survival implications" suggested by the major UFO hypotheses. If the global incidence of UFOs is imaginary, he reasons, then a human mental aberration of alarming proportions would appear to be developing. If UFOs are hallucinations, he believes man's ability to distinguish reality from fantasy is brought into question. If UFOs are secret earthly projects, then the ability of our early-warning systems to correctly diagnose an air attack is in doubt. If UFOs are extraterrestrial, the analyst feels their source is probably our technological superior, and our planet is subject to conquest. All these hypotheses, he says, "have serious survival implications."

For the moment, UFOs are poised in a kind of scientific limbo, caught somewhere between the alarmist views of an anonymous intelligence analyst and the pooh-poohing of critics. No one will deny that the greater part of the phenomenon is illusory, i.e., IFOs, but this admission is not reason enough to lose track of the phenomenon's essential feature: whatever UFOs turn out to be, something extraordinary is happening.

CHAPTER 7

Writ of Habeas Corpus Extraterrestrial

Larry W. Bryant has been a "UFO friend" since my childhood. Though employed as a writer-editor for the Pentagon for much of his career, he managed to wage his battle against UFO secrecy on his own time. Retired now since 1994, Bryant continues to prod the government from his home/office in Alexandria, Virginia.

In 1983 Bryant filed an unusual pro se lawsuit that had both serious and amusing implications. It cried out: "Write me!" So I did, after getting Pamela Weintraub, the Antimatter editor at OMNI, interested in the story.

I wrote the story straight, so that those who wanted to take it seriously could, and those who wanted to laugh could do so as well. It appeared without a title in the "UFO Updates" section of those hard-to-read red Antimatter pages in the June 1984 issue of OMNI.

✳

"We wanted the court to consider the constitutional rights of visitors to this planet," says Larry W. Bryant, a career civil servant and an administrator for the group Citizens Against UFO Secrecy (CAUS). "According to the government's own documents [extraterrestrials] have been detained illegally and denied due process of law." So last summer Bryant decided to file a petition for a writ of habeas corpus extraterrestrial, claiming that the Air Force maintained custody over one or more occupants, "dead or alive" of crashed flying saucers.

"This was my latest attempt to break open the Cosmic Watergate," says Bryant, who has tried for the past 25 years to blow the lid off the government's alleged cover-up of UFOs. His petition held that "the capture and internment of any of the UFO crewmen constitutes an unwarranted deprivation of their freedom to travel" and that any postmortem on their corpses "violated their right to privacy and their right to be claimed intact by their relatives." As evidence, Bryant cited an authentic FBI memo, dated March 22, 1950, which notes that the Air force had recovered three flying saucers in New Mexico, each of which contained the bodies of three-foot-tall humanoids dressed in a fine metallic cloth.

"The Air Force treated the petition as a serious matter," says its spokesman, Captain John Whitaker, "just as we would any other court summons." Whitaker checked with the foreign-technology division at Wright-Patterson Air Force Base and the space-systems division at the Pentagon before reporting that "we do not now have, nor have we ever had, any extraterrestrial beings or spacecraft."

Despite these denials, the case appeared in U.S. District Court, in Washington, D.C., on a hot July afternoon. During the hearing, Bryant stated that the issue at stake "may transcend anything else this court will ever see." He called the evidence a smoking gun. But the judge was skeptical and asked: "Do you have anything except smoke?"

Bryant explained that the people in the military who had seen the crashed saucers and retrieved occupants were not coming forward because they had not been released from the oaths of secrecy they had taken while in service.

Royce Lamberth, the assistant U.S. attorney appearing on behalf of the Air Force, moved that the petition be denied on technical grounds. "The person bringing the writ, or his attorney, has to be authorized," he says, "and obviously since they have never talked to these extraterrestrials or met with them, they cannot represent them."

The judge, septuagenarian Oliver Gasch, ruled in favor of the defendant. "I didn't think the case had any merit," explains Gasch, "though it was imaginative, and it did create quite a bit of interest."

The judgment left Bryant unfazed. "It's just a momentary set-back," says the fierce civil libertarian, who is planning a renewed legal attack. So the ETs, if they exist, will just have to cool their heels in the federal icebox until Bryant gets another day in court.

✳

Postscript:

Larry W. Bryant was not discouraged by the outcome of this 1983 UFO-related lawsuit. In the decades to follow, he would file seven more such lawsuits against various government agencies.

In the mid-eighties Bryant began publishing advertisements in various military base newspapers soliciting evidence from "UFO-coverup whistleblowers." When officials at Peterson Air Force Base in Colorado balked at his ad submission, he filed a suit under the U.S. Privacy Act seeking access to employer-related records on himself generated at Peterson AFB. The judge in this 1986 action against the Air Force, which was filed in U. S. District Court for the District of Columbia, dismissed the case on the grounds that the records were being maintained in a system of records outside the purview of the Privacy Act.

Not surprisingly, Bryant's UFO-ad campaign touched off a countercampaign by Bryant's employer, the secretary of the Army's Office of Public Affairs. His superiors at the Pentagon not only conspired to have certain base public affairs officers impede his ad submissions but also targeted his official job performance ratings in order to muzzle him. Unfazed, Bryant counterpunched with a two-count suit against the Secretary of Defense Caspar W. Weinberger et al., filed in U. S. District Court for the Eastern District of Virginia (Alexandria) in 1986. On count one, Bryant reached a "consent order" by which the defendants agreed to cease interfering with Bryant's ad submissions. The other count of this First Amendment action—whether Bryant was entitled to "equitable relief" against the alleged on-the-job harassment by his employer—initially was won by the government, but subsequently was overturned via a review by the U. S. Supreme Court. A trial ensued on the merits of his reprisal claim, but Bryant failed to present enough evidence to convince Judge Claude Hilton that any reprisal had occurred.

Two years later Bryant was back in court. The issue this time was an FBI memorandum dated March 22, 1950, in which an informant had revealed the crash-landing and USAF retrieval of three occupied "flying saucers" in New Mexico. Bryant's 1988 Freedom of Information Act (FOIA) suit against the U. S. Department of Justice sought to compel the Federal Bureau of Investigation to disclose the censored part of its FOIA-released memorandum. This time the government argued, successfully, that to reveal the censored information would constitute an "unwarranted invasion of privacy," even though all the principals probably were deceased.

Bryant's next lawsuit again targeted the Justice Department. When world-renowned UFO researcher Stanton T. Friedman encountered a stone wall upon requesting a copy of his F.B.I. dossier, Bryant stepped in to assist the Canadian resident. But the judge in this 1989 suit, filed in U. S. District Court for the Eastern District of Virginia (Alexandria), accepted the FBI's summary-judgment affidavit without conducting an in-camera inspection of Friedman's classified dossier. The judge stated that he was not going to second-guess the Bureau in this matter of "national security."

Four years later, the CIA would feel the brunt of Bryant's litigious crusade against government UFO secrecy.

The lawsuit centered on a 1973 memo, released through the FOIA, about the Agency's 1965 effort to recruit UFO researcher Richard H. Hall. Bryant wanted to know the identity of the person(s) referred to in the memo: "[deleted] is not going to pursue the matter, however, [deleted] in their telephone conversation, suggested that we had not heard the last from Mr. Bryant." The judge in this 1990 case, filed in the U. S. District Court for the District of Columbia, sided with the Agency and its obligation to protect the privacy of its personnel and informants.

Shortly before his retirement from federal civil service, Bryant began submitting "UFO-coverup whistleblower" letters-to-the-editor to two Army-owned weekly newspapers in Washington, D.C. This effort, essentially a follow-up to his UFO ad campaign of the 1980s, continued Bryant's unrelenting pursuit of what he calls "the smoking gun of the Cosmic Watergate." When the newspapers refused to publish his letters-to-the-editor, Bryant went back to court. His reasoning? "Such a 'commercial enterprise newspaper'" said Bryant, "constitutes a 'designated public forum,' open to all comers regardless of message."

But the judge in this 1993 case against the secretary of the Army agreed in part and disagreed in part. His decision declared "facially invalid" an Army regulation's provision that "Commentaries and editorials may not extend to material not in consonance with policies of the Department of the Army." But he let stand the Army's arbitrary, content-based rejection of Bryant's letters, noting that "there is no evidence in the record to support the Plaintiff's allegation that these regulations have been unconstitutionally applied...."

Bryant's latest lawsuit represents yet another effort to force the government's hand on the UFO issue. In 2000 Bryant filed a Petition for a Writ of Mandamus against

Gov. James S. Gilmore III in the Circuit Court of the City of Alexandria, Va. The suit centered on the Virginia chief executive's constitutional and statutory duty to "protect the general welfare" of the state's citizenry—a duty which Bryant interprets as also helping to repel the invasive presence of so-called "flying triangles" as well as incidents of UFO-related abductions by perpetrators yet to be fully identified, apprehended, and brought to justice. After a brief hearing on the governor's motion to dismiss the case, the judge did so, noting that any such gubernatorial duty remains a matter of discretionary function.

Larry W. Bryant continues to be a thorn in the side of the U.S. government. We have indeed not heard the last from Mr. Bryant.

CHAPTER 8

The Hudson Valley UFO

Here is one UFO I saw myself. I was in Boston the year that most of the sightings occurred over Westchester County, New York, but in the years that followed I would see the Hudson Valley UFO more than once. One evening while living in Lake Peekskill, I heard a loud, low drone. By the time I went outdoors to see what was happening, the sound had stopped, but there, right overhead was a circle of lights—I don't remember exactly how many—moving slowly in perfect silence. It was an awesome sight.

THIS IS IT, I thought at first. But as I kept watching, eventually the droning sound started up again and the lights split off in different directions. I could tell at this point that this UFO was nothing more than a bunch of small planes—perhaps ultralights—flying in formation. I doubt this explains all the Hudson Valley sightings, but I'll bet it explains a lot of them. Once people look up expecting to see a UFO, more often than not they WILL see a UFO.

This was my second UFO story for OMNI and the beginning of a ten-year stint writing on the subject exclusively for the magazine. The untitled story appeared as a "UFO Update" in the Antimatter section of the February 1988 issue of OMNI.

✳

It has been called the most spectacular display in UFO history. During 1983 and 1984 more than 5,000 people living in the counties just north of New York City witnessed a huge, brilliantly lit, boomerang-shaped object parading over their cars, homes, and neighborhoods. The excitement was such that a conference held in Brewster, New York, drew more than 1,500 people and a horde of reporters from across the country. There was a palpable hunger for an explanation: What was seen in the sky?

The answers satisfied no one. If the UFO was a secret experimental aircraft, why was it flying over such a heavily populated area? If it was an extraterrestrial spaceship, why were government officials being so lackadaisical? And if it was nothing more than a bunch of sneaky stunt pilots flying their Cessnas in formation, as police suggested, why wasn't the Federal Aviation Administration raising a stink about it?

Afterward, the UFO fever that had gripped the Hudson Valley subsided. Then, last year, as Whitley Strieber's tale of his encounters with intelligent non-humans, *Communion,* hit the best seller lists, Peter Gersten, the attorney who had organized the original Brewster conference, decided it was time for another. "Strieber's abduction occurred in this area at about the same time that all these sightings had taken place," says Gersten. "I wanted to see if we could uncover any other abduction experiences."

Philip Imbrogno, a high-school science teacher and the primary investigator of the sightings in the area, says he has only about a dozen cases involving contact with aliens. "What is more interesting," he says, "is that some of the people who had close encounters with the object felt they were being probed. They were afraid of being caught. They felt an intelligence, a presence, there."

Meanwhile, as investigations continue, the boomerang itself has returned. It was seen in Waterbury, Connecticut, last summer and appeared in Dutchess County, New York, in the fall. Once again observers described the culprit as a "huge object with twenty to thirty lights." Actually, the UFO never really went away, according to Imbrogno, who has some 200 sighting reports on file for both 1985 and 1986.

Yet the critics long ago wrote off the Westchester flap. One of those, Jerry Clark, editor of the *International UFO Reporter,* is convinced that many of the sightings can be attributed to the "guys flying those planes." But, he adds cautiously, "I would be foolish if I declared that there was no real UFO sighting involved. I'm just saying that because the whole subject of UFOs is so controversial already, you cannot go to the scientific community with evidence that you yourself have to agree is contaminated. You need pure stuff, and this material is just not it."

But those who have seen the object may no longer care about proof or answers. Some 800 people turned up for the most recent Brewster conference, and everyone knew better than to believe speaker John Keel, author of *UFOs: Operation Trojan Horse,* when he said, "I'm going to tell you the secret of the flying saucers; then you can all go home." Everyone laughed. No one went home.

CHAPTER 9

Aliens 'R' Us

A veritable alien fever swept the country in the summer of 1987, following the release of Whitley Strieber's best selling book, COMMUNION. These frail beings with black, wrap-around eyes would soon become firmly entrenched in our cultural consciousness. Since I was now on the UFO beat for OMNI, I managed to wrangle a trip out to an annual gathering of abductees and contactees at the University of Wyoming.

The plane that flew me from Denver to Laramie was so small that the snack consisted of the co-pilot handing a bag of potato chips to the four passengers behind him. With me on the plane was University of Connecticut psychologist Ken Ring, who would go on to write THE OMEGA PROJECT, linking the abduction phenomenon to near death experiences.

When we arrived at the conference, it was clear that this was a gathering of believers. There was nary a trace of skepticism anywhere. But then where else would I have the opportunity to have a personal one-on-one with an alien? This untitled article appeared as a "UFO Update" in the Antimatter section of the April 1988 issue of OMNI.

✳

Aliens made all the headlines that week. But they were Mexicans. I was after aliens of another sort—the non-human kind. A good place to start, I thought, would be a conference of contactees and abductees held at the University of Wyoming. So I packed a tape recorder and an open mind and headed off for Laramie.

I was not disappointed. The highlight came in the course of introductions, when several people insisted I should talk to Ida

Kannenberg. We had something in common, they said. So I met Ida.

Ida is a pleasant, somewhat serious elderly woman who claims to have met the aliens in 1940 on Highway 10, near Desert Center, California. Later, under regressive hypnosis, she learned that two beings had come to her car and guided her to a "round cabin." Implants were placed in her nose, ears, and brain to let "them" hear and see through her. For eight years Ida has been in constant telepathic contact with one of those aliens.

When I introduced myself to Ida, she was startled. The reason? Her alien and I had strikingly similar names. My last name is Huyghe. His name is Hweig. I was born with mine. He had made up his from random letters. Ida then told me her alien would be interested in talking to me, and she offered to channel him for me. I accepted without hesitation.

So it was that at 11:45 on the night of July 12, 1987, I went to room 1720 of the Wyo Motel in Laramie and conversed, through Ida, with an alien with a name like mine. Huyghe meets Hweig.

His first word, "Hello," was spoken in a voice more measured and slightly deeper than Ida's. Following chitchat about our names, he asked if I had any questions.

I did, though I felt quite silly asking them. Where do UFOs come from? I began. He explained that they come from different planets, from interdimensional worlds, as well as from Earth. The latter are "pseudo-UFOs," he said. They are manufactured in Brazil by German refugees and are manned by depraved and power-hungry alien renegades who have interbred with the natives.

Should we fear the space people? He replied: "Some of the space people are here more for their own purposes and interests than they are to help Earth people. They are more clinically and scientifically minded. They do not have the compassion and emotions of Earth people. They are therefore ruthless in their abductions and examinations. But mostly you have to fear people of the earth."

I asked how to contact the space people, forgetting that he was one of them. He didn't catch the slip. "Don't call us, we'll call you.

You are acceptable. You will be contacted," he replied. Thanks. *Acceptable* is such a flattering word.

I had one last question: Does the government know about you? "We have worked with the U.S. government since 1926 in various ways. They don't know all about us—no one does. We have had occasions to give them information but never information that will lead to weapons or warfare."

At the end, Hweig said we would meet again. Later Ida told me more about Hweig. He looks like we do, she said, and for good reason. Hweig is half human. His mother is Russian, and he was born on Earth.

CHAPTER 10

A UFO Carjacking in Australia

When I took a three week vacation to Australia in January 1988 with my wife-to-be, I thought I was about as far from the UFO beat as I could possibly get. Wrong. On the day before our return to New York, I was relaxing by the hotel swimming pool when I opened up the day's newspaper and saw, splashed on the front page, a story about a UFO carjacking of all things.

The incident had occurred clear across the country in southwestern Australia, and I was on the northeast coast, which put a kibosh on any thoughts of personal investigation. So I did the next best thing and picked up copies of all the day's newspapers to see how the incident was being covered. The story also ran on radio and television stations.

When I returned home I called my editor at OMNI, who gave me the go-ahead to write up the story for the magazine. To get the latest scoop on the case, I had a long international phone conversation with one of the primary investigators of the incident. This untitled article appeared as a "UFO Update" in the Antimatter section of the June 1988 issue of OMNI.

✳

During the Australian bicentennial, Faye Knowles, forty-eight, and her three sons left their home in Perth for a holiday in Melbourne. Last January 20, at three A.M., the foursome were driving along the Erie Highway near Mundrabilia in the southern Australian desert when they noticed a strange light in the sky.

According to front-page newspaper stories published the next day, the brilliant, egg-shaped object terrorized the family for an hour and a half. It descended on their car, hoisted it into the air, then dropped it onto the road. The family scrambled into some roadside bushes and hid until the object departed. Then, after changing a tire and driving to Ceduna, they reported the incident to the police.

The Australians had a field day with the story. One cartoonist depicted the family running from their car as an alien in a UFO shouts, "Racists!" A UFO buff wanted to hypnotize the Knowleses to uncover a possible abduction. Charles Morgan of the Sydney Observatory believed the car had been hit by "a large carbonous meteorite shower." Peter Schwerdtfergger, a professor of meteorology at Flinders University, thought the family had run into a "dry thunderstorm."

One tire company took out a full-page ad in *The Australian*. Above a humorous sketch of a UFO lifting the car were the words IF ONLY THEY HAD STUCK WITH DUNLOP.

Meanwhile, representatives from Channel 7, a television station in Adelaide, had met the Knowleses and negotiated an exclusive contract for their story. But Keith Basterfield, field investigator for UFO Research-Australia, managed to sit in as the Knowleses told their story. Family members, he says, were still so distressed 36 hours after the episode that they could recall only a string of details: Sean, twenty-one, had been driving when a bright light approached the car. The family heard a thump on the roof and thought the light had landed there. No one remembered looking up and seeing anything protruding from the car top, nor did anyone remember looking out the window and seeing the road while the car was supposedly in the air. The luggage that had been strapped to the roof was gone.

Researchers from the Australian Mineral Development Laboratory examined the car for Channel 7 and concluded that the marks on the roof of the car were old and due to normal wear and tear.

Basterfield believes the Knowleses told "the truth as they saw it," but he thinks the facts point to a more mundane series of events: The family had been driving nonstop and became mesmerized by a light in the sky. A blowout occurred while Sean was driving. The family heard a thump as the luggage jolted loose. The right rear end of the car struck the ground, and Sean hit the brakes hard. The car vibrated as he tried to pull it off the road. The dogs barked. The Knowleses rolled down their windows and smelled a nasty smoke from the strained front brakes. The frightened family headed for the bushes.

The light remains a mystery, admits Basterfield, but this UFO probably did not pump iron. People make mistakes, just like the ad agency for the tire company. It turns out that the Knowleses' tires were Dunlops.

CHAPTER 11

NASA's Role in UFO Research

There are no secrets. Everything comes out eventually. You just have to be in the right place at the right time when the word comes out. In June of 1988 I was attending the annual meeting of the Society for Scientific Exploration, which is comprised of scientists who have an interest in anomalous topics such as UFOs, ESP, etc. One of the presenters was a professor of astronomy named Richard Henry and he was speaking out about NASA's involvement with UFOs. Henry could speak authoritatively on the subject because he was there when NASA decided how it would handle the UFO situation. My story appeared as an untitled "UFO Update" in the Antimatter section of the December 1988 issue of OMNI.

*

Question: Which government agency investigates physical evidence from UFOs? Answer: NASA.

"We stand ready to respond to any bona fide physical evidence from credible sources," says David Williamson, NASA's special assistant for policy integration and its point man on UFOs. That has been the policy, but NASA has not been terribly busy at it. In fact, they have analyzed only a few items, all of which proved to be as ordinary as the bottom of a cola bottle; one item sent in turned out to be just that.

"We never found anything non-terrestrial," says Williamson, "anything that was so extraordinarily different, or anything unavailable on Earth."

NASA got involved in the UFO business in 1977, when Frank Press, the science adviser to President Carter, asked the agency to take over all the UFO mail pouring in to the White House. Press also had wondered whether NASA shouldn't investigate any new findings on the subject since the last official investigation in 1969.

Richard Henry, now a professor of astronomy at Johns Hopkins University, has recently provided a behind-the-scenes look at just how NASA handled this sensitive request. Henry knows, because back then he worked in the Office of Space Science, the NASA branch that made the decision. Henry recalls that it was David Williamson, assistant for special projects, who eventually drafted the NASA reply to Frank Press's request.

In an early memo Williamson had weighed NASA's options: If NASA refused there would be charges of a cover-up. But any NASA commitment to some review of the phenomenon, Williamson realized, would not satisfy the believers if the results were negative or the critics if the results were positive. Besides, such a task might place considerable demands on NASA manpower and finances.

The final proposal: NASA would not "establish a research activity in this area," yet it would analyze any hard evidence on UFOs offered to it.

Is NASA's ambivalent attitude part of an organized cover-up? Henry doesn't think so. "I think it's just that officials at NASA had other, more important things to do," he says.

Williamson explains the reason behind the final decision this way: "NASA didn't try to figure out whether UFOs should be studied," he says, "but whether they could be studied at all." NASA decided that they could not. But if physical evidence comes in from credible people, then it should be NASA's responsibility to look it over. "There must be someplace," Williamson explains, "where an analysis of such material can be trusted."

Williamson's knowledge and open-mindedness on the subject puzzle people. It turns out, however, that back in the winter of 1952-53, Williamson, while on night guard duty at Fort Leonard Wood, Missouri, saw a white light cross his line of sight, stop, and then suddenly zip away, "almost like in a cartoon." He was later grilled on his sighting by "intelligence types." One admitted that radar had picked up the same object. And to this day, Williamson says, the sighting is listed as "unidentified."

CHAPTER 12

First Communion

At the same conference where I heard the NASA story, I ran into Jungian scholar Dennis Stillings, who happened to mention that Whitley Strieber's experiences in COMMUNION reminded him of an episode in the life of psychologist Carl Jung. What he found when he looked into it was worth a short mention in the Antimatter section of the December 1988 issue of OMNI.

*

Just about everyone now knows of Whitley Strieber's nighttime encounter with small entities and UFOs from his best seller *Communion.* "Very much like Strieber's experience, but largely unmentioned," notes researcher Dennis Stillings, is what a world-renowned psychologist encountered some 60 years earlier in Switzerland and recounted in his autobiography *Memories, Dreams, Reflections.*

The psychologist was Carl Jung. One night in the spring of 1924 he woke up hearing noises outside his secluded home in Bolligen. He looked out the window and saw no one, so he returned to bed and went back to sleep. But once more Jung said he heard footsteps, talk, laughter, and music and had "the visual image of several hundred dark-clad figures." He thought they might be boys in their Sunday clothes. He got up again and saw a "deathly still moonlit night." Said Jung, "I felt obliged to consider the possibility of its reality."

Years later, in October 1958, Jung dreamed of two gleaming discs "flying directly toward me." One came within four or five hundred yards. When Jung awoke, he thought, *We always think that the UFOs are projections of ours. Now it turns out that we are their projections.*

All this led Stillings, a Jungian scholar in Minnesota, to wonder if Jung had believed in extraterrestiral craft manned by intelligent beings. So he contacted Marie-Louise von Franz, a colleague who had worked with Jung for 40 years. "The answer," said Stillings, "was a definitive and straightforward no."

CHAPTER 13

Enfant Terrible

All but four of the UFO stories that I ever wrote for OMNI appeared in the magazine. This is one that never did. The story concerns one of the mystery men of UFOlogy, Richard Doty, a USAF sergeant assigned to the Air Force Office of Special Investigations. In the mid-1980s, Doty had close ties to William Moore, a UFO researcher who in 1989 publicly admitted to having had a long career as a "controlled informant" to the U.S. government on UFOs. Doty's then parent agency, the Air Force Office of Special Investigations, serves as a counter-intelligence organization whose personnel have long been suspected of helping execute disinformation activities in the UFO field. What remains unclear is whether Doty's UFO-related activities in this regard had official sanction, or simply represented the private hobby of a renegade. Inquiring minds want to know—including some in the CIA apparently. (More about this in the postscript to this story and later in this book.) This may well be turn out to be the story of a cat chasing its own tail.

✳

If *People* magazine had an interest in UFOs, Richard C. Doty would be on the cover. When he first came to the attention of UFO researchers nearly a decade ago, Doty was serving as a special agent for the Air Force Office of Special Investigations (AFOSI). A series of unidentified aerial lights had appeared over the restricted test range of Kirtland Air Force Base outside Albuquerque, New Mexico, during August of 1980, and Doty, who was stationed there, had prepared the official report on the incident.

Three years earlier Doty had been at Ellsworth Air Force Base in

South Dakota when an alleged Air Force document dated November 1977 told of a shootout between UFO aliens and Ellsworth security guards. When New York attorney Peter Gersten met with Doty in 1983, Doty reportedly impressed upon Gersten the significance of this case. Not true, says Doty. "I never heard of that incident until after I left Ellsworth. It's a complete hoax."

In 1983 Denver television producer and animal mutilation researcher Linda Howe met with Doty at Kirtland to gather information for a documentary she was putting together on UFOs for HBO. She says that during their conversation Doty showed her a "Briefing Paper for the President of the United States" on UFOs. The content, she recalls, involved crashed UFOs, the retrieval of extraterrestrial bodies, and direct contact with the aliens.

Doty denies this scenario also. "The only thing I showed her," he says, "was a Project Blue Book report. It did admit that there were a number of unexplained sightings, and it did say that each president had been briefed on Blue Book, but that's all it says." Blue Book is the name of the Air Force project charged with investigating UFOs until 1969. The fact that Doty has an uncle who was an investigator for Blue Book has raised more than a few eyebrows among UFO researchers.

Suspicions seem to hound Doty. In 1981 a UFO group received an anonymous letter from a person claiming to be an airman at Kirtland. The informant related the story of a visiting air cadet, Craig R. Weitzel, who had photographed a landed UFO and seen an individual in a metallic suit leave the craft. The letter mentions that Doty investigated the case.

When interviewed about the sighting years later, the air cadet pointed out that the letter's account bore no resemblance to the real story. He claimed only to have seen a hovering object the size of a dime held at arm's length. Barry Greenwood of Citizens Against UFO Secrecy suspects Doty's involvement in the letter. The typewriter used to produce the "leaked" letter is thought to be the same as the one used to produce the 1980 Kirtland report signed by Doty.

Doty admits that the air cadet reported a sighting to him, but absolutely denies having written the anonymous letter. He knows the typefaces are dissimilar, he says, because it's been the subject of a government investigation. "All this has caused me trouble at work," he says. "I was investigated by the FBI a number of times. I've had to take polygraph examinations. But I passed every one of them. I've been exonerated."

In the fall of 1987 Doty retired from the Air Force, having spent his last two years of service as a "food service specialist," a position totally outside his career field in security and counterintelligence. "The Air Force people I spoke to felt that this meant he was being punished," says Greenwood, "and they dumped him in food services to ride out his term."

Not so, says James Bennett, then assistant chief of personnel at Kirtland, who signed Doty's release papers. "A few years ago," he explains, "security police was so over-manned and food services had such a shortage that they had an involuntary retraining."

Doty has yet another explanation. He says he accepted the position after being asked to leave AFOSI for his having performed "unauthorized" actions in a counterespionage operation in West Germany in 1986.

Such explanations do little do dispel the mystery surrounding Doty, who became a sergeant in the New Mexico State Police after his retirement from the Air Force. Doty's personal belief in UFOs also leaves much left unsaid. "If I should base my decision on information that I had access to during my government service, I would have to say, yes, Earth has been visited. However," he adds, "I am not 100-percent certain that the information I had access to was entirely accurate."

✳

Postscript:
Like the Energizer bunny the Doty stories go on and on and on.

It turns out that Doty played a key role in the sad case of government contractor Paul Bennewitz. His family owned Thunder Scientific Corporation, which provides Kirtland Air Force Base in Albuquerque, New Mexico with "humidity generation, calibration and measurement instruments," according to the sign outside their office. In the late 1970s Bennewitz filmed mysterious lights in the sky and became convinced that he was monitoring electromagnetic signals that extraterrestrials were using to control the people they had abducted. He also became convinced that the aliens had underground bases near Albuquerque and others near Dulce, New Mexico. Being a good citizen, Bennewitz eventually went to the Air Force with his suspicions and that's where he met Special Agent Richard Doty of the Office of Special Investigations.

Doty realized that Bennewitz had "accidentally tapped into a supposedly secure communications system at Kirtland," according to Jim Moseley, the editor of SAUCER SMEAR, the wonderfully trashy gossip rag of the UFO community. "The coded messages he was receiving were genuine, but he was grossly misinterpreting them. It was Doty's job to misdirect Bennewitz into continuing to believe the messages were actually for the aliens." Doty admitted all this in a telephone call with Moseley in the spring of 2000.

Doty has also been more specific about his knowledge of UFOs. In a subsequent letter to the editor of SAUCER SMEAR, Doty wrote: "I don't have the belief that some might think. The truth is this: Two alien spacecraft crashed in the desert of New Mexico in the summer of 1947. Our Government recovered five bodies and one live alien. That alien lived until 1952. The recovered spacecraft were transported to Wright-Patterson for examination and then on to several secret locations. That is it. To the best of my knowledge we have not been visited since. We don't have any UFOs at Area 51. We might still have some remnant of the crashed craft from 1947. The bodies were preserved but I have no knowledge as to their location.

"During my OSI days, I did perform disinformation operations against many different targets, but everything I did was sanctioned by our Government. I never did anything as a maverick."

What are we to make of Doty? In an interview with Joan d'Arc for PARANOIA magazine, Dan T. Smith, a physicist turned metaphysician and eschatologist in the Washington, D.C. area, stated: "Rick Doty has probably contributed more to the UFO-government conspiracy rumors than everyone else combined. He has done so while in the government employ, and maintaining high level contacts in the intelligence community."

One of Doty's contacts was a mysterious "DIA man" in Washington,D.C. It is widely believed that this man was Lt. Col. Roland B. Evans, who as a Defense Intelligence Agency officer wrote the glowing evaluation of a 1976 case involving a Iranian jet's encounter with a UFO. Evans is also thought to be the one who handed NICAP the Loring Air Force Base documents of 1975. After leaving the DIA, Evans was transferred to the Strategic Air Command HQ in Omaha. Some suspect Evans of being the mastermind behind several hoaxed government UFO documents, though this makes no sense given his access to real UFO documents.

In the late 1990s Ron Pandolfi, the CIA's "keeper of the weird" asked Dan Smith and a low-key UFO researcher by the name of Bill LaParl to collect all the data available on Rick Doty and his alleged source, the "raven." LaParl's dozen page report with its supporting documents was apparently quite thorough. This report was circulated in some pretty high offices, perhaps even to the commander-in-chief, according to rumor. The situation led Smith to wonder: "How can one staff sergeant cause so much heart burn....?"

CHAPTER 14

Cancer and UFOs

Does exposure to UFOs cause cancer? Not exactly. But I thought that the notion suggested by a leading Canadian experimental neuropsychologist in an issue of the monthly MUFON UFO JOURNAL, the field's premier periodical while edited by Dennis Stacy, had some merit. After all, cancer and UFOs sounded like quite a volatile mix of topics, though certainly more in the flavor of the NATIONAL ENQUIRER than of the NEW ENGLAND JOURNAL OF MEDICINE. My story appeared untitled as a "UFO Update" in the Antimatter section of the February 1989 issue of OMNI.

✳

These days, cancer seems to lurk behind everything we eat, drink, and do. So it should come as no surprise that investigating UFOs may bring on the disease as well. That, at least, is the warning issued by Canadian neuropsychologist Michael Persinger, one of the world's leading authorities on the effects of magnetic fields.

According to Persinger, a professor at Laurentian University of Sudbury in Ontario, the danger does not come from extraterrestrial weapons or from deadly green rays but rather from intense natural electromagneitc fields. That's because most UFOs, says Persinger, are simply "luminous phenomena produced by extremely energetic geo-physical forces," such as the movement of the earth's crust.

Similar low-frequency fields, Persinger says, are routinely expe-rienced by electrical engineers and technicians and by those living near overhead power lines. And studies of these groups indicate that they are likely to suffer a higher risk of brain tumors and leukemia, as well as depression and suicide, than the normal population.

These complications are also a concern for the UFO buff, adds Persinger, "particularly for those who spend literally hours, if not days, out in the field."

Persinger is not suggesting that people stop investigating UFOs. Nor does he suggest that all those who investigate UFOs will develop brain tumors or other cancers. (Not everyone who smokes, he notes, gets lung cancer.) But, he warns, UFO researchers should take precautions like bringing detection equipment to do the dirty work and try to keep exposures down.

Persinger's evidence for the UFO-cancer theory, many critics believe, is slim. It's true that at least two UFOlogists—including J. Allen Hynek, the father of the field—have died of brain tumors. And at least two others are known to have committed suicide.

But UFO researchers are not impressed with these examples. "I think it's just a crazy coincidence," says John Keel, author of *Disneyland of the Gods,* who spent four years in the field investigating UFOs in the mid-Sixties. "Probably just as many UFOlogists have died of appendicitis."

And Mutual UFO Network (MUFON) director Walt Andrus, who first published Persinger's warning in the *MUFON UFO Journal,* says: "I was afraid to even publish the article, because I thought it might scare people away. But that has not occurred." MUFON has about 1,000 investigators across the country, Andrus adds, and no one has resigned due to the recent report.

Persinger, however, counters that while many researchers write about UFOs, few actually spend much time in the field. This lack of exposure, he adds, means that UFO researchers may not be the best population in which to demonstrate his hypothesis.

Toward that end, Persinger has begun examining cancer records in areas that have been repeatedly exposed to the luminous displays otherwise known as UFOs. If he is correct, Persinger says, these areas should show a rise in cancers and depressive disorders within five years of the time a spate of sightings occurs.

CHAPTER 15

Past-Life Aliens

Much discussion has taken place trying to explain why, if aliens exist and have visited our planet, they have yet to take over the Earth. While I was out at the Laramie UFO conference in the summer of 1987, I came across the wildest explanation yet, though it's probably as good as any if you are prepared to accept the basic premise. This short item, titled "Past-Life Aliens," appeared in the Antimatter section of the February 1989 issue of OMNI.

✳

Why do so many UFO abductees and contactees believe in reincarnation? Why, if there are extraterrestrials (ETs), have they not taken over the Earth? Those are the kinds of questions being pondered by James Deardorff, a retired professor of atmospheric sciences at Oregon State University.

Deardorff first noticed that the belief in reincarnation is far more widespread among abductees and contactees than among the general population. "The level in the general population is about twenty-three percent," says Deardorff. "Those who know abductees well, however, claim that they essentially all believe in it."

In many cases, adds Deardorff, people report flashbacks from their past lives in the years following their abductions. Still others learn that they were themselves aliens in a past life.

But it didn't dawn on Deardorff why reincarnation beliefs would go hand in hand with alien contact until he began thinking that the ETs themselves just might hold the same beliefs. He now thinks that a reincarnation ethic would explain why planet Earth hasn't been invaded by UFOs.

"Killing everyone on the planet would be bad Karma," explains Deardorff. "Besides the souls would live on. And what if those human souls were to reincarnate as ETs? Would they really want that?"

CHAPTER 16

B-2 or not 2-B?

Secret government devices probably rank as the
leading contender for explaining UFOs—after the more
popular belief that UFOs are piloted by alien ETs. Those
large, dark, wing-shaped UFOs certainly resemble the
stealth aircraft that the Air Force has been producing of
late. It's also worth noting that the number of wing-shaped
(or boomerang-shaped or triangular) UFOs being reporting
has skyrocketed since the late 1970s, eclipsing the
traditional "flying saucer," which clearly must be an
earlier model. But if that's the case, how could the Air
Force's wing-shaped aircraft be responsible for the
sightings that started it all back in 1947? My story
appeared as an untitled "UFO Update" in the Antimatter
section of the April 1989 issue of OMNI.

✳

It made its official debut in Palmdale, Califomia, on November 22,
1988. A wing-shaped airplane with a black underside and no tail,
this supersecret B-2 Stealth bomber was so new, the Air Force said,
that it had yet to fly.

Or had it? "Very definitely the Stealth has been seen here," says
Dan Gordon, the news and sports director for radio station WYVE-
AM in Wytheville, Virginia. "I've got twenty-twenty vision, and I saw
it fly over my car."

To make himself heard, Gordon has just written a book called
Don't Look Up, about the more than 3,000 reports of UFOs over this
small town in the mountains of Virginia since October 1987. Most of
the sightings have been of dark, wing-shaped craft resembling the
Stealth bomber. Says Gordon, "Unless someone has five hundred million dollars to produce a similar craft, there's no way this flying wing
could be anything else."

Gordon's claims would be easy to dismiss if Virginia were the only state in the nation plagued by wing-shaped UFOs. But similar reports have emerged elsewhere with surprising regularity. More than a decade ago, for instance, the Lumberton, North Carolina, area was swamped with reports of V-shaped craft. And in recent years similar objects were reported in the skies of central Ohio and Westchester County, New York.

Could any of these UFO reports be attributed to surreptitious test flights of the B-2? "The B-2 has not flown, period," says an exasperated Major Pat Mullaney of Air Force public affairs. "I have dealt with that question time and time again. As soon as we acknowledged the existence of the flying wing, even though it hadn't been rolled out of the hangar yet, we've had people say, 'Oh, I've seen that thing flying.' Absolutely no way."

The Air Force did, of course, fly such craft in 1946, when the then-secret XB-35 and its jet-powered counterpart, the YB- 49, were tested in the skies over Southern California. These craft were the culmination of a decade of flying-wing development by the Northrop Corporation, the same company that is responsible for the B-2 bomber today.

UFO activist Peter Gersten, however, points out that the early Northrop flying wings were being tested just as the UFO era got under way. Keeping this in mind, Gersten, a New York attorney, has been trying to link the development of the XB-35 and other experimental craft to those first UFO reports of 40 years ago.

Central to Gersten's theory: the notion that at least one of the objects seen by Kenneth Arnold over Washington State on June 24, 1947, was a Northrop flying wing. According to Gersten, Arnold's original account refers to nine "bright objects" without "tails" that fluttered and tipped their "wings." Arnold's illustration of one of the craft even indicates that it was crescent-shaped. "The clincher," says Gersten, "is a photograph taken in the late Forties showing nine of these flying wings on a runway in California. Arnold himself thought he saw something the government was testing. That was everybody's first thought."

CHAPTER 17

Fly That Saucer

If I had to point to a year when the UFO business got completely out of hand, I would have to say 1989. Like cream rising to the top, all the wacky stories suddenly rose to the fore, obscuring all other UFO matters completely. Before 1989 you had a crash story or two, rumor of an alien body here or there, or an unusually wooly UFO encounter. But now you had dozens of crashes, dead aliens everywhere, government collusion with ETs, humans test-flying alien craft, underground alien bases farming human body parts, soul-sucking aliens in humongous motherships, and on and on and on. There was now a "can you top this" quality to UFO stories. The following story epitomizes this trend. It appeared as an untitled "UFO Update" in the Antimatter section of the September 1989 issue of OMNI.

✳

John Lear loves to fly. A captain for a major charter airline, he's flown airliners, seaplanes, fighters, gliders, gyroplanes, and heli-copters—160 different types of aircraft all told, including the Learjet designed by his father, William P. Lear, Sr. But he has never flown a flying saucer, and he says he's jealous of those who have.

Lear believes that since 1947 the U.S. government has recovered at least 30 flying saucers belonging to alien civilizations. And, he claims, some of these have been test-flown by U.S. government personnel from Groom Lake, Nevada, under a secret program called Project Redlight. What's more, he declares, the United States government currently has at least 30 frozen alien bodies, representing three different alien civiliza-tions, in storage at Wright-Patterson Air Force Base, Homestead Air Force Base, and CIA headquarters in Langley, Virginia.

But not all the aliens the government deals with are dead. "The U.S. government has been in business with little gray extraterrestrials for about twenty years," says Lear, who gets his information from published UFO literature, personal contacts in the intelligence community, and government documents both genuine and alleged. In fact, he says, by the early seventies, the United States had made a deal with these creatures: "In exchange for technology we promised to ignore their abduction of humans and mutilation of cattle."

The government, says Lear, was led to believe that these activities were simply part of an ongoing effort to monitor our developing civilization. This was not the case. Instead, he says, the aliens, whose digestive systems have atrophied, extract hormones and enzymes and feed themselves by applying a solution of this material directly on their skin.

The human and animal body parts are processed in huge underground alien bases on Earth, says Lear. New Mexico, the "Land of Enchantment," is thought by some of Lear's intelligence sources to be the home of three of these bases, located near Dulce, Datil, and Sunspot. Witnesses, adds Lear, report seeing hundreds of huge vats with human body parts floating in an amber fluid. "We are in deep, serious trouble," says Lear, "and the public needs to know about it now."

These bold statements have made Lear an extremely controversial figure in the UFO field. "I don't wish to repudiate his claims," says Leonard Stringfield, who has spent decades researching reports of UFO crashes and retrievals. "But I would rather be cautious and refer to those sorts of things as rumor rather than fact."

Walt Andrus, international director of the Mutual UFO Network, comments, "Some people say it's way-out material. But it might be true. Who knows?"

"He's a very colorful character," says Jim Moseley, editor of *Saucer Smear*, "who has capitalized to some degree on his father's name. I don't happen to believe a word of what he says, but it's a lot of fun."

As for Lear, he says he saw U.S. government personnel "test an alien spacecraft" last March. It was his first personal encounter with the alien force.

CHAPTER 18

UFOs Framed

Physicist Bruce Maccabee, who just happens to work for the Navy, is an expert at analyzing UFO photographs. His work is widely respected, or at least it was until he came down in favor of the reality of the Gulf Breeze UFO photographs.

You'll notice that the skeptic quoted in this story about a Maccabee UFO photo analysis is Phil Klass. He has appeared in many of my UFO stories over the years, for several reasons. Since American journalism strives for balance and "fairness," both sides of a controversy must appear in the story. In other words, editors require an opposing point of view. Sometimes the requirement goes to the extreme, but often, on the subject of UFOs, it's a good idea.

Now, the reason I went to Phil Klass repeatedly over the years is that there are so few skeptics actually qualified to speak on the subject. Most skeptics just exude hot air; they simply don't know the subject. Klass, for the most part, does. He even publishes a newsletter on the subject called the SUN (Skeptics UFO Newsletter). But I had one other reason for using Klass as my skeptic: his sense of humor. This little item, titled "UFOs Framed," appeared in the September 1989 issue of OMNI.

✳

The notion that pictures are worth a thousand words doesn't apply to UFOs. For one thing, bright smudges of light against a dark background don't allow experts to pin a size on the so-called objects. For another, the obscure images might be a few inches or tens of miles from the lens. But now, some experts say, the photos taken by the controversial "Mr. Ed" of Gulf Breeze, Florida, are an exception. Since last November, Mr. Ed has taken dozens of Polaroid shots and a videotape of UFOs. Some of these photos were taken by special cameras provided or suggested by such UFO investigators as Maryland physicist Bruce Maccabee, an expert in optics. Particularly revealing for Maccabee are a pair of frames from a set of stereo photographs taken by dual Polaroid Sun cameras. Maccabee's analysis measured one cylindrical UFO in the photographs to be more than 20 feet wide. A second object was judged to be smaller, about two and a half feet long.

"This small object could indicate that there are six-inch aliens or that ten-foot aliens have remotely piloted vehicles," says Maccabee, anticipating jokes about "tight quarters." But he believes that "the probability of a hoax is smaller than the probability that it's real."

Skeptic Phil Klass, who examined the most suspicious of the photographs rather than the best, believes otherwise. "I'm convinced that the photos are ninety percent authentic and ten percent hoax," he says. "The authentic parts are the trees, the bushes, and the light pole. The hoax part is the UFO."

CHAPTER 19

AWOL in UFO Heaven

My editor at OMNI approved just about every UFO story I proposed, and just about all the stories I wrote for the magazine actually appeared in print. But there were a few exceptions—including this one—and I have no idea why. The mix of UFOs and politics certainly seemed worthy, and my reporting on it managed to beat all the published accounts hands-down.

You will note that I never personally interviewed the participants in this escapade. Their lawyer disallowed it. Perhaps they were keeping the story for themselves, in order to better capitalize on it later on. Indeed, a few years later, one of the key players, Vance Davis, did just that, writing UNBROKEN PROMISES: A TRUE STORY OF COURAGE AND BELIEF (with Brian Blashaw). The appendix of their book reproduces a number of INSCOM documents on the case which were freed-up by the FOIA.

✳

At three o'clock in the morning on July 14, 1990, police pulled over a 1971 Volkswagen van with a set of broken tail lights. It was just the sort of incident that David Lynch, creator of "Twin Peaks," might have used to kickoff one of his bizarre celluloid melodramas. But this was real life. The place was Gulf Breeze, a little Florida beach town that has been a hotbed of UFO activity for the past couple of years.

Police officers running a check on the driver of the "improperly equipped" vehicle learned that Pfc. Michael Hueckstaedt was a wanted man and placed him under arrest. Husckstaedt, it turns out, was one of six soldiers with top-level security clearances absent without leave, or AWOL, from an intelligence unit at an electronic listening post in Augsburg, West Germany.

Shortly afterwards, according to Gulf Breeze police chief Jerry Brown, the Army, FBI, and CIA swooped into town. "They wanted them mighty bad," he says. The sole female member of the group, Sgt. Annette Eccleston, was arrested at a nearby campground, and the other four, including Spec. Kenneth Beason, were found at the home of Anna Foster in nearby Pensacola. Beason had met Foster, a local psychic, the previous year during his training in cryptology at the Navy's Cory Station in Pensacola. Federal authorities suspected the soldiers of espionage and decided to confiscate Foster's computer and floppy disks.

Beason, it seems, was the group's leader. He had told Stan Johnson, a friend of his with a photography business back home in eastern Tennessee, that they were coming to Gulf Breeze to prepare for the end of the world and the second coming of Jesus Christ. The group, which was portrayed as a cult in some press accounts, believed Christ to be an alien who would return in a spaceship, landing in Gulf Breeze to rescue believers before the Earth is destroyed eight years hence. The beginning of the end, Beason told Johnson in July, would come on August 4th, when Lebanon invades Israel.

The "Augsburg 6" had left their posts with the 713th Military Intelligence Battalion in West Germany using forged leave papers and rendezvoused in Gulf Breeze. After their arrests, they were transferred to Fort Benning, Georgia, the nearest Army installation, and later were brought, under MP escort, to Fort Knox, Tennessee, one of four "personnel containment facilities" in the United States. There they were processed as deserters.

A subsequent investigation by the U.S. Army Intelligence and Security Command, however, cleared the soldiers of espionage. "These were not troublemakers," says Maj. Ron Mazzia with Army Public Affairs at Fort Knox. "This was the first blemish on their records." As a result, their desertion charges were downgraded to AWOL, and in lieu of a court martial, they were offered "Article 15," a non-judicial punishment involving a loss of rank and a half-month's pay. The six were then discharged from the Army.

The bizarre little episode raised many questions and provided ample grist for the rumor mill. "It kind of shakes your faith in the Army's psychological screening of the folks who do military intelligence jobs," says Chuck Vinch, a reporter who covered the story for *The Stars and Stripes* military newspapers. "But nobody really knows what was at the core of this. There were rumors that they were on some kind of spy mission and the whole thing was concocted to let the Army absolve themselves of responsibility. This was bolstered in some people's minds by the fact that they got such light sentences. They were basically told to just slide out of the Army and forget about it."

But the six did not get off easily, insists Mazzia. "By virtue of their positions and their jobs they got hit a lot harder than if they had been normal soldiers and gone AWOL," he explains. If they had not had access to secret information, a sergeant might have just "chewed their butts out and given them some extra work." They were given a quick discharge in part because they expressed no remorse. "They didn't think they had done anything wrong," says Mazzia, "and even indicated that they probably would have done it again."

Since their release the Augsburg 6 have refused all requests to be interviewed. But Johnson reports that Beason now has changed his story somewhat. He's apparently playing down the alien and spiritual angle, but continues to believe that their initial prediction was—but for minor details—essentially correct. The big event happened on the 2nd of August, not the 4th; and it was Iraq invading Kuwait, not Lebanon invading Israel.

This curious bit of information, explains Johnson, had been channeled psychically through Spec. Vance Davis. But since their jobs in West Germany involved intercepting and decoding enemy communications, it seems more likely that one or more of the six might have come across some scrap of intelligence while on duty that led them to believe that something of this sort would be happening shortly in the Middle East.

Upon discharge the six were issued travel tickets home, but at least three of them returned immediately to Gulf Breeze instead. Police chief Jerry Brown admits to keeping an eye on them. "It's not that they've done anything wrong and we have no charges pending against them. It's more or less just to see what they are doing." Brown believes that the military made a mistake telling everyone they were part of a cult. He prefers to dismiss the whole affair, saying: "They were just here to rest and regroup before heading out west." Clearly, Brown would be glad to see the UFO hysteria that has swept his little town go west as well.

CHAPTER 20

Superqualified Observers

I've often been fooled into thinking that something unusual I've seen in the sky might be THE REAL THING. Not Coca-Cola, but an honest-to-goodness flying saucer from outer space. All but one time was I able to explain what I saw. That exception occurred when I was nine years old. One evening I saw a curious object flying perpendicular to the flight path into Langley Air Force Base in Virginia. As an airplane buff at the time, I could identify what kind of plane was flying overhead merely from the sound it made as it passed over our house.

This one made no sound. It was orange-colored, probably because of the late afternoon sun. It made no unusual moves and I cannot recall how it disappeared. It was not all that unusual, just that I could not identify it in the limited amount of time that I had to observe it. So, yes, I saw a "UFO." But I'll never in a million years claim that it was the real thing.

That parable, then, helps reiterate a simple point: not every UFO is an alien craft. And even the most trained observers can make mistakes. The following story appeared as an untitled "UFO Update" in the Antimatter section of the August 1990 issue of OMNI.

✳

You can't ask for a more qualified observer than Patricia Reiff, senior research scientist in the department of space physics and astronomy at Rice University. Early one night last summer she spotted a small, very bright cloud in the clear western skies over Hickley,

Texas. She called it to the attention of her family, and within five minutes the cloud had expanded fourfold and dimmed considerably.

More than 50 people in five separate cities more than 200 miles apart saw it as well. Virtually every witness reported an object in the same shape and in about the same position—roughly halfway between the stars Arcturus and Spica. Reiff calculated the cloud to be at least 700 miles away and nearly 350 miles up.

The cloud resembled a gas release from a sounding rocket, but a launch, Reiff thought, was unlikely to have been scheduled on a Saturday night with scattered thunderstorms forecast around the country. She called the White Sands Missile Range in New Mexico and learned that no missiles had been fired than night and that a test laser, developed by the star-wars program to shoot down aircraft drones and low-flying objects, was not functioning at the time. Checks with NASA/Goddard Space Flight Center, Vandenberg Air Force Base, and others failed to resolve the mystery.

"It's also unlikely that it could have been the aftermath of a fireball-type meteor," says Reifff, "since most meteors disintegrate at lower altitudes. But none of the observers reported a meteor at the time. It's clear that there was something in the sky, but the question remains: What?"

James Oberg, an engineer in the space shuttle program, has made a second career out of explaining aerial mysteries. But after looking into the Reiff sighting, he, too, has come up empty-handed. "It has all the characteristics of a gas release from a sounding rocket," he asserts, "but whoever launched it has not come forward. We checked with those who would know and they have no record of any suborbital launches. But then, there is no international convention on registering such things. You only find out years later."

Strangely enough, Oberg had his own mystery cloud sighting just a couple of months after Reiff's. Oberg was trick-or-treating with the kids on Halloween when, he says, they saw "quite a strange visual phenomenon. There were a lot of clouds in the sky, and the object looked to me like a spotlight projecting on the bottom of the cloud deck."

Initially, other reports from the area confirmed that the object was far away. But then "a very good observer" just north of Oberg said that as he topped a rise in the highway, he could see a refinery burn-off on the ground; it was, he observed, lighting up the clouds directly above.

The story holds a simple lesson. "It stresses the importance of watching for anomalous phenomena," says Oberg. "The more that people come forward, the easier it is to find a solution."

CHAPTER 21

What the Government Knows

What does the government know about UFOs? That's what everyone wants to know, of course. Some think the government knows—and is hiding—it all. I'm not so sure. I'm willing to concede that they may be hiding something from us, but what they well may be hiding is their lack of knowledge of the subject—or worse, their lack of interest. This article, titled "What the Government Isn't Saying About UFOs," appeared in the December 1990 issue of OMNI.

✳

Deep in the bowels of the Pentagon a secret meeting is in progress. Seated at the conference table are three Air Force generals, an Army colonel, several scientists from the Defense Intelligence Agency (DIA), and personnel from both the Central Intelligence Agency and the National Security Agency. The colonel, Harold E. Phillips, is running the show. The idea for this cozy gathering known as the UFO Working Group was all his.

Phillips has convened this session to discuss the "perfect" UFO incident. The case, he says, involved a whole town full of witnesses. He wants the CIA to send an investigative team. But a CIA representative at the table balks. The agency cannot legally conduct domestic activities, he says. A discussion ensues. Eventually an exception to the rule is found, and two CIA agents, posing as NASA engineers, are sent to investigate the UFO sightings over Elmwood, Wisconsin.

The existence of the 17-member UFO Working Group was revealed for the first time this fall by investigative reporter Howard Blum in his new book *Out There*. According to the former *New York*

Times journalist, the group was established in February 1987 to coordinate a review of the evidence for UFOs and the search for extraterrestrial life.

The DIA, of course, denies that the UFO Working Group exists at all. To UFO researchers, the government team is less than impressive. "They seem like a loose-knit, unofficial discussion group called together on the authority of Phillips, a self-appointed UFO guru within the agency," says Larry W. Bryant, who directs the Washington, D.C., office of Citizens Against UFO Secrecy (CAUS). Others wonder how the group could have been impressed by the sightings over Elmwood, the proposed home of a welcome center for ETs. David Jacobs, a history professor at Temple University and the author of *The UFO Controversy* in America, thinks it can mean only one thing. "They're amateurs," he says.

Blum maintains that the group is official DIA business. But he doesn't think the government is harboring any secrets. "They're covering up not what they know, but what they don't know," he says. "They're embarrassed, and even a little frightened, by their inability to explain certain phenomena." Blum's view that the government knows little more than we do about UFOs is a decidedly "lite" version of the cover-up. The more sinister, traditional view holds that the government has evidence of alien visitations and has for decades kept this knowledge from the public. This "high calorie" version of the cover-up as government conspiracy has been around for decades.

The first to raise a stink about it was Donald Keyhoe, a retired major in the Marine Corps and a former aide to Charles Lindbergh. With the 1950 publication of *Flying Saucers Are Real,* Keyhoe became the first prominent individual to champion the notion that the government was hiding the existence of UFOs. Keyhoe had such troubles prying UFO information from the Air Force that he quickly became convinced a massive cover-up was taking place. The Air Force was aware that flying saucers were from another planet, said Kehoe, but they were covering up the fact to prevent a public panic.

Today many of the arguments for or against a government cover-up hinge on a single case. On the evening of July 6, 1947, a large glowing disc was seen over the New Mexico desert. A sheep rancher, who heard an explosion at the time, went out the next morning to find an area of his ranch covered with strange wreckage. Days later the public information officer at the nearby Roswell Army Air Field created a sensation by announcing they were in possession of a crashed flying disc.

Shortly afterward, however, a retraction appeared: The wreckage, officials declared, was actually a "weather balloon." This much is history. Less well-known are reports that a thorough search of the area in the days that followed led to the discovery, miles away, of the main portion of the crashed disc. Inside, supposedly, were several small beings who had died in the crash. The military is said to have whisked away the wreckage and its occupants. During the past decade more and more people have come forward claiming to have seen the craft and the aliens themselves.

If there is a cover-up, then Roswell is where it all began. "Once Roswell came along, the government had real justification for keeping something under wraps," says Bruce Maccabee, a physicist who directs the Fund for UFO Studies in Mount Rainier, Maryland. "Assuming the Roswell case is true, there must be some groups keeping track of that stuff, keeping it under guard."

Witnesses of the Roswell incident were intimidated, contends Stanton Friedman, a nuclear physicist in Fredericton, New Brunswick, Canada, who has interviewed many of the eyewitness and other participants. "People were told not to talk," he says, "no question about it. One officer was told by the acting head of the Strategic Air Command, 'I don't want you to talk about this ever again.' I even have a man who handled the bodies on official assignment down there, and not only was he personally threatened, but he was told that if he talked about this, they'd get his family, too."

More convincing is the lack of official documentation on the case. "We know something crashed," says Barry Greenwood, research director of CAUS. "We know material was gathered. We know that it was shipped out somewhere. So where is the paperwork? Where is the analysis? We just don't see it." But Greenwood, unlike Friedman, is not convinced that Roswell represents the crash of an extraterrestrial spacecraft and its occupants. He takes the "lite" view and thinks the government is just as baffled by the UFO phenomenon as the rest of us.

Thousands of pages of UFO documents generated by the CIA, the FBI, the Air Force, the State Department, and other agencies have been released under the Freedom of Information Act. But these, says Maccabee, offer only indirect evidence of a cover-up: They point to an accumulation of information that wouldn't be there if no one were interested. "It's hard to believe that all those reports would pour into government agencies and no one paid any attention," he says. "It's hard to believe the government would be so stupid." Maccabee believes the government is covering up the existence of UFOs, covering up that it really doesn't know what's going on, and covering up that it doesn't know what to do about it, namely what would happen if it went public with all this.

Government agencies still have hundreds of UFO documents that they refuse to release to UFO researchers. The National Security Agency (NSA) admits to withholding more than 100 UFO-related documents, the CIA refuses to release about 50, and the DIA says it's withholding six. This is black-and-white proof of a cover-up, says Greenwood. "In a literal sense, information is being covered up in being withheld."

The most tantalizing of all the withheld UFO documents are those belonging to the NSA, the super secret agency whose primary job is eavesdropping on military communications. No one really knows what UFO information its documents contain, but Friedman has an idea what one may be about. Someone working for the agency told Friedman that in March 1967 a listening post picked up communications between Cuban radar installations and two MiG-21 jets sent to intercept a mysterious, bright metallic sphere in Cuban airspace. When the MiG pilots failed to make contact with the object, they were instructed to shoot it down. "Suddenly there was this shrieking from the pilot in the second plane," says Friedman. "The first plane had disintegrated." Friedman's contact says that NSA headquarters was sent a report on the incident.

UFO researchers took the NSA to court for its UFO documents in 1980, but federal district court judge Gerhard Gesell, the same judge who presided over the Oliver North case, ruled in the NSA's favor. The agency refuses to release any of its UFO-related documents because to do so would reveal sources and methods, and that would be a violation of national security. But Friedman believes that there is something about the phenomenon itself that the agency regards as a threat to national security. These objects are violating our airspace, he points out, and they show the powerless response of our military systems to such intrusions. Friedman has a name for all this. He calls it the Cosmic Watergate.

Philip J. Klass, an aerospace journalist and the field's foremost skeptic, says there is no such thing. He points out that many of the communications intercepted by the NSA come from potentially hostile nations and many of them are coded. So the agency's rationale for not making these documents public is actually quite simple. "They might reveal the location of certain listening posts," he explains, "and even more important, they would reveal that we have cracked and were able to decipher certain codes."

So if the question is whether the withheld documents contain any answers to the UFO mystery, the answer is, Probably not. "Long ago a lot of us used to think that the government was covering up a knowledge of extraterrestrials and their craft," says Greenwood, who six years ago co-authored *Clear Intent: The Government Coverup of the UFO Experience.* "But we've had a change of attitude. We just don't see the government as having any answers. If they knew what UFOs were all about, I think history would have been a little different than what we now see."

This argument gains power, oddly enough, from the Roswell incident itself. "If it was a UFO that crashed in Roswell," says Jacobs, "a whole series of events would have been set in motion in the government. There would be major studies of it. Hundreds of scientists would have been involved with it over the past forty years. The government would be acting very differently about UFOs than they do now. All of UFO history makes sense if there was not a crash, and none of UFO history makes sense if there was a crash." Jacobs adds, "It's still possible that one could have crashed and there's an entirely different scenario at work."

If the craft at Roswell had been an ET craft, insists Klass, then the United States would have wanted to know just how many of these craft were passing overhead. At the very least, he says, we would have established a space-surveillance system similar to the one that was set up three years after the launch of Sputnik. Klass cannot imagine the government doing nothing and simply hoping the aliens are friendly.

Never in his 24 years of UFO investigation has Klass encountered a government cover-up of significant information. If you think there's a cover-up, he says, call your local air base and report that a saucer has just landed in your backyard and that strange-looking creatures are getting out of it. If the government really were trying to keep things under wraps, he says, the voice on the other end would ask for your address and a SWAT team would be there within minutes. Instead, what will happen, says Klass, is that the voice on the other end will simply thank you for calling and suggest that you report your sighting to the local police department or to one of the national UFO groups.

That's too simplistic, says Bryant. If they really have hard evidence about aliens and flying saucers, what would they care about what's in your backyard? For the past several years Bryant, who happens to be a Pentagon employee, has been placing ads in military newspapers encouraging anyone with UFO information to come forth and blow the whistle on the government cover-up. So far no one has come forward to reveal what he calls the "ultimate secret" that will motivate the general public, the press, and Congress to resolve the issue. He's not surprised. "So few people in the government really know about UFOs," he says. "And those who don't know are covering up because it's just the way of doing things. It's the bureaucratic way. When in doubt, don't let it out. Don't even let out that you don't know."

CHAPTER 22

What the Dolphins Know

For the past 10 years crashed saucers have been the holy grail of UFOlogy. People would go to amazing lengths to uncover an alien craft. Some even tried to find out what dolphins know on the subject. I kid you not.

Such trolling in UFO waters would be just funny if the person attempting dolphin communications on this subject, C. B. Scott Jones, wasn't somebody. In fact he served for several years as Special Assistant to Senator Claiborne Pell of Rhode Island, Chairman of the Senate Foreign Relations Committee and one of the most senior politicians on Capitol Hill. Jones seems to have devoted himself entirely to paranormal topics. His interest in UFOs comes from a personal sighting as a Naval fighter pilot during the Korean War. This short report appeared under the title "Dolphin Operators" in the January 1989 issue of OMNI.

*

Dolphins have now been recruited in the search for extraterrestrial life. Scott Jones, director of the Center for Applied Anomalous Phenomena in Falls Church, Virginia, is trying to establish telepathic contact with dolphins in the hopes that they will lead him to an unknown underwater object such as a crashed saucer.

Jones began his project in 1984, after an experiment indicated that Jan Northup, a Washington, D.C., businesswoman, was communicating telepathically with dolphins in a circular holding pen. Last summer Northup and Jones began working with a pod of dolphins in the open ocean.

If the information exchange was not extensive, Jones says, it is probably because "we hadn't yet been fully accepted into the pod. It appears that we have an apprenticeship to fulfill. We did however, manage to outline our research with them, and we anticipate working with the pod again."

CHAPTER 23

A Curious Hypersensitivity

One of the first questions that comes to mind on the subject of UFO abductions is: What's wrong with these people? Are they mentally ill? Several studies have been conducted on the subject and the general consensus seems to be that, no, abductees are quite normal and much like ordinary people, though perhaps a little more fantasy prone than the average. But is this the chicken or the egg? The study by psychologist Ken Ring discussed here indicates that those who have had near-death experiences are in the same boat as abductees—whatever boat that happens to be. This story appeared as an untitled "UFO Update" in the Antimatter section of the February 1991 issue of OMNI.

✳

Are altered-state experiences in adulthood tied to childhood trauma and stress? Yes, says psychologist Ken Ring of the University of Connecticut in Storrs. Ring's latest study shows that people who report a UFO experience or claim a near-death experience (NDE) as adults are especially likely to have suffered abuse when young.

Ring's study profiled 170 people reporting UFOs and NDEs. Subjects filled out a detailed questionnaire, dredging up information on childhood homes, religious beliefs, and other factors. Ring then compared their answers with those of a control group not subject to altered states.

Some results from the study were not that surprising. The survey revealed, for instance, that people reporting UFO abductions were psychologically similar to those reporting merely UFO sightings or NDEs. Ring also found that no matter what the nature of the altered state, those prone to such heightened experiences often became more spiritually oriented and sometimes even embraced a cosmic interpretation of events on Earth.

But the most controversial aspect of Ring's survey is the high incidence of disturbed childhoods—including physical mistreatment, sexual abuse, and neglect—among those reporting UFOs and NDEs. It turns out that these people were also more likely than others to recall psychic episodes from their childhood.

Ring has proposed a daring interpretation of these findings. It's well known, he says, that children exposed to physical violence, sexual abuse, or a negative home atmosphere are strongly motivated to "tune out" those aspects of their world, to dissociate themselves from the source of their troubles. "By doing so," Ring says, "they are more likely to tune in to other realities where they can feel safe regardless of what is happening to them." So this sensitivity to "alternate realities," brought on by childhood difficulties, might actually attune people to UFOs and NDEs as adults. If so, Ring says, their "extended range of perception" could be regarded as a "compensatory gift" for the physical and psychological "wounds" they suffered in childhood.

Ring's interpretation does not sit well with some child abuse experts. "Is it a hyperperception of reality or a distortion of reality?" asks a recognized authority on child abuse who does not wish to be quoted on "outrageous science" topics. "I'm more inclined to see these people as more susceptible to fantasy creation as a strategy of coping with pain, rather than a hypersensitivity to things that are really out there in an objective sense."

Byron Egeland, a professor of child development at the University of Minnesota who has done a lot of research on the causes and consequences of child abuse, concedes only that "it might be the case that somebody who had experienced a lot of hurt as a child is more sensitive as an adult." But the reason these people experience these bizarre phenomena, he says, "is not because they are more sensitive to them, but because they are very confused about what's real and what's fantasy. I can guarantee you that the majority of individuals who have those kinds of experiences are fairly disturbed individuals. I think their experiences are the result of the abuse."

Ring objects. "I do *not* want to pathologize these people," he says. "Survey participants reporting UFOs or NDEs are no more fantasy-prone as a group than grocery store clerks or anyone else."

CHAPTER 24

Blaming the Japanese for Roswell

We return here to the matter of context. Often it's impossible to establish the actual context of an event until many years later. The now ridiculously famous Roswell event (Hey, it appeared on the cover of TIME, for goodness's sake!) provides a case in point. In the past decade or so, numerous explanations have been put forth for that event. But regardless of what you think of the one suggested here by John Keel—who covered the UFO beat as no other during the sixties—the crashed saucer explanation remains probably the worst of the lot. This story, which bore the title "UFO Update: Was a Japanese balloon responsible for the most publicized UFO report of all time?" appeared in the May 1991 issue of OMNI.

✳

UFO researcher John Keel believes that the most famous UFO incident of all time is just a lot of hot air. According to Keel, the infamous wreckage reported near Roswell, New Mexico, in 1947 was not a flying saucer, as UFO buffs claim. Nor was it a weather balloon, as the U.S. Air Force says. Rather, says Keel, the debris found in the New Mexico desert came from a Fu-Go balloon, a type of Japanese bomber used during World War II.

Though it's not well known, the Japanese did launch an aerial attack on the continental United States during World War II. For a period of six months, beginning on November 3, 1944, the Japanese sent aloft 9,300 unmanned balloons, each armed with a payload of 50 pounds or so, from several sites in Japan. Hundreds of these balloons were carried by the upper atmospheric air currents of the jet stream over the 6,500-mile-wide Pacific Ocean and into North America.

The Fu-Go balloon bombs caused 285 incidents on this side of the Pacific between November 4, 1944, and August 8, 1945, according to a report prepared by the Smithsonian Institution in 1973. The balloons peppered 18 states, from Hawaii and California in the West to Michigan in the East. Remarkably, however, they caused very little damage. Only one incident resulted in casualties: five children and a woman picnicking near Lakeview, Oregon, were killed when a balloon bomb they were dragging out of the woods exploded.

As for the Japanese, they listened eagerly for news of widespread destruction in the United States. But the U.S. Office of Censorship had asked the media to withhold all reports of balloon incidents. Because newspaper editors and radio broadcasters largely complied, the Japanese assumed their Fu-Gos had failed.

"But one of the places a Fu-Go landed was in Roswell, New Mexico." Keel declares. "The witnesses to it—and there were only a couple—described in detail what Fu-Go debris looked like: a lot of paper, twisted little pieces of metal, and pieces of plastic. Like a lot of people who found these things, they thought it might be from outer space."

Keel believes that upper atmospheric air currents had kept this one balloon airborne longer than most. Then, when the rubber cement holding the balloon panels together fell apart, the whole thing came crashing down in the New Mexico desert. Debris from the balloon and its instrumentation would later be discovered by a rancher thinking he had come across the crashed remains of one of the flying discs, which, at the time, were just beginning to make the news.

Edward Doty, a meteorologist who established the Air Force's Balloon Branch at nearby Holloman Air Force Base in New Mexico beginning in 1948, calls the Japanese Fu-Go balloons "a very fine technical job with limited resources." But "no way could one of these balloons explain the Roswell episode," says Doty, "because they could not possibly have stayed aloft for two years."

Kevin Randle, who is co-author with Donald Schmitt of *UFO*

Crash at Roswell: The Military Cover-up, also dismisses Keel's Fu-Go explanation. "His entire hypothesis hinges on the fact that the balloon bombs were secret in 1947," he says. "And that's simply not true."

New York attorney Peter Gersten is also investigating the Roswell incident and, like Keel, is convinced of a terrestrial explanation. "It seems to me that Keel's explanation has to be closer to the truth," he says, "than those who believe in alien spaceships."

CHAPTER 25

On the Russian UFO Scene

Most of the UFO-research community consists of talkers. Few are doers, and understandably so. Funding is as rare as blue diamonds, and few people manage to support their UFO interests—or habit, as the case may be.

One of the doers happens to be French-born astronomer Jacques Vallee. He has played a major role in UFO affairs in the United States. For an excellent behind-the-scenes-look, read his FORBIDDEN SCIENCE. Vallee also published what is perhaps the earliest, if not the best, scientific examination of UFOs in his 1965 book, ANATOMY OF A PHENOMENON, and its 1966 companion, CHALLENGE TO SCIENCE.

By being a doer, however, Vallee has exposed himself to lots of flak from the UFO gallery because some people dislike the conclusions he draws. I suspect that Vallee has completely tired of it all at this point. The following article appeared under the title "Russia's Alien Ideas" in the Antimatter section of the July 1992 issue of OMNI, after the release of one of his last books.

✳

Westerners were intrigued back in 1989 when the Soviet news agency, Tass, reported the claims of some school children from the city of Voronezh. A spectacular UFO had landed in town, the children insisted, along with its ten-foot-tall occupant toting a tube-shaped gun. Scrutinizing the Tass report, the Western press assumed the Russians were letting off steam after years of censorship. Some UFO buffs in the United States called the episode a hoax, but one Western scientist ignored the ridicule and left for Moscow instead.

In January of 1990, Jacques Vallee, a computer scientist regarded by many as the world's major UFO researcher, held a week-long series of meetings with the Soviet Union's leading UFO lights. He met with a scientist who'd studied the mysterious explosion that had rattled the Tunguska region of Russia in 1908 and with an ex-Soviet Naval officer who detailed his UFO sightings by Navy personnel. But according to Vallee, the most compelling sighting was the one in Voronezh itself.

In his book, *UFO Chronicles of the Soviet Union,* Vallee describes the cast of dozens—adults as well as children—who reportedly witnessed the spherical Voronezh craft, its three-eyed giant, and an accompanying robot. He also cites engineers who examined an imprint allegedly left by the craft, an object they claimed weighed 11 tons.

While Vladimir Migulin, a member of the Soviet Academy of Sciences, attributed the markings to a rocket launched from Volvograd, Vallee does not agree. "Migulin's skeptical attitude," he says, "is not very different from what you would get from our own National Academy of Science."

Why does Vallee believe the Soviet sightings are for real? The weight of the craft, he notes, was "in the range of estimates reached by French scientists studying physical markings left by UFO landings in France." And though the beings bore no resemblance to the familiar, short, Hollywood-style UFOnauts, they were similar to aliens reportedly seen "in a very similar case in Argentina in 1978."

Vallee's sojourn—and his ideas—have taken fellow UFOlogists by surprise. Some wonder how scientific the Russians really are, given that they regularly use dousing to gather information about UFO sites. "With all due respect," says Michael Swords, a professor at Western Michigan University and editor of the *Journal of UFO Studies,* "some Russians are questionable in terms of UFO research. They tend not to be very well disciplined, nor are they good at documenting their work."

As for Vallee's book, Swords says "it sounds like 'What I Did on My Last Vacation.' Vallee may have met a lot of interesting people and heard a lot of interesting tales, but he doesn't document things properly, and if he has, he never seems to share it with anybody."

But Vallee insists the Russian findings are significant, in part because of the region's weak cover-up system. "With the chaos spreading over the Soviet Union," Vallee explains, "I felt there was genuine information coming out from the witnesses."

Vallee supporter and experimental psychologist Richard Haines agrees that the French researcher is onto something real. Explaining the misunderstanding about Vallee's work, Haines says, "He's a theoretician. He doesn't claim to be a field investigator. And I think he has some very challenging ideas."

CHAPTER 26

On the Mars UFO Scene

The number of failures that have occurred with our Mars bound spacecraft gets more remarkable by the day (as I write this, the Mars Lander touches down on the Red Planet and promptly fails to report in). The circumstances surrounding an earlier failure, that of the Russian Phobos 2, left some people to suspect that a Martian UFO was involved. The paranoia actually served to fuel an open-minded examination of the incident by an independent astronomer, and led to an unexpected payoff as yet unacknowledged by mainstream science. I wrote this article after seeing Tom Van Flandern's presentation on the subject at the annual meeting of the Society for Scientific Exploration in Princeton in 1992. The story appeared as a "UFO Update" titled "Martian Mystery" in the May 1993 issue of OMNI.

✳

When a Soviet probe spun out of control near Phobos, one of two Martian moons, experts called the accident an unavoidable hazard of venturing on high. But to some members of the UFO community, the crash was the evil handiwork of aliens based on Phobos for years.

Fueling this otherworldly rumor, it seems, was a statement by none other than Alexander Dunayev, chairman of the Soviet Space organization responsible for the space probe, named *Phobos 2*. The doomed craft, Dunayev stated, had photographed the image of an odd-shaped object between itself and Mars. The object could have been "debris in the orbit of Phobos," Dunayev suggested, or perhaps the spacecraft's jettisoned "autonomous propulsion sub-system." But his tone of uncertainty—and the fact that the Russians never released the spacecraft's final photograph—left saucer buffs guessing the mysterious object had been a genuine UFO.

Their suspicions were heightened just recently when retired Soviet Col. Marina Popovich made a trip to the United States. Speaking at a press conference in Los Angeles, UFO advocate Popovich stated that the object had measured a whopping 25 kilometers, or 15.5 miles, in length. A former test pilot and the wife of a highly decorated cosmonaut, Gen. Pavel Popovich, the visiting colonel said she had received the alarming photo itself from cosmonaut Alexei Leonov, her friend.

But if Washington, D.C., astronomer Tom Van Flandern, formerly of the U.S. Naval Observatory and now head of his own group, Meta Research Inc., is correct, the failure of the probe was no mystery at all. The Soviets had long said that the craft had spun out of control because of an erroneous ground command on March 27, Van Flandern discovered, yet the photo of the mystery object had been dated March 25. "It was unlikely," he explains, "that the object in the photo had anything to do with the spacecraft's demise."

To determine the identity of the object, however, Van Flandern analyzed the picture. "The first thing that struck me," he explains, "is that the object was similar in brightness to Phobos, an asteroid-like body that is carbonaceous and dark." It did not reflect light as a metallic, artificial object would.

Van Flandern also examined the timing of the *Phobos 2* camera, set to track the motion of the Martian moon. Anything not matching the moon's relative motion would appear to streak or trail across the photographic page. Thus, the "streak," thought to be 25 kilometers long, was, in fact, a much smaller object imprinting its motion, not its length, across the image. Only the very end of the elongated streak hints at the object's true shape: rounded but irregular, with one end narrower than the other. To Van Flandern, the clues suggest the mystery object was a moonlet, or a third, miniature Martian moon.

Of course, Van Flandern's conclusion has not pleased everybody. One German researcher says the image is just an artifact produced by the malfunction of the *Phobos 2* camera in space. And Popovich contends the object may be an alien craft. To make her point, she has even given a copy of the telling photo to Don Ecker, director of research for *UFO Magazine,* based in Los Angeles. Ecker, deferring to "the facts as presented by the Russians," favors the notion of a Mars-based UFO.

But Van Flandern contends the lack of alien involvement in the image should not detract from its importance. "It is an exciting astronomical discovery, " he contends, "and means that instead of just two moons revolving around Mars, we may have three."

CHAPTER 27

The Dark Side

In their efforts to keep UFOlogy out of the hands of paranormalists, certain key players in the field would like to deny that the UFO phenomenon has quite a bit in common with ghosts and other paranormal topics. Certainly those who undergo a UFO abduction experience report much the same consequences as those who undergo near death experiences, for example, and therapists who end up seeing such people tend to lump them together in any case.

Though the UFO experience is not the sole concern of the following story, it certainly is the primary one. As far as I'm aware the organization featured here, TREAT, no longer exists, or at least remains moribund, though the number of therapists that now handle these topics has no doubt increased. Note also that the telephone number for the Spiritual Emergency Network has been updated in the story; the BULLETIN OF ANOMALOUS EXPERIENCE is no longer being published.

The story, which contains one of my favorite quotes ("belief is not evidence"), appeared under the title "Dark Side of the Unknown" in the September 1993 issue of OMNI.

✳

Tell us about it. Terrorized by little gray creatures with large black eyes who whisk you away from your bedroom at night? Plagued by poltergeists rattling the bookshelf and hurling pictures from the wall? Haunted by the ghost of a loved one, say, or precognitive dreams that turn suddenly real? Whatever the nature of your encounter with the unknown, you may have been left physically drained or emotionally scarred. Chances are, you've confided in no one, fearful friends and relatives would consider you insane. So where do you turn?

Actually, you have some options. You might, for instance, place your trust in someone who makes a business out of the unknown. You saw the movie; you know the tune. Who you gonna call? Ghostbusters! If it's psychic troubles you've had, you call a parapsychologist. And when it comes to possessions and visions and such, there's always the minister, rabbi, or parish priest. On the plus side, you can be fairly confident these people will believe you. On the other hand, if your trouble is even partially psychological, how much help would they be?

That's where mainstream psychologists and psychiatrists come in. If you're hallucinating, they might have a treatment or cure. But don't expect them to believe you. They'll dismiss your story as a raving fantasy, and if you can't shake the episode, you may end up diagnosed with schizophrenia and on anti-psychotic drugs.

Not what you had in mind? Then consider your third option: the new breed of mental-health professional now contending that such other worldly experiences are legitimate and commonplace among the sane. That's not to say they accept the reality of alien abductors or precognition or ghosts—though much to the horror of their colleagues, a few of them have. But what many of these therapists have come to believe over the past five years is that such experiences—regardless of their cause—are common among normal, healthy people, and that those who find themselves traumatized by such episodes are just as deserving of psychological ministrations as those who suffer anxiety, depression, or the trauma that follows a plane crash or a rape.

To signal the birth of this new discipline, some dedicated professionals have even formed a group known as TREAT, for clinicians and physical and behavioral scientists interested in the Treatment and Research of Experienced Anomalous Trauma. TREAT, which holds a conference each spring, deals with everything from reports of UFO abduction and precognition to near-death episodes, satanic possession, and alleged contact with the dead. Another favorite TREAT area is kundalini—often perceived as a burning, vibrating, or electrifying sensation associated with meditation or any other heavy-duty spiritual chore. By all indicators, TREAT is a movement whose time has come. Indeed, every national poll on the paranormal confirms just how widespread such experiences are. A 1992 survey by the Roper Organization, for instance, suggests that 2 percent of the population, or 1 of every 50 adult Americans, exhibits the symptoms that sometimes mask a UFO abduction experience. A 1987 study conducted by Andrew Greeley and colleagues at the University of Chicago showed that 42 percent of American adults reported contact with the dead, 67 percent claimed ESP experiences, and 31 percent reported clairvoyance. And a 1981 Gallup poll showed that an extraordinary 15 percent of all people revived from the cusp of death reported the spectacle of the near-death experience in which they glimpsed such generic signposts as beckoning loved ones or a tunnel of light.

One must not, of course, mistake these experiences for proof of their reality. "Truth should not be defined by what people believe," warns Harold Goldstein, a psychologist in the division of epidemiology and services research branch of the National Institutes of Mental Health. "Facts are facts. Now it may turn out that there are aliens and such things, but there needs to be evidence for it, and belief is not evidence."

Then again, say the professionals on the frontier of the new psychology, beliefs should not be dismissed. "Paranormal experiences are so common in the general population," psychiatrists Colin Ross of Dallas and Shaun Joshi of Winnipeg, Canada, said in a recent issue of the *Journal of Nervous and Mental Disease,* "that no theory of normal psychology or psychopathology which does not take them into account can be comprehensive." Such experiences, they say, could be studied scientifically, "in the same way as anxiety, depression, or any other set of experiences" without making "any decision as to whether some, all, or none of them are objectively real."

That may sound good in theory, but some observers wonder whether it's really possible in practice. Therapists, it turns out, are no more immune to the potent lure of the unknown than anyone else. Unwary specialists of the human mind may, in fact, be particularly prone to accepting the reality of their patients' fascinating tales. And enchantment can lead to obsession. The psychoanalyst Robert Lindner admitted as much in 1955 after coming under the spell of a patient who provided detailed accounts of visits into the future reality of another planet. To help the patient, Lindner studied the mass of written records Kirk had prepared, noted the inconsistencies, and confronted him with the errors. That effort forced cracks in the fantasy and led, eventually, to Kirk's recovery. But Lindner, meanwhile, become so absorbed in the story that he had difficulty extricating himself from its grip. In his classic book, *The Fifty Minute Hour,* he admits to skirting "the edges of the abyss." Now, some 35 years later, the latest mental-health professionals to flirt with UFO abduction, the near-death experience, and psychic phenomena face this danger as well.

One mental-health worker to dive headlong into the dark pit of the unknown in recent years is psychiatrist Rima Laibow. Her sprawling office in the upscale Westchester County town of Hastings-on-Hudson, New York, is ringed with the big fluffy pillows she uses in holding therapy, originally designed to repair early attachment deficits in autistic children but now used with other serious childhood and adult problems as well. Dressed in blue slacks and a blouse, her frizzy hair tossed to one side, Laibow recalls her first professional journey through the looking glass. "It was 1988," she explains, "and a patient whom I had known for many years came to me in a state of anxiety and panic because, out of the corner of her eye, she had caught sight of the cover of *Communion.*"

The patient, a 43-year-old cardiologist, had never read this 1987 best-seller by horror novelist Whitley Strieber, didn't know that it concerned alleged encounters with UFO entities, and had never been interested in the subject of alien abduction at all. Despite all this, after glimpsing the cover of *Communion,* she claimed terrifying memory fragments of encounters with creatures like those on the book's cover.

"Such notions had always struck me as psychotic," Laibow

explains, "but this patient taught me otherwise." Convinced that her patient showed no sign of major psychopathology, in fact, Laibow came up with a different diagnosis for the sudden breakdown the cardiologist experienced following recall of an alleged alien encounter: posttraumatic stress disorder, or PTSD.

According to the most recent *Diagnostic and Statistical Manual of Mental Disorders,* PTSD is a stress reaction triggered by various external events "outside the range of usual human experience." Triggering events, the American Psychiatric Association's manual goes on to say, include such atrocities as rape, war, and natural disasters like earthquakes or floods, which are "usually experienced with intense fear, terror, and helplessness." In fact, Laibow's patient met all the criteria for PTSD but one. "There had been no known trauma," recalls Laibow, "so I thought, how could she have PTSD when we all know there couldn't possibly be an external event like an alien abduction—could there?"

Over the weeks that followed, Laibow worked to quell her patient's anxiety and panic. But the doctor herself remained genuinely puzzled. In search of answers, she read all the literature she could find on reported alien abductions and spoke to the primary investigators in the field: New York artist Budd Hopkins, who had written two books on the topic, and Temple University historian David Jacobs, who, like Hopkins, had become a kind of folk guru and de facto therapist for UFO abduction victims.

"What I found," Laibow states, "left me both impressed and appalled." She was impressed, she says, because "there's a substantial body of data suggesting that under some circumstances, at some times, for some reason, there are things in the atmosphere we call UFOs that appear to have external physical reality." But she was appalled because from her "sad and shocking experience, UFOlogy as it exists today is little more than a collection of belief systems vying for dominance. The field is plagued by the notion that just collecting neat stuff is the same as doing research. If I were the National Science Foundation, I wouldn't fund this research, either."

Hoping to change all that, Laibow began by giving UFO abduction and the whole gamut of experience with unexplained phenomena a new, more respectable name. "Experienced anomalous trauma," she called it, so that "professionals, who would otherwise stop listening because you've mentioned UFOs, parapsychology, and other weird things would now stop and process those three words in relation to each other and ask, 'Like what?'"

The strategy worked. In fact, with the name *experienced anomalous trauma* as a draw, Laibow found dozens of psychiatrists and Ph.D. psychologists intrigued by her ideas. To take advantage of the momentum, she formed an umbrella organization for the Treatment and Research of Experienced Anomalous Trauma, or TREAT, and held the group's first meeting in May 1989. TREAT quickly attracted some big guns in the mental-health community. One was John Wilson. A professor of psychology at Cleveland State University, Wilson is one of the pioneers in the field of posttraumatic stress disorder. He helped both to coin the term and to formulate a definition of the disorder as far back as 1980. In the past two decades, Wilson has listened patiently to more than 10,000 people traumatized by some major life event and has conducted major studies of PTSD in Vietnam combat veterans and victims of toxic exposure.

Wilson's own curiosity with the unknown dates back to childhood, when a neighbor of his worked for Project Blue Book, the notorious Air Force effort responsible for investigating UFOs. When the abduction phenomenon emerged, he began to wonder what symptoms the alleged victims would report. "The most obvious answer," he says, "is that they would have PTSD." According to Wilson, in fact, those who report memories of UFO abduction find themselves in the same sort of psychologically stressful dilemma as those who have been exposed to invisible toxic contaminants such as hydrogen sulfide. "They aren't sure about it," he explains, "not sure anybody is going to believe them, don't know how to stop it, and don't know how long it has gone on. But the big difference is that those claiming a UFO abduction don't even know if it occurred for sure. If you've been exposed to a toxic chemical, you can usually have a toxicologist come and study your house, and they'll say, yeah, it's there, or it's not. But someone who's had a UFO abduction experience can't point to the flying saucer or the little gray guy with the almond-shaped eyes. That puts them in a really psychologically ensnaring position." In fact, Wilson places UFO abductions and exposure to invisible toxic contaminants in the same general category of traumatic experiences as childhood sexual abuse and psychological torture, calling them examples of "hidden events" that may lead to PTSD but which often can't be proven real.

Wilson isn't surprised by his colleagues' slow reception to anomalous trauma. "Fifty years ago, mental-health professionals didn't believe in childhood abuse," Wilson notes. "When kids or adults would report incest experiences, sexual molestation, or rape and went to see a mental-health professional, they were told, 'That's a fantasy; that doesn't happen; it can't be real.' It wasn't until the sixties that the American College of Pediatrics even did a study to find out what was going on. And then, *voilá*, it was out of the closet, and today we have hard data on childhood sexual abuse. There is a parallel here to anomalous experience; whether it's UFO abduction or demon possession, our culture says no."

But as far as Wilson is concerned, the cultural disbelief system will change as anomalous trauma becomes a diagnostic subcategory of PTSD. "American culture is on the leading edge of this material," he says, "and my prediction is that within five to ten years, the idea of experienced anomalous trauma will get the serious consideration it deserves."

Indeed, with Wilson's stamp of approval and Laibow's promotional drive, other psychiatrists and psychologists have begun to come around. One already going that route is kundalini expert Bonnie Greenwell, a California-based psychotherapist and author of *Energies of Transformation.* This "energy phenomenon," as Greenwell calls it, has been described by Hindu mystics and practitioners of Yoga as an "awakening" of spiritual energy that supposedly "sleeps" at the base of the spine. But kundalini awakenings, considered the beginning of the process of enlightenment by masters of the technique, can result in serious psychological disturbance as well.

And that's where Greenwell comes in. Even those seeking the kundalini experience can find it painful, she explains, and for those not expecting it, the experience can be a nightmare. Indeed, those undergoing the kundalini experience don't seem to know what hit them because they are unaware that it might be triggered by anything from a physical trauma or emotional shock to a long-term spiritual practice or dose of LSD. What's more, says Greenwell, the experience may be accompanied by visions and trances, the sensation of leaving the body, and alternating periods of ecstasy and despair, symptoms that could lead to pathological diagnoses by conventional shrinks. But Western medicine is not alone in its ignorance of kundalini, according to Greenwell. Many spiritual teachers don't have a clue what to do with it, either. "Some teachers will tell them it can't be kundalini or it would feel good," she says. "Others tell these people they're having a breakdown. There are even cases in Buddhist retreats where people have been taken to psychiatric hospitals when they had a kundalini opening. Many people who teach yoga or meditation are not developed to the extent that they have gone through this process themselves. It's very unfortunate, and it's one of the major reasons I started doing what I do."

Greenwell's craft includes helping those troubled by kundalini tap the positive aspects of the phenomenon while discarding the negative as quickly as they can. "Once they understand the process as essentially positive in the long run," Greenwell says, "they are no longer afraid of it and can often work it out quite effectively on their own."

One person Greenwell saw overcome the problems of kundalini was Sarah, born after her father's death in 1918. During childhood, Sarah spent numerous hours communing with her deceased father and as an adult used that same impulse to meditate. Listening to high-frequency sound and visualizing the inside of her body, Sarah began feeling waves of kundalini along with terrifying visions: In one, she was cut up piece by piece, and in another, her body was invaded by swords. In the end, Sarah managed to control her terrors by expressing the creative energy of kundalini in the form of dreams, dance, movement, and art.

Other clients, Greenwell adds, have been far more distressed by kundalini energy than Sarah. In these severe cases, she notes, "the person struggles to get control of a body which involuntarily forces them into motions or freezes them in action, locks pain into the back and shoulders or into the site of any preexisting injury, and flushes them with intense heat and cold. Such subjects occasionally fall into trance or report that they are leaving their body. They may be blinded by lights upon entering a dark room or feel they're being electrocuted in bed."

Depending upon who these people consult, says Greenwell, they may be diagnosed with any number of disturbances from schizophrenia to grand mal epilepsy. That's just what happened to Cathy, who experienced periods of intense, trance-like states, extreme sensations of cold, and "unusual energy flows" moving upward from her feet to her hands. Given medication for everything from psychosis to seizures, Cathy finally decided to abandon all conventional treatment and accept her symptoms as "spiritual" in nature, coming from energies beyond. It was this acceptance, Greenwell claims, that resulted in an immediate improvement in Cathy's health and enabled her to give up anti-seizure drugs and integrate her experiences in a positive way into her life.

Greenwell probably sees more patients with kundalini problems than therapists on the East coast, perhaps because kundalini is largely a California phenomenon. The high percentage of meditators out West, she concedes, means "you have a lot of people primed for the experiences." Those who suffer from spiritual traumas, kundalini or otherwise, can also access another West Coast resource—the California-based Spiritual Emergence Network, or SEN, a telephone referral service (415-648-2610) founded by Christina Grof, who with her husband, Stanislav, pioneered research on the altered state.

"We get about 150 calls a month," says Deane Brown, a therapist and the Network's program director. "People call us when something is happening that they don't understand. The volunteers who answer the phone come from a variety of backgrounds, and many of them have experienced some critical or frightening period of spiritual emergence of their own. So they can truthfully say to the caller, 'I know what you're going through; I've been there.' What we do, essentially, is listen. That's the greatest gift that we can give to a caller. We don't judge the content of what they say. We respond to the feeling rather than the content. We never diagnose."

After talking to the caller for a while, SEN volunteers provide the name and number of one of the 500 people in the SEN database. These people range from psychiatrists and psychologists who are familiar with the SEN philosophy of "spiritual emergence" to shamans, psychics, healers, or clergy in the troubled caller's area.

"The types of calls seem to go in cycles," notes Brown. "We will often get a lot of the same calls at about the same time from all over. For a while we may get a lot of kundalini calls. Then we may get a lot of psychic opening, including out-of-body experiences, telepathy, and uncanny coincidences. Other callers report possession, psychic attack by demons, and the like."

Despite the common goals of workers like Greenwell and Laibow, however, the TREAT movement has run into some trouble of its own. The reason: Laibow's strong resistance to the pioneering group of workers *without professional credentials* who aided the spiritually traumatized in the first place, years before it became fashionable for those with degrees. The biggest rift was caused by her refusal to accept artist Budd Hopkins, author of the classic volumes *Missing Time* and *Intruders,* and the individual who brought the plight of UFO abductees to the attention of physicians and the general public when everyone else was ignoring them or calling them insane. Laibow's beef: Hopkins and others had been hypnotizing the alleged abductees to elicit their tales, and they had no business doing so "since their formal training amounted to just about nil." Such "wannabe clinicians," she believes, can be very dangerous, indeed.

Says Laibow, "There's a huge difference in being able to induce a hypnotic trance and being a clinician who knows what to do when you've got a trance, who knows how to not contaminate the material, and who knows how to facilitate recovery rather than cause retraumatization—because people can be retraumatized by the unconscious repetition of their material. And what do you do if a UFO investigator does you clinical harm by taking on clinical responsibilities? Where is his malpractice liability, and how are you going to be protected? People who are not willing to take the time and the effort to become clinicians should not be stomping around in the unconscious."

Though many professionals agreed with Laibow's argument, others felt it was unjust to throw out those who had brought the phenomenon to their attention in the first place. As Hopkins himself said, "Where have all the mental-health professionals been all these years while these people were clamoring for help." In fact, the dispute has done little to diminish Hopkins' influence, who continues to bring mental-health professionals into the fold.

One of Hopkins' recruits is Harvard Medical School psychiatrist John Mack, author of the 1977 Pulitzer Prize-winning biography of Lawrence of Arabia. Though he is the most prominent and respected member of the mental-health profession to take an interest in anomalous experiences in recent years, Mack is not a pretentious man. The photo from a *Boston Globe* profile shows him standing in a field wearing corduroy slacks and a plaid shirt, his soft gray-green eyes staring calmly at the camera. Unlike most therapists who take an interest in these matters, Mack makes no attempt to hide the fact that he is "open to what these people are telling us."

Mack met Budd Hopkins in January 1990, and was impressed both by the man and the case histories of alleged UFO abductions he had collected over the years. "The stories didn't sound at all like dreams or fantasies to me," says Mack, his voice resonant with authority. "It sounded like something real was happening. And I thought, well, if this is real, what is it? Then Budd asked if I wanted to see some of these people, and I realized I was crossing some kind of line, but I said yes."

Since then, Mack has heard abduction stories from people of all walks of life. "Forty years of psychiatry," he says, "has given me no way to explain what I'm encountering in my interviews and hypnosis sessions of these individuals. Something is going on; something is happening to these people. I'm convinced of it."

In fact, Mack has done as much as TREAT to bring anomalous trauma to center stage in the professional domain. He has spoken freely with the media about his interest and has given talks and participated in private conferences on the subject. Colleagues who hear him speak often raise the issue of whether UFO abduction stories might not be covers for episodes of sexual abuse and incest in childhood. But according to Mack, the reverse has been the case. "There is not a single known case of the thousands that have been investigated where exploring or looking into the abduction story revealed behind it an incest or sexual-abuse history," he says, "but therapists looking for incest stories have come up with UFO abduction memories instead."

Mack understands his colleagues' reluctance to delve into the subject. "It's so shocking to the paradigm of psychology and psychiatry, which tend to look for the source of the experience in the psyches of the people who are affected rather than to acknowledge that something mysterious is happening to these people. The phenomenon is not simply a product of their mental condition but has some kind of objective reality. Whether you call it extraterrestrial or other-dimensional, what it really means is that we may live in a rather different universe from the one Western science has told us we live in."

Mack speaks of vast philosophical implications for this phenomenon and human identity in the cosmos. "There's really a great fear of opening up our world beyond what we know," he says. "But we need to get out of the box we're in and see ourselves in relationship to the universe, and I think this phenomenon could be very important in expanding our sense of ourselves."

Mack's daring views are not shared by all therapists involved in the dark side of the unknown. "If aliens are coming and invading us and abusing us in a very literal sense," argues Toronto psychotherapist David Gotlib, "then it's difficult for me to understand how a significant portion of those who are taken could find it curious or enlightening. If you compare it to the Holocaust or the Vietnam War or any kind of traumatic event, then sure you can learn to grow through it, but only after a lot of pain and soul searching, and not right away. So it discourages me from subscribing to a literal explanation. It also suggests to me that the phenomenon may be dependent on who's experiencing it as well as on what's happening."

Gotlib has thought a lot about UFOs since 1988, when he began treating a woman who had been turned down by other therapists because she claimed her anxiety was due to an alien abduction. He has now seen 40 such patients and publishes the *Bulletin of Anomalous Experience* so that his 150 subscribers in the mental-health professions can network and exchange ideas on UFO abduction reports and related phenomena. "I don't expect to solve the puzzle or have the puzzle solved in my lifetime," notes Gotlib. "These kinds of things have been going on for hundreds of years. I think if we start trying to solve the question definitively, then we're chasing our tail. What I'm most concerned about is, how can we help these people?"

Gotlib sees his next patient and 50 minutes later calls back to answer his own question. "Basically, what we have to do is listen to them without judgment. You let them know that there are a lot of other people who have had these kinds of experiences, that they are not crazy, they are not psychotic, they are not mentally ill, they aren't losing their minds, and this has the effect of empowering them. You talk about the different ways that people understand this experience, and you explore it with them. One patient left saying that his fear had been transformed into curiosity. If I can do that, then I think I've met my therapeutic objective."

It's not a surprise, of course, that Mack, Laibow, and other mental-health professionals championing the anomalous have faced a growing barrage of criticism both from colleagues and outsiders. Are these therapists, critics wonder, clinging to the myth of their own mental impregnability and being drawn into the abyss by the magnetic pull of their patients' experiences? "One needs to monitor one's own reaction to what it is that goes on," cautions NIMH psychologist Harold Goldstein. "You can be sympathetic, you can be empathic, you can be understanding, but your goal as a therapist is not to leap into the same pit as the patient, but to be there to help pull someone out. I think that when physicians or psychologists endorse these things, or appear to endorse them, we do real damage to issues of rationality and realistic evidence. When we reach a point that what's true is what people believe, then we've sunk to a very dangerous situation."

Bill Ellis, a researcher in contemporary legends at Pennsylvania State University in Hazleton, applauds mental-health professionals for coming to grips with anomalous experiences, but, like Goldstein, thinks a little more objectivity is in order. "I think we forget how easily, even if unintentionally, therapists can communicate through body language what they want from their patients," he says. "It's the clever Hans phenomenon. It's like the horse that could come up with the square root of 360, but what it had really learned to do was keep pawing the ground until its trainer relaxed. The trainer was not doing it deliberately. The trainer was convinced that the horse could add and subtract and do square roots. But eventually, somebody who was smart enough to figure out what was going on stopped watching the horse and started watching the trainer. I think we should have more people watching the therapists."

Doing just that is Robert Baker, a retired professor of psychology who taught at the Massachusetts Institute of Technology and the University of Kentucky. And Baker doesn't like what he sees. "I hope we can do something about this nonsense, because it's getting to the point where it's almost a national panic disorder," he says. "We have to do something about therapists who really don't know what they're doing. The therapists who commit themselves to this nonsense are not aware of major areas of human behavior and just do not understand the way the human nervous system works."

One thing that fools therapists, says Baker, is cryptoamnesia, a series of false memories that form a fantasy with a few minor elements of truth thrown in. "The fact is, we do not remember things exactly," he explains. "We change, arrange, and distort the memories we have stored to better serve our needs and desires. We fill the gaps in memory with events that never happened or with events that did not happen the way we imagine, and the results can be bizarre."

The other major cause of the wild stories people tell, according to Baker, is sleep paralysis, a sleep disorder accompanied by hallucinations that affects about 5 percent of the population. In sleep paralysis, Baker explains, "people wake up in the middle of the night and can't move. They feel like they're wide awake, but they continue dreaming and in the dreams often see such things as demons, aliens, or ghosts. Since they're partly awake, however, they may think the dream really happened when, in fact, it didn't. It's no wonder that people find this terrifying, and that's what's responsible for the post-traumatic stress disorder that therapists are talking about."

But Baker has no explanation for the wild stories told by the therapists themselves, unless, he notes, they're "simply seeking attention." Laibow, for instance, claims to have personally experienced anomalous "healing," an event she says cannot be explained by conventional medical science. As Laibow recalls, it was a muggy day in August 1991 when she "trucked on down to Brooklyn to an un-air-conditioned high-school auditorium filled with lots of Polish and Russian émigrés." She sat for three hours, she says, watching Kiev-based psychiatrist and self-proclaimed healer Anatoly Kashperovsky dance to New Age Gypsy music and thought, "What's a nice girl like me doing in a place like this?"

Anyway, there was Laibow, watching Kashperovsky's performance, impatient and skeptical and thinking, "This wouldn't work well at the AMA," when suddenly," she says, "this Caesarean scar that I had, which was thick and ropey and very prominent because I'd gotten an infection immediately after the delivery of my son, began to tingle." As soon as she could decorously take a peek, she hiked up her skirt and found to her surprise that the scar was gone. She immediately made an appointment with her gynecologist, "the head of reproductive medicine at a major university," who, Laibow claims, was shocked when all he could find was a very fine *hairline* scar. The gynecologist, whom she will not name, was excited by her story. "Imagine if we could do that," Laibow says he exclaimed. Laibow adds that the gynecologist may be interested in collaborating on a future study of healing. One possible subject: a Japanese healer who Laibow says "seems to have some very substantial powers."

As founder of TREAT and raconteur of stories both marvelous and strange, Laibow is controversial to say the least. But are the doctor and her colleagues merely misguided, marrying their fortunes to the winds of culture, much like those who touted fairies and dragons in eras past? Or are they onto something new? Will their quest lead more people to come forward with anomalous experiences and encounters, providing the data necessary for proper scrutiny—perhaps even authentication—by the scientific and medical communities at large? In short, are these mental-health professionals fooling themselves, or are they forging extraordinary paths through the byways of consciousness and the murky outback of the unknown? To answer these questions, of course, is to know the nature of the unknown, and that is something we humans have ceaselessly attempted for thousands of years—so far, without much success.

CHAPTER 28

Alien Writing

Undeciphered scripts fascinate me as much as UFOs, if not more. It was through my interest in epigraphy, in fact, that I became interested in pre-Columbian contacts with the New World and how I came to write COLUMBUS WAS LAST. This story brings epigraphy and UFOlogy together. The man whose work is featured in this story, Mario Pazzaglini, died in 1998. He had a fascinating background. Beginning in 1967 he did ethnographic studies on neighborhoods and the kinds of drugs they use, and traveled all over the world in the process. In 1969 he ran one of the drug clinics at Woodstock. His interest in the subject of street drugs stemmed from a fascination with images—the same subject that eventually led him to study "alien writing." This story appeared in the February 1994 issue of OMNI.

✳

Have aliens visited our planet, leaving messages of hope or despair imprinted in the mind of man? Mario Pazzaglini, a Newark, Delaware-based clinical psychologist, aims to find out. His controversial evidence: More than a hundred samples of "alien writing," including symbols reportedly seen on alien craft, scripts read by abductees in so-called alien books, and material said to be psychically transmitted directly into human brains.

According to Pazzaglini, author of the new book, *Symbolic Messages: An Introduction to the Study of Alien Writing,* the concept of alien writing is hardly new. Throughout history, he says. whole systems of writing have been attributed to gods, angels, spirits, and, most recently, extraterrestrial beings. The god Thoth supposedly gave Egyptians the gift of writing. And Quetzelcoatl, the feathered serpent, is said to have handed some Mexican cultures their symbol systems. The incredible number of "alien" scripts are only the latest part of the pattern. "Certainly, something is happening at psychological, sociological, and perhaps even physical levels," Pazzaglini says. "Either we're desperately trying to tell ourselves something, or someone is trying to get through to us."

Despite this insight, Pazzaglini brushes aside the possibility that the many alien scripts he describes are actually different species trying to communicate with us. "They cannot all be real or of true alien origin," he says.

One problem is hoaxing. "There's a lot of it," Pazzaglini explains, "One person tried to pass off an exact copy of a page from the *Book of Mormon*. Other alien scripts are simply too mundane; it's unlikely, for example, that an alien writing system would contain exactly the same letters as our own alphabet unless they were writing specifically for us in English."

After eliminating obviously forged scripts as well as those without enough symbols for true evaluation, Pazzaglini was left with five samples to put to the test. "These five scripts are promising," he says, "because each displays a limited number of symbols in patterns suggestive of grammar." Three of the five even seem to share some symbols and may be part of a single writing system.

But Pazzaglini won't commit himself on that point. "It's like comparing your handwriting and my handwriting and someone else's printing," he says. "If you were totally unfamiliar with a language, and that language was more complex than ours, it would be pretty hard for you to tell if those represented the same system or different ones."

While researchers are normally hush-hush when it comes to alien scripts for fear that dissemination may contaminate future responses, Pazzaglini will reveal this: One of his favorite candidates looks like Gregg shorthand. But unlike shorthand, the structure appears to be syllabic, somewhat like Sanskrit.

Despite all the theories, Pazzaglini, is unwilling to rule out psychological interpretations for the "alien" writing he has seen. "The psyche may be capable of some incredible unconscious maneuvers," he explains, "including devising symbol-sound systems with inherent syntax and grammar. We could be neurologicaly wired to do this." Still, he can't help but wonder if those few promising scripts might not be evidence that "something truly unknown is at hand."

CHAPTER 29

Manhattan Transfer

Every once in a while a magazine will utterly botch a story—or at least their lawyers will, as happened here. Apparently OMNI's attorneys were uncomfortable that this abduction story allegedly involved some high-profile political figures. The Antimatter section of OMNI attracted the most lawsuits, I was told, so perhaps their concern was justified. But despite their efforts to eliminate the sensitive names from the story, they did not completely succeed, and so ended up damaging a major story.

In the first paragraph of the story, next to the words "major political figure" they inserted the phrase "who will remain unnamed." Curiously, however, the man's name— Javier Pérez de Cuéllar—does appear later in the story. And the other major political figure who IS named in the story—Mikhail Gorbachev—was only peripherally involved in the events, but they deleted the paragraph that explained his very tenuous tie to the story, no doubt leaving readers totally confused.

OMNI was not alone going through ridiculous lengths to avoid naming names. In fact, the primary investigator in this case, Budd Hopkins, later wrote an entire book on the case, WITNESSED, without naming Javier Pérez de Cuéllar, even though Hopkins considered this the "case of the century" because of the latter's alleged involvement! Hopkins even used a pseudonym for the central witness in the book, even though her real name had long before been revealed. Since she has become a public figure, even a celebrity of sorts, talking at various UFO conferences across the country, everyone now knows that Linda Cortille is actually Linda Napolitano.

In an attempt to set things straight, I have edited the

original OMNI story in such a way as to reveal these gaffs and correct them at the same time. The words changed or inserted by the editors/lawyers are now in italics within brackets, and the critical paragraph the lawyers cut out now appears in its proper place in italics.

I should add that Budd Hopkins was unhappy with my story—but for entirely different reasons. He felt that my story was far too skeptical. I disagree; I presented his rejoinder to almost all the critical points. Hopkins was particularly peeved because he had been so revealing with me off-the-record. While I honored his off-the-record requests, I felt that, given the public facts of the case, I could reach no conclusion other than the one presented. To conclude otherwise would have been unfair to the reader.

Besides, Hopkins apparently just wanted to save these tidbits for his own book, where anyone now can read about them and pass judgment on their significance. One of these aspects concerns a gift—an old diving helmet—allegedly given to the central witness's son by the major political figure. I do not believe now—I did not believe then—that such unproven tangential material substantiates the basic story—or the major political figure's involvement in it.

My article for OMNI was titled "The Great High-Rise Abduction" and appeared in the April 1994 issue.

✳

It was cold and clear, about 3:00 a.m., when the car stalled near the South Street seaport in Manhattan. Glimpsing up, the passengers—a major political figure *[who will remain unnamed]* and two government agents—spied a glowing oval object hovering over a building a couple of blocks away. As the lights on the heavenly vision changed from red-orange to a bright bluish-white, a woman in a nightgown floated out of a twelfth-story window and hovered midair. The awe-struck witnesses watched as the woman, surrounded by several small creatures, ascended effortlessly into the bottom of the craft. The object zipped over the Brooklyn Bridge and finally plunged into the East River. Or so the story goes.

"It's an extraordinary case," says Budd Hopkins, a world-class modern artist who has recently become known for his books, *Missing Time* and *Intruders*, detailing his 18 years of investigation into claims that thousands of people have been abducted by UFOs. A trip to Hopkins' studio on Manhattan's West Side reveals the profound influence these so-called abductions have had on his art. Scattered around the room are colorful, profile-shaped paintings he calls "guardians" that evoke nothing if not the aliens in question. Indeed, as Hopkins describes his work, his dark, thick eyebrows dance with enthusiasm; these days, it is the bizarre tales of UFOs and the nasty creatures who inhabit them, plucking innocents from their homes in the middle of the night, that consume most of his time.

If Hopkins seems excited, he explains, it's because he has found a case that might convince the army of skeptics who have hounded him for years. Unlike the thousands of other abduction cases on record, he explains, this is the first time independent witnesses have come forward claiming to have seen the event take place. Even more significant, one of these witnesses is said, in the vernacular, to be a Very Important Person. "The implication," Hopkins speculates, "is that this was deliberate, a demonstration of alien power and intent."

Hopkins has never had trouble drawing dramatic conclusions about UFO abductions, a phenomenon that emerged, it should be noted, without him. The first bizarre story came to public attention in 1966 and involved the now-notorious New England couple, Betty and Barney Hill. Under hypnosis, the Hills recalled being snatched from their car and examined by small creatures aboard a flying saucer. But it would take another decade, a few more headline-grabbing abduction tales, and, finally, the television broadcast of the Hills' own story before tales of alien encounters became embedded in the popular consciousness at large.

The stage was now set for Hopkins to emerge as the leading authority on abductions. It happened in 1981 with the publication of his book *Missing Time,* in which he suggested that the abduction experience was much more widespread than anyone had imagined. For Hopkins, the plight of the abductee became a personal crusade, and before long, he would be lecturing on the subject across the country, appearing on one talk show after another, and finally writing *Intruders,* a 1987 best-seller that was turned into a television miniseries in 1992. Clearly, no one has done more than Hopkins to bring this strange phenomenon to public awareness. Even more to the point, no one has had greater success in getting scientists and mental-health professionals to take a serious look at abductions.

So it's no surprise that when Hopkins began touting his latest case as the strongest evidence yet for UFOs, their alien occupants, and their systematic abduction of human beings, people listened. But as the pieces of the puzzle were revealed, critics began charging that rather than prove his point, Hopkins had fallen victim to the elaborate fantasy of a bored housewife or a complex hoax. Indeed, said his detractors, so outrageous was the tale and so fragile the evidence for it, it had backfired, destroying his credibility and bringing down his body of work like a house of cards.

The story certainly is a humdinger, with more twists and turns than California's Highway 1 and more mystery characters than a Le Carre spy thriller. "It's a crazy, endless saga," says Hopkins, including such elements as secret agents, attempted murder, and two high-level political figures, Mikhail Gorbachev one of them. The central character in the case is Linda. She does not want her last name revealed. She lives in Lower Manhattan, and on the very hot spring day I went to meet her, I came to appreciate why the aliens had decided to grab her through the window. It certainly beats penetrating a locked gate and the scrutiny of a guard, then taking an elevator up 12 stories and winding your way through a corridor to her place. When I knocked on the door, I was greeted by an attractive, fortyish woman with brown, almond-shaped eyes and long, flowing brown hair. We sat down on her couch, and as her air conditioner blasted arctic air and she smoked a dozen cigarettes, I was treated to one mind-boggling tale.

It started early in 1988. Linda had just bought Kitty Kelly's biography of Frank Sinatra and another book, which she took to be a mystery. The other book was *Intruders* by Budd Hopkins. By the end of the first chapter, she was stumped: Aliens had left mysterious implants in people's brains and noses, and that last little bit bothered her. Thirteen years before, she had found a lump on the side of her nose and had gone to a specialist who said it was built-up cartilage left over from a surgical scar. But she had never had any such surgery, even as a child, she said. Linda then took my finger and put it on her nose: Yes, I could feel a very slight bump on her upper right nostril. But there had to be more than this, I thought. There was.

A year later, Linda finally contacted Hopkins, who decided to explore Linda's past with his favorite tool—hypnosis. "It felt kind of strange," Linda says. "I'm just a wife and mother. I'm just Linda. UFOs? Naw."

Hopkins says he learned otherwise. He regressed Linda to age 8, enabling her to recall an episode in which she thought she glimpsed the cartoon character Casper, of *Casper the Friendly Ghost* fame. But under hypnosis, her memory of Casper turned out to be a large, top-shaped object that she'd seen flying above the apartment building across the street from her childhood home in Manhattan. Hopkins came to suspect that she had been abducted by aliens, and by June of 1989 had invited her to join his support group for abductees. "I remember sitting there bug-eyed listening to these people," says Linda. "I felt strange the first time, but after that I felt better."

Then, on November 30, 1989, a very agitated Linda called Hopkins to report she had been abducted again. She had gone to bed quite late, at about ten minutes before 3:00 a.m., because she'd been up doing the laundry. Towels and blue jeans for four take eons to dry in her small dryer, she explained. Her husband, who normally worked nights, was on jury duty that week and so was home and asleep in the bedroom. She showered, got into bed, and lying on her back, clasped her hands and began reciting "Our Father" to herself, a habit she carried over into adulthood from her Roman Catholic upbringing. Then she felt a presence in the room.

"I was awake but had my eyes closed," she recalls. "I was afraid. I knew it wasn't my husband; he was snoring away. Then I lay there wondering, *Did I lock the door? Is it one of the kids?*" She called out the names of her two boys and finally reached out for her husband. "Wake up," she said, "there's somebody in the room."

He didn't answer, and she began to feel a numbness crawl up from her toes. After months in the support group exploring her past abductions, she recognized what that meant. *It's now or never*, she thought and opened her eyes. At the foot of the bed, says Linda, stood a small creature with a large head and huge black eyes. "I screamed and yelled," she says, "and then threw my pillow. The creature fell back." After that, she has only fragments of conscious memory—a white fabric going over her eyes; little alien hands pounding up and down her back; suddenly falling back into bed.

It was a quarter to 5:00 in the morning when Linda jumped out of bed, ran into the kids' room, and discovered, she says, that "they weren't breathing." Hysterical, she retrieved a small mirror from the bathroom and placed it under their noses. Suddenly, a mist formed on the mirror, she says, and she heard her husband snoring in the other room. They were all alive. Linda, in shock, sat on the floor in the hallway between the two bedrooms until dawn. Later she called Hopkins.

Under hypnosis, Linda revealed that there had actually been five creatures in the apartment. They had led her from the bedroom through the living room and out a closed window, she declared, where, floating in midair, she saw a bright bluish-white light. She was afraid of falling and embarrassed, thinking her nightgown had gone over her head. She moved up into the craft and then found herself sitting on a table. The creatures around her, she says, were scraping her arms—"like taking skin samples," she speculates, and pounding with an instrument up and down her spine—all typical abduction fare, to say the least.

Quite atypical is what allegedly happened 15 months later. In

February 1991, Hopkins received a typewritten letter from two people claiming to be police officers. Late in 1989, the letter said, the two had witnessed a "little girl or woman wearing a full white nightgown" floating out of a twelfth-floor apartment window, escorted by three "ugly but small humanlike creatures" into a very large hovering oval that eventually turned reddish orange. The object, the letter added, flew over their heads, over the Brooklyn Bridge, and plunged into the East River. They wondered if the woman was alive, though they wished to remain anonymous to protect their careers. They signed the letter with first names only—Richard and Dan.

Hopkins was astonished. "I realized immediately that the woman they had seen was none other than Linda," he said. "The account seemed to corroborate the time, date, and details of her abduction. Here, finally, were independent, seemingly reputable witnesses to an abduction."

When Hopkins first called Linda to tell her, she replied, "That can't be possible." Then she wondered if she and Budd were the victims of a cruel joke. But all suspicions vanished one evening a few weeks later, she says, when Richard and Dan showed up at her door.

"Police," they announced. Linda looked through the peephole and saw two men in plain clothes flashing a gold badge. "So I let them in," said Linda, "and they looked at me kind of funny. When they introduced themselves as Dan and Richard, my stomach dropped to the floor." Both were tall, well-built, attractive men in their forties, she says. Dan sat on the couch, put his head in his hand, and said, "My God, it's really her." Richard had tears in his eyes and hugged her, expressing relief that she was alive.

"Budd had warned me not to discuss the incident with anyone," Linda says now, "so all I could do was tell them to talk to Budd."

In the year that followed, Linda claims, she had numerous encounters with the mystery duo—at bus stops, outside her dentist's office, even at church. Hopkins himself never had the pleasure of meeting the pair, though, he says, he did eventually receive three more letters from Dan and four letters and an audiocassette from Richard.

In one letter, says Hopkins, Dan explained his need to remain anonymous: He and Richard were not New York City cops, he said, nor on that fateful November night had they been alone. They were, in fact, government security agents and had been escorting an important political figure, whom they would not name, to a downtown heliport; suddenly their car's engine died and the headlights went out. They had seen Linda's abduction unfold after they pushed the car to safety under the elevated FDR Drive.

Dan and Richard just couldn't stay away. One morning, after Linda had walked her youngest son to the school bus at 7:15, she claims she was approached by Richard, who asked her to take a ride in his car. She refused, but Richard's grip firmed on her shoulder. "You can go quietly or you can go kicking and screaming," Linda claims Richard told her. As he dragged her to the open rear door of his black Mercedes, he tickled her, Linda states. "That's how he got me in the car."

"They drove me around for about three hours," says Linda, "asking me all sorts of questions." Did she work for the government? Was she herself an alien? They even demanded she prove herself human by taking off her shoes. Aliens, they would claim in a letter to Hopkins, lacked toes. She called Hopkins as soon as they dropped her off at home.

"Hopkins told me to call the police," Linda now explains, "but I refused. Who would have believed me?" The notion of surveillance by Richard and Dan eventually spooked her so much that she quit her secretarial job and simply stayed home. To ease Linda's isolation, Hopkins found a benefactor who paid for Linda's limited use of a bodyguard so she could go out.

Unfortunately, the bodyguard was not around for what Linda says was her second major encounter with Richard and Dan. On October 15, 1991, Linda reports, Dan accosted her on the street and pulled her into a red Jaguar. As they drove along, he sometimes put his hand on her knee—"to distract me," Linda suggests, "from following the route to a three-story beach house which I assume was on Long Island." Inside, Dan started a pot of coffee and gave Linda a present: a nightgown, she says, "the kind a woman might wear if she didn't have any children, especially sons." Dan asked her to put it on so he could photograph her in it as she appeared mid-abduction, floating over New York. She refused but finally agreed to put it on over her clothes. As Dan's behavior became increasingly strange, she decided to flee, running out the door and onto the beach.

"Dan caught me and picked me up, shaking me like a toy," she says. There was mud on my face, so he dunked me in the water once, twice, three times. I don't think he was trying to drown me, but he kept me under too long." This behavior, which critics of this strange tale have termed "attempted murder," finally ceased. Instead, Dan pulled off Linda's wet jeans and, she says, pulled her down on his lap in the water, rocking her like a baby. Shortly after, Linda reports, "Richard showed up, apologized for Dan, and drove me home."

Linda went straight to Hopkins. "She left sand all over my house," Hopkins says. "A few weeks later, I received a half dozen photographs of Linda, in the nightgown, running along the beach."

That November, the saga became stranger still. While lunching with Linda, a relative who was also a doctor insisted she go to the hospital to x-ray the lump in her nose. The x-ray Linda now presents shows a profile of her head; clearly visible is a quarter-inch-long cylinder apparently embedded in her nose.

"It was weird," says Hopkins' friend Paul Cooper, professor of neurosurgery at New York University, who has examined the x-ray. "I've never seen anything like it." But even Cooper admits the x-ray could have been faked by taping a little something to the outside of Linda's nose.

Moreover, as usually happens in UFO stories, this tantalizing bit of evidence vanished as quickly as it had appeared. Soon after getting the x-ray, Linda told Hopkins she'd awakened with a bloody nose. Under hypnosis, Hopkins says, Linda revealed that the aliens had again whisked her away. Later, with Cooper's help, Hopkins had further x-rays taken, but the implant was nowhere to be seen.

Meanwhile, another alleged witness to Linda's spectacular abduction came forward. That same month, Hopkins received a large manila envelope from a woman living in upstate New York. On the outside, in large letters, appeared the words, *Confidential, Re: Brooklyn Bridge.*

On the evening of November 29, 1989, the woman—Hopkins calls her "Janet Kimble"—had been in Brooklyn at a retirement party for her boss. When she headed home via the Brooklyn Bridge around 3:00 a.m., she told Hopkins, her car came to a dead stop in the middle of the bridge and her headlights blinked out. The same thing, she states, happened to the cars coming up behind her. Suddenly, she saw what she thought was "a building on fire" about a quarter of a mile away. The light was so bright that she had to shield her eyes, she said. Then she realized what she was seeing: Four "balls" had floated out of an apartment window and, midair, unrolled into three "rickets-stricken" children and a fourth, taller, "normal girl-child" wearing a white gown. "While I watched," she wrote, "I could hear the screams of the people parked in their cars behind me." The "children" were then whisked up into the object, whereupon it flew over the Brooklyn Bridge and disappeared when her view was obscured by a walkway.

Hopkins says he telephoned "Janet Kimble" immediately and later had lunch with her. The tale told by this "widow of about sixty who once worked as a telephone operator" corroborates stories told by Richard and Linda, he says, ruling out the possibility of a hoax.

In fact, if Hopkins is to be believed, another witness to the Linda abduction was actually the first. That person, he states, is a UFO abductee as well, a woman in her early thirties who claims to have been abducted from her Manhattan bedroom in the middle of the night. She consciously remembers being outside at some point, moving along the streets involuntarily, and seeing 15 to 20 other women all moving zombie-like toward a UFO on the banks of the East River.

When Hopkins tells me this, I can't help but guffaw. He finds my reaction perfectly understandable. "What can I say?" he says. For Hopkins, who is in the midst of investigating another mass abduction in New York City involving a hundred humans, this woman's story is only "a little more bizarre than most."

In any event, says Hopkins, this woman at one point looks down the East River and sees two other UFOs in the sky, one a bright orange object at the southern end of Manhattan, ostensibly the one that abducted Linda.

The two cases, if believed and taken in concert, shed an ominous light on the humorous name that some critics have bestowed on the Linda case: "Manhattan Transfer." Were the aliens out that night abducting Manhattanites like Linda in droves?

By December of 1991, the end of Linda's saga was nowhere in sight. She was now struggling with an obviously disturbed and persistent human named Dan, who, according to Richard, had been admitted to a "rest home." At Christmas, she received a card and note from Dan. It was a love letter, actually. He told her he planned to leave the "rest home" soon and asked her to pack her toothbrush—he was coming for her. He wanted to learn her alien ways and her special language. "You'll make a beautiful bride," he teased. Linda, however, was not amused.

Dan apparently tried to get Linda in February of 1992, but she was rescued from this dragon by Richard, whom Linda now regards as a knight in shining armor. Linda says that Richard, upon returning from a "mission" abroad, had gone to visit Dan at the rest home, found him missing, and had come looking for him in New York. When he learned that Dan had prepared a passport for Linda and booked two tickets to England, he immediately sought out Linda and managed to spirit her away just in time.

Linda's last contact with the aliens occurred a few months afterward. On Memorial Day 1992, she, her husband, two sons, and one of their guests all awakened at about 4:30 in the morning with nosebleeds. Hopkins says he has subsequently confirmed, through hypnosis, that the incident was UFO related.

"I really don't try to convince anybody," says Linda, having come to the end of her story. "I don't expect anyone to believe this because, to tell you the truth, if the shoe were on the other foot, I wouldn't believe it either. But it happened. It happened."

If it really did, I thought, the independent witnesses would confirm it. The prize witness obviously was the VIP, and the word in the UFO community is that Hopkins thinks it was Javier Pérez de Cuéllar, secretary-general of the United Nations from 1982 to 1991. "I will not deny or confirm that," says Hopkins. "I won't say who he is, but I can say this: All the letters from Richard and Dan refer to the fact that there was a third man in the car. And he's written one letter to me, which was signed, *The Third Man*. I can't make the things he said public, though clearly he's letting me know between the lines who he is."

Actually, rumor has it that this third party may be central to the Linda case. According to anonymous sources close to Hopkins, Richard, Dan, and their passenger were *all* abducted on that fateful day of November 30, 1989, right along with Linda. Their delayed recall of this event supposedly would explain why it took 15 months for them to write to Hopkins, why they were so interested in Linda, and why they are so reluctant to come forward now.

But all that is certain about Pérez de Cuéllar is that he was in New York City on the days in question. Did he really witness the Linda abduction? Joe Sills, spokesman for the secretary-general at the United Nations, was nice enough to check with the security people but came up empty-handed. "No one that I spoke to," he says, "was aware of him ever being in that part of town at that hour of the morning. It's just not in the kind of schedule that he kept." What's more, he added, Pérez de Cuéllar could not have been heading for the heliport since he always went to the airport via limousine. U.N. spokesperson Juan Carlos Brandt checked with Pérez de Cuéllar directly. "He says he never witnessed any incident," says Brandt.

And adding insult to injury, Hopkins can't even prove that the two government security agents, Richard and Dan, are real. He has never met or spoken to them, and all efforts to identify them have proved fruitless. In March of 1991, for instance, Linda looked through six hours of clips of news programs showing security agents at events in New York City. The clips belong to one of Hopkins' contacts in government law enforcement. *[Near the end of the six hours, Linda spotted a man whom she identified as "Dan." Despite the fact that the images were taken from a distance, involved crowds and the bustling chaos that accompanies visiting dignitaries, she apparently had no trouble making her identification. Those who have viewed the tapes have seen a man who appears to be taking part in official business, and who is in no way out of place or unusual.]*

Near the end of the six hours, while watching a Peter Jennings broadcast of Gorbachev's visit to New York in December of 1988, Linda believes she spotted the person she knew as "Dan." He first appears in a sequence at the United Nations, where he immediately precedes the entourage of Gorbachev and Pérez de Cuéllar walking down one of the UN's lengthy corridors. He is tall, has short dark hair, wears a blue suit and blue tie, and like others in the security detail, sports a white rectangular ID card on his lapel. He appears again at the end of a sequence on Governor's Island. Here Dan opens the limousine door for Gorbachev, then as Ronald Reagan shakes hands with the translator, Gorbachev shakes hands with Dan before stepping inside the limousine. Upon seeing this, Linda called Hopkins in a panic, thinking Dan must be KGB. "I said it can't be KGB," says Hopkins, "because Gorbachev would never turn to his own man and shake hands with him. It would be like shaking hands with your own chauffeur. He has to be assigned to the security detail. He has to be American."

In the months that followed, Hopkins and Linda made the rounds with their pictures of "Dan" in hand. They went to United Nations security and the State Department, Secret Service, and Russian delegation offices in New York. At times, Hopkins and Linda would use a cover story so as not to arouse suspicion: "Sometimes we said we were husband and wife and that this was a friend we had met a couple of years ago in Cape Cod and he had said to look him up here when we came to New York," Hopkins explains. But the ploy didn't work. "I've been all over with these pictures," says Hopkins, "and nobody recognizes him."

Then there is the woman on the bridge, "Janet Kimble." She is a real person but apparently, after being ridiculed by her own family, wants no part of Hopkins' story. When Hopkins tried to arrange an interview for me, she told him, "I can't help you anymore with this." The final independent witness is the woman up the East River who claims to have participated in the mass abduction of women that very night. But she's another abductee and not truly impartial in the matter.

With no independent witnesses willing to come forward, the case, not surprisingly, has come under intense criticism. Curiously, two of those most critical of the case initially became involved at Linda's request. By early 1992, Linda was feeling so helpless at the hands of her human kidnappers that she decided to seek additional expert help. At the suggestion of New York journalist and UFO researcher Antonio Huneeus, she contacted Richard Butler, a former law-enforcement and security specialist for the Air Force and a fellow abductee, whom Linda had met at Hopkins' support group. Butler met with Linda on February 1, 1992, and brought with him Joe Stefula, a former special agent for the U.S. Army's Criminal Investigations Command and current head of security for a drug company in New Jersey. During the meeting, Linda asked for safety tips on how to protect herself from the dangerous duo, and Butler and Stefula, in order to give useful advice, asked Linda a few questions of their own.

Several months later, after Hopkins made the case public at the 1992 Mutual UFO Network annual meeting in Albuquerque, Stefula, Butler, and a friend of theirs, parapsychologist George Hansen, decided the case needed a thorough investigation and began poking around Linda's neighborhood. They spoke to the security guard and supervisor at Linda's building, went to the offices of the *New York Post* nearby, and simply interviewed residents to see if they remembered anything amiss. No one did.

Afterward, Hansen, already the author of a number of stinging critiques of both psi research and its critics, wrote a lengthy skeptical report. The central issue, say the skeptics, is the lack of large numbers of witnesses to this spectacular event. After all, New York never sleeps; there are people out and about even in the middle of the night.

Why did none of the truck drivers at the loading dock of the *New York Post* just a short distance from Linda's apartment see this blindingly bright object? Why haven't all those other people whose cars were supposedly stalled on the Brooklyn Bridge come forward?

To such questions, Hopkins has a two-fold reply: "The unwillingness of people to report such fantastic experiences is not new. People do not like to be ridiculed," he says. Then there's the invisibility issue, "which just seems to be part of the phenomenon. Many people who you think should have seen these things just don't," Hopkins explains.

But Hopkins can't explain everything. For instance, how could "Janet Kimble" know that the words Brooklyn Bridge written on the outside of her envelope would attract Hopkins' attention unless she knew or was related to one of the people in the Hopkins support group, all of whom had heard about the case? The answer, replies Hopkins, is ridiculously simple: "She saw the abduction from the Brooklyn Bridge and thought that the others who had been stalled on the bridge that night might have contacted me about it."

But Butler says the likelier explanation is that Linda fabricated the whole story after reading *Nighteyes,* a science-fiction novel by Garfield Reeves-Stevens published in April of 1989, just months before her alleged abduction. The novel charts the abductions of an FBI team staking out a beach house in California while a mother and daughter undergo a series of abductions in and around New York City. It concludes with an apocalyptic finale. Butler claims that Linda was very intrigued when the book was brought up at the Hopkins support-group meetings. "I guarantee you that's where she got the basis for her story," he says.

Butler admits the book's storyline is different from Linda's but says there are too many parallels to be coincidence. Both Linda and the novel's Sarah were abducted into a UFO hovering over a high-rise apartment building in New York City. Linda was kidnapped and thrown into a car by Richard and Dan; one of the novel's central characters, Wendy, was kidnapped and thrown into a van by two mystery men. Dan is supposed to be a security and intelligence agent, while one of the book's central characters is an FBI agent. Both Dan and an agent in the novel were hospitalized for emotional trauma. Both Linda and the novel's Wendy were taken to a "safe house" on the beach. The list of such parallels goes on and on.

"But similarity does not prove relationship," replies Hopkins. Without an important political figure witnessing the abduction—the very essence of the Linda case, he notes—the comparison with the book is meaningless.

Hopkins is not alone in his support of the case. Walt Andrus, international director of the Mutual UFO Network (MUFON), is "absolutely convinced the case is authentic." And David Jacobs, a history professor at Temple University and another researcher on the abduction scene, says the critics debunking the case have twisted the facts. "Over the past several years, I have been a confidant of Hopkins' and, at times, of Linda's. I can tell you that when Hopkins' report comes out, the inaccuracy of the critics will be apparent and the case will stand or fall on its own merits."

For Hansen, of course, those merits are slim. And, he says, the hoaxing he believes occurred is the least of it. "For me," he says, "the worst infraction is the reaction of the leadership of UFOlogy. I think this has given us great insight into the mentality—and the gullibility—of Budd Hopkins, Walt Andrus, and David Jacobs, the people who really control much of what people actually read about UFOs."

Hansen is particularly upset that, given charges of kidnapping and attempted murder, the leadership did not go to the police. "I recognize there is government cover-up on UFOs," he says, "but covering up a so-called attempted murder and kidnapping, as these guys apparently say they've done—that's quite something else."

Hoping to right the wrong, Hansen has, in fact, sent a letter to the inspector-general's office, Department of the Treasury, requesting that Linda's claims of kidnapping and attempted murder by federal agents be investigated. In February of 1992, the Secret Service contacted Linda and she and Hopkins went down to their World Trade Center offices to speak to Special Agent Peggy Fleming and her supervisor.

Hopkins and Linda told Fleming the story and explained that they didn't know who Hanson was or why he was involved. Linda also objected to what she perceived as Hansen's insinuation that she was against the government. She was not, she said: "I'm a Bush Republican."

When I called the Secret Service about their investigation, I was referred to Special Agent James Kaiser, media representative in the New York field office. After reviewing the file on the case, titled "Special Agent Alleged Misconduct, February 10, 1993," Kaiser told me that Linda "was, in fact, interviewed at our office, and it was determined that her allegations regarding U.S. Secret Service agents having any contact with her whatsoever prior to that day were unfounded and baseless. It never happened. She may have been mistaking us for some other agency or organization. Case closed."

The case is also closed as far as Hansen, Stefula, and Butler are concerned. They truly believe that Linda is involved in a hoax. "I think she started out with a small lie," speculates Hansen, "a tall tale that grew in the three years that followed. She's been a typist and temporary secretary, so she has had access to a lot of different typewriters undoubtedly. It would not surprise me if there were someone else hoaxing Hopkins as well."

Hopkins flatly rejects the hoax scenario. "An efficient hoax has a minimum of moving parts," he says. "You don't want to go into too many details. This has more moving parts than one could possibly imagine."

As for Linda, when asked if she had made up this whole scenario, she replied simply, "No. How could this be a hoax? There are too many people involved. In fact," she added, "I take the suggestion as a compliment. They must think I'm pretty intelligent to pull off such a thing."

Some details of the case frankly do make me suspicious. For one, the drawings of the abduction that Hopkins received from Richard and the woman on the bridge not only look like they might have been prepared by the same person, despite the stylistic and perspective differences, which Hopkins has duly noted, but more importantly, both were done in crayons and used the same colors.

What's more, to actually meet Linda and hear her talk is to be transported to a world where reality is inverted, where all we have ever known is flipped on its head. Strain your ears, and you can almost hear the chords from *Twilight Zone* kick in as the underlying chaos of the universe takes control. Fact is, outrageous as I find Linda's story, Linda herself seems sincere. Her emotions—fright, anxiety, and anger—appear genuine.

I'm not alone in these impressions. John Mack, a professor of psychiatry at Harvard University Medical School, whom Hopkins confided in as the story unfolded and who now knows Linda well, insists that "there is nothing unauthentic or devious" about her.

Gibbs Williams, a New York psychoanalytic psychotherapist with a quarter century of experience, has tested Linda and also dismisses any notion that Linda might be hoaxing the whole affair. "You would have to have the kind of conspiratorial mentality of Richard Nixon and be able to think sixty-two moves ahead," Williams says. "Quite frankly, Linda doesn't appear to have that kind of mind; she does not have that kind of abstracting capacity." He notes further that her emotive capacity—her anger, crying, and tendency to get carried away—is not consistent with the psychopathic cool mentality of the hoaxer and liar. "My conclusion," he says, "is that from her perspective, she is telling her truth."

Perhaps Jerome Clark, vice president of the Center for UFO Studies (CUFOS) and editor of the *International UFO Reporter,* sums up the controversy best: "This is an absolutely extraordinary claim, and the evidence that you need to marshal to support such a claim simply is not there."

Hopkins promises it will be when his book appears. Until then, Linda stands alone, ambivalent about her fame. On the one hand, she seems to revel in the notoriety. She attends national UFO meetings obviously dressed to impress. "To tell you the truth, it wouldn't be that bad if I didn't have a family," she admits to me.

Yet she also feels victimized. "There are a lot of Italian Americans and Chinese in my neighborhood, and many of them even laugh at joggers," she says. "Imagine if anyone in the area heard that I was abducted by aliens."

"Worst of all," she continues, "those critics took away the safety of my family by taking my real name and publishing it. We are sitting ducks for any crackpot in the UFO community. They know where I live. They know what I look like." She has already taken her name off her intercom system, and she fully expects to move when Hopkins' book on the case comes out. "I don't know what's worse," she says finally, "what Richard and Dan did, what these three stooges from New Jersey did, or what the aliens did." Or what Hopkins has done, I might add. After all, he promised so much and has delivered so little.

Poor Linda.

CHAPTER 30

Extraterrestrial Transfer

Taken to its limits, the ancient astronauts scenario holds that ETs' interaction with humans dates far back in history and that they are responsible for at least inspiring all works of human greatness. Eric von Daniken wrote a best-seller on the subject years ago, but in the United States he was criticized back into obscurity. This is a follow-up look at CHARIOTS OF THE GODS a quarter of a century later. The story, titled "The rise, fall, and afterlife of Erich von Daniken's theory of extraterrestrial gods," ran in the "UFO Update" section of Antimatter, in the May 1994 issue of OMNI.

✳

A little more than 25 years ago, the manager of a first-class Swiss hotel wrote a worldwide best seller titled *Chariots of the Gods?* Its author, Erich von Daniken, captured the public imagination with a dramatic presentation of the idea that extraterrestrials had left physical traces of their presence throughout the world. *Chariots* held, for instance, that the giant stone faces on Easter Island off the coast of Chile were probably constructed with the help of extraterrestrials; the long Nazca lines, criss-crossing the plains of Peru and only visible from the air, von Daniken said, were probably landing strips for their craft.

By the late 1970s, however, von Daniken's "ancient astronaut" theory was crumbling under an avalanche of criticism from archaeologists and astronomers. Today, few believe these extraterrestrial gods ever existed. But don't tell that to the 350 people who met in Las Vegas last August to attend the twentieth-anniversary conference of the Ancient Astronaut Society, or to any of the Society's 10,000 members in 93 countries worldwide. Twenty speakers, including numerous

Ph.D.'s, engineers, and writers gave presentations that touched on everything from the "spaceships" of the Biblical prophet Ezekiel to the notorious "face on Mars."

Von Daniken's largest base of supporters, however, is not in the United States, but rather in Germany and other nations of Europe. In 1993, for instance, Europeans saw von Daniken star in a 25-part biweekly TV series titled *On the Trace of the Almighty*. And touring the cities of Europe, von Daniken still manages to fill 2,000-seat auditoriums. His last nine books, all best sellers in Germany, have also appeared in Italy, France, Holland, Spain, Greece—everywhere, it seems, but in the United States, England, and Australia. "I must be blacklisted in America," says the 58-year-old author with a chuckle.

Despite such slights, von Daniken's belief in the ancient-astronaut theory remains firm. "Each and every one of my books has had to be better than the one before," he says. "We have had to come up with stronger proof each time out."

Of note are the new translations of some ancient Asian Indian texts von Daniken has commissioned. "They describe gigantic space cities that surrounded our planet thousands of years in the past," he says with great enthusiasm. "And from these cities, extraterrestrials used small vehicles to descend to Earth."

Carl Sagan, a major critic of von Daniken in the 1970s, says he has not changed his mind. One of Sagan's original objections was the underlying assumption that our ancestors were apparently too stupid to create the monumental architecture of our past. "But it's never been my idea," von Daniken objects, "that ancient astronauts had constructed great buildings and temples. Mankind did. But why? Mythology and religion say they were dealing with the teachers that had descended from heaven."

Von Daniken's protestations are unlikely to sway his critics. "The whole ancient-astronauts hypothesis was based more on pseudo-history and pseudo-archaeology than any reasonable hypothesis of extraterrestrial intelligence," says Kendrick Frazier, editor of the *Skeptical Inquirer*. "I just don't know anybody who takes this seriously anymore."

CHAPTER 31

Secret Agent Man

Put Bruce Maccabee on stage and he will speak for hours on his favorite subject—UFOs—perhaps even after everyone has left the room. A physicist with a specialty in optics, Maccabee has been the man UFO organizations turn to for analyzing a UFO photograph or video, as I noted earlier. No question about it, the man knows his UFOs. So much so, in fact, that when President Clinton's science advisor needed a backgrounder on UFOs in preparation for a meeting several years ago with Laurance Rockefeller (who was asking the government to come clean with its knowledge of UFOs), to whom did the CIA turn for UFO information? Bruce Maccabee. Such hob-nobbing with "the enemy" has not exactly made him popular with some UFO believers. Maybe he should stick to the piano, which he plays quite well. My story, which was titled "Secret Agent Man," appeared as a "UFO Update" in the Antimatter section of OMNI for August 1994.

*

Physicist Bruce Maccabee has been one of the leading lights of UFOlogy for more than a decade. Back in 1979, he helped establish the Fund for UFO Research, which supports research into the reality of the phenomenon. But now Maccabee faces charges from within the UFO community he has helped to build.

According to a 12-page paper issued by the so-called Associate Investigators Group, Maccabee has been holding secret meetings with the CIA. The paper, sarcastically titled "The Fund for CIA Research?" claims that "Maccabee first approached the CIA in 1979" to discuss UFOs and has continued briefing the organization ever since. The report also states that "Maccabee's public support" for some highly controversial cases might have been encouraged by intelligence contacts who wanted to use him as a mole.

According to W. Todd Zechel, an author of the paper and one of the people to get the CIA to release UFO documents back in 1979, Maccabee has shown "a lack of judgment." His relationship with the CIA represents "a conflict of interest," Zechel declares. "The public has been misled," he says.

But Maccabee insists he has done nothing wrong: "My contacts with the agency have been informal lunchtime lectures for employees. Besides, the CIA people I've talked to tend to be skeptical about the whole thing."

According to Maccabee, his relationship with the spy group began in 1979 when he was asked to brief the CIA on some highly publicized sightings from New Zealand three months before. "I was a little leery," recalls Maccabee, "They were the bad guys: they had just released a thousand pages on UFOs after claiming for years they had no information at all. But I figured they would have technical experts who could comment on the case, and I felt nothing ventured, nothing gained."

His next contact with the CIA came in 1984 via intelligence officer Ronald Pandolfi, who was interested in Maccabee's work for the Navy. But in the course of their professional relationship, Maccabee and Pandolfi also discussed UFOs. So after the Mutual UFO Network held its conference in Washington, D.C., in 1987, Pandoffi asked Maccabee to present a lunchtime talk on UFOs to CIA employees. Maccabee surprised everyone by talking about UFO documents which the CIA itself had released. "The employees were apparently unfamiliar with these papers," says Maccabee, "and afterward, some people even tried to find more CIA UFO documents on their own."

Maccabee's most recent talk at the CIA took place last year, in May of 1993, two months after resigning as chairman of the Fund for UFO Research. The resignation, Maccabee adds, had nothing to do with the CIA: he'd simply moved out of town.

Maccabee's relationship with the CIA is likely to persist. "Bruce has been a friend for quite a few years," states Pandolfi. "The brown-bag luncheon meetings are popular with the staff."

As for colleagues at the Fund for UFO Research, they have long accepted Maccabee's relationship with the CIA. "We were hungry for official information and took Bruce's word that he was in control of the situation," states Larry W. Bryant, a former member of the Fund's executive committee. "I don't think Maccabee ever jeopardized that trust."

The relationship, Maccabee contends, has yielded fruit. "These contacts managed to help me get translations of Soviet newspaper articles," he notes. But the enlightening part has been this: "I have yet to run into anybody who knows a heck of a lot more about UFOs than I do."

CHAPTER 32

Would Someone Please Tell the President?

A lot happens behind-the-scenes in the UFO community—or rather, doesn't happen—which the public, for the most part, never hears about. The previous piece about Bruce Maccabee and his CIA connections doesn't even come close to telling the whole story. Much has happened since, and in preparing this book I felt the need to flesh out this "behind-the-scenes" angle a little. The following story involves a stellar cast of characters—the CIA's own Fox Mulder, one of the richest men in America, and the President himself—as well as some not-so-stellar characters. The following sequence of events is the best I could piece together given that everyone involved, or on the periphery, seems to disagree on exactly what happened and when it happened. This piece, written in January of 2001, has not appeared anywhere previously.

✳

Shortly after Bill Clinton became president in 1992 a number of well-connected people attempted to have the new man-in-charge reveal the government's long-held UFO secrets. Two of these people were Laurance S. Rockefeller, the 86-year-old philanthropist and grandson of John D. Rockefeller, and Scott Jones, a retired naval intelligence officer who worked as a consultant to the Defense Nuclear Agency (1981–1985) then as a Special Assistant on "paranormal interests" to Senator Claiborne Pell (1985–1991).

Rockefeller and Jones wanted to get UFO disclosure on the president's agenda. To accomplish this goal Rockefeller employed Washington lawyer Melvin Laird, who had been the Secretary of

Defense for Richard Nixon in the early 1970s, to approach then Secretary of Defense Les Aspin. Laird did so and Aspin in turn tossed the ball to the White House science advisor, John "Jack" Gibbons. Gibbons, who claimed not to know a thing about UFOs, then asked the CIA White House liaison for information on the subject. That led to Ron Pandolfi, apparently the CIA's real X-Files man. But Pandolfi didn't have someone within the agency prepare the UFO briefing paper. Instead he turned to Navy physicist and UFO buff Bruce Maccabee for the task. And that's just what Maccabee did in April of 1993.

Pandolfi provides some insight into how all this came about in an email posted on physicist Jack Sarfatti's stardrive.org site on the internet. "I had one and only one conversation with Jack [Gibbons] on the issue of UFOs," writes Pandolfi. "Jack was concerned with how to respond to requests from Rockefeller. Jack asked why in the world someone like Rockefeller would believe such nonsense. My response was that only a fellow believer could answer such a question. I offered to ask Bruce to respond, and Jack accepted. The entire conversation lasted about 30 seconds. I called Bruce and he agreed to work that evening on a briefing book. Bruce delivered the briefing book to Jack the following morning before his meeting with Rockefeller. My understanding is that Jack gave the briefing book to Rockfeller. I have no reason to believe Jack read the briefing book or made a copy."

Why would Jack give the briefing book to Rockfeller? Macabee provides some insight into the matter on Sarfatti's website: "My real hope for having the briefing read was based on the requirement that it be available to Gibbons before the Rocky "Horror" Scott show [this is how Maccabee refers to the Rockeffeler-Scott Jones effort, which he abbreviates elsewhere as RHS]. I assumed that my effort would bear fruit if I kept to the timeline and transmitted my briefing on time (I was at home and had to wait for a nearby store to open before I could fax the document at 8AM). Little did I know that my effort had been undercut by the decision of Gibbons and the others to set the RHS show before my briefing could get there. Then of course, after the

RHS show was over Gibbons had disposed of the problem and had no reason to read the briefing."

And what did Maccabee put in this briefing paper? Information that, he says, "would or should be startling to anyone who had never encountered the subject or who had dismissed it out of hand. Hence my inclusion of the SAC base flyovers in 1975, the Iranian Jet case in 1976, and even the Coast Guard case in 1988. My intent was to, at the very least, put a question in his mind. Could this be true?"

But it was all for naught. Gibbons wanted to shield the president from the "nuts" and apparently did a good job of it. The briefing document probably never made it into the White House, and if it did, it probably stopped at the desk of Mack McClarty, the Chief of Staff to the President.

Some believe the real briefing for Gibbons was conducted by Christopher "Kit" Green, a General Motors executive formerly of the CIA with an interest in such matters, but Green denies ever briefing the president himself on UFOs. On this subject Pandolfi comments: "Kit mentioned several short UFO-related conversations he had with Jack [Gibbons] during breaks in meetings on completely unrelated subjects. You can call these 'mini-briefings' if you want, but as I recall it was just Jack expressing frustration with how to avoid confrontation with Rockefeller on what Jack perceived to be a non-issue."

The pressure from below continued on those above in September of 1993 when John Peterson, a futurist who runs the Arlington Institute, a beltway think tank for the military, presented James Woolsey, a friend of his who was then director of the CIA, with a package of heavily sanitized CIA documents on UFOs that UFOlogist and nuclear physicist Stanton T. Friedman likes to brandish about during his UFO lectures. Peterson, whose book *Out of the Blue* discusses the potentially huge impact of human contact with extraterrestrial intelligence, wanted to know why the documents were so heavily sanitized and Woolsey agreed to look into the matter.

Then on December 13, 1993, Steven Greer, an emergency room physician in North Carolina and avid UFO believer who runs a UFO organization called CSETI, and his wife flew to Washington D.C. to have dinner with then CIA director James Woolsey and his wife, who was then the Chief Operating Officer of the National Academy of Sciences. The host of the dinner part was none other John Peterson. Greer viewed the event as a UFO briefing for the CIA director. In his book *Extraterrestrial Contact: The Evidence and Implications,* Greer claims that at the meeting Woolsey and his wife recounted having seen a UFO in New Hampshire in the late 1960s, and that after about 15 minutes of Greer's UFO presentation Woolsey had said in effect, "Yes, I know they exist." Woolsey subsequently called Greer's recollection of the dinner inaccurate. Woolsey and Peterson called it a dinner party. Greer says the dinner party was a cover story for the briefing. Perhaps it was a serious conversation over dinner, but who ever heard of a briefing over wine with spouses?

Peterson's efforts paid off to some extent. At the end of 1993 Woolsey commissioned Gerald K. Haines, the National Reconnaissance Office historian, to prepare a historical review of the CIA's UFO involvement. The Haines report entitled "A Die-Hard Issue: CIA's Role in the Study of UFOs, 1947-90" was later unclassified and published in a 1997 issue of the CIA journal *Studies in Intelligence.*

In the introduction Haines explains how he had come to his task. "In late 1993, after being pressured by UFOlogists for the release of additional CIA information on UFOs, DCI R. James Woolsey ordered another review of all Agency files on UFOs. Using CIA records compiled from that review, this study traces CIA interest and involvement in the UFO controversy from the late 1940s to 1990. It chronologically examines the Agency's efforts to solve the mystery of UFOs, its programs that had an impact on UFO sightings, and its attempts to conceal CIA involvement in the entire UFO issue. What emerges from this examination is that, while Agency concern over UFOs was substantial until the early 1950s, CIA has since paid only limited and peripheral attention to the phenomena." Haines says that CIA officials wanted to keep the public unaware of the agency's interested in UFOs, fearing that it would just fuel the already heated controversy over the subject. "This concealment of CIA interest contributed greatly to later charges of a CIA conspiracy and cover," wrote Haines.

One should note that Woolsey, frustrated by his lack of access to the president, would not be in his post as CIA director for long. Andrew Cockburn, writing in the July 23, 2000, issue of the *New York Times Magazine,* stated: "When a deranged pilot crashed a small plane into the White House grounds in the fall of 1994, the isolated CIA chief bitterly repeated a joke that this was Woolsey making a desperate attempt to see the president. In December 1994, convinced that he would never get support from above, he announced he was quitting." Not only had the president failed to back him, but Woolsey encountered disloyalty within the agency itself. Lying and deception, he discovered, were institutionalized within the agency bureaucracy.

For this reason, I wonder if Woolsey ever really discussed UFOs with Clinton, despite rumors to the contrary on the internet. The mysterious Dan Smith recounts the following story: "Ron [Pandolfi] and I are driving back from Front Royal after my briefing a special forces Colonel, a devout Catholic, on UFOs, eschatons and messiahs, with Ron observing. So I ask Ron about briefing the next President. And he said that if Geo W. [Bush] wanted a briefing he could just ask his dad about it. Ok, and what would his dad tell him, Ron? Well, his dad could tell him that he had tasked Jim Woolsey to find out and get back to him. Oh, really! And what was the result, Ron? Well, Jim came back and told the President that he just didn't need to know."

Smith then mentions a subsequent get-together with Pandolfi: "The point of the dinner meeting was to see if Ron would confirm or not deny his original statement to me that Woolsey had told Pres. Bush that he did not have a need to know about the 'visitor' situation. If he would not deny it, [documentary producer] Gus Russo was prepared to take the story to [*New York Times* investigative reporter] Sy Hersh. Ron did deny it..."

Meanwhile Rockefeller kept pressing Clinton. Finally, during the weekend of August 19-20, 1995, Rockefeller got his chance to make his

UFO pitch to the president. Bill and Hilary Clinton and Jack Gibbons had come out to Rockefeller's Wyoming ranch in the Grand Tetons for the weekend. Clinton subsequently instructed Webster Hubbell, his associate attorney general, to look into UFOs. Hubbell disclosed the president's request in his book, *Friends in High Places*. But despite the president's request, Hubbell was unable to learn anything about the subject. At least nothing that satisfied Clinton's curiosity.

It's likely that the back-door full court press will continue. During the 1968 Congressional Hearings on UFOs, it was Donald Rumsfeld, now President George W. Bush's new Defense Secretary (and President Ford's Defense Secretary as well), who introduced astronomer and Project Blue Book scientific advisor J. Allen Hynek. Rumsfeld was Hynek's congressman at the time. Rumsfeld should expect a knock on the door any day now.

Vice-President Dick Cheney has already been quizzed on his knowledge. On April 11, 2001, while appearing on the Diane Rehm radio show on WAMU, Grant Cameron called-in this question: "There is a vicious story circulating in the UFO community that you have been "read into" the UFO program. My question is, in any of the government jobs you have had, have you ever been briefed on the subject of UFOs? If so, when was it, and what were you told?"

Cheney replied: "If I had been briefed on that, I'm sure it was probably classified and I couldn't talk about it." Rehm then posed a follow-up question, asking if there was any investigation within this administration with regards to UFOs. Cheney answered with a chuckle: "I have not come across the subject since I've been back in government, since January 20th [2001]. I've been in a lot of meetings, but I don't recall one on UFOs."

Eventually UFO buffs will grow up and stop trying to collar the president (or the next best thing). When it comes to UFOs, it's obvious he doesn't know much more than the rest of us. Of course, some people claim that the president is deliberately kept out of the loop when it comes to UFOs, that those few in-the-know are controlling the information and misinformation, its secrecy and release, and have done so for the past half century. This close-knit group is supposedly called MJ-12. But the documents supposedly revealing the existence of this super top-secret group are not convincing and are probably a hoax—at best part of the misinformation being spread on the subject. There never was such a group and no such group of insiders who knows "the truth" about UFOs exists today. It's a fantasy. And not a very good one at that.

But if I'm wrong, would someone please tell the president?

CHAPTER 33

Fast Walkers

I was not the only person on the UFO beat for OMNI magazine. OMNI was running more and more UFO stories and Dennis Stacy, who also edited the monthly MUFON UFO JOURNAL at the time, would write articles on the subject for the magazine as well. In fact, in 1993 OMNI asked Stacy to write a six-part article on the "Cosmic Conspiracy." We managed pretty much to stay out of each other's way until a conflict arose as Stacy was due to begin writing Part 5 of the series, on the 1980s. I had been talking to Joe Stefula, who knows more about UFOs than most so-called experts on the subject, and he had mentioned a remarkable incident that had been recorded by one of our defense satellites.

When I proposed an article on this subject to my OMNI editor, Pamela Weintraub, she quickly said yes. But she called back shortly afterward saying that since Stacy was working on the 1980s and this incident had occurred in 1984, she wanted to take the story away from me and give it to Stacy to write up for that part of the Cosmic Conspiracy series. Since I had been hot after this story and already had begun the interviews, I was not just disappointed, but a little upset. I then suggested that perhaps we could co-author the story. Weintraub had no problems with that, and neither did Stacy, as it turns out. In fact, it helped cement a growing friendship that eventually led to sharing the editorship of a journal we both wanted to publish, called THE ANOMALIST.

So Stacy and I split up the duties. I did most, but not all, of the interviewing, and he did most, but not all, of the writing. Editor Weintraub provided the glue that made it work for the series and the co-authored story appeared under the title "Cosmic Conspiracy: Six Decades of Government UFO Cover-Ups: Part Five," in the August 1994 issue of OMNI. Following the published story, I have appended an update.

✳

From their vantage point 22,300 miles above the Earth's surface, a fleet of supersecret military satellites monitors our planet for missile launches and nuclear detonations. On a clear day, these satellites can see forever, so it's no surprise when they also pick up erupting volcanoes, oil-well fires, incoming meteors, sunlight reflections off the ocean, and a host of other heat sources, including those that still remain unexplained.

Since 1985, all this data has been beamed down in near real-time to the U.S. Space Command's Missile Warning Center, operating from within Cheyenne Mountain, near Colorado Springs. The purpose: coordinating satellite-based early warning systems for the Army, Navy, Air Force, and Marines. Whether harmless or threatening, the information has always been a guarded national secret. But suddenly, in 1993, with the Cold War over, the Defense Department agreed to declassify some satellite information not related to intercontinental ballistic missile (ICBM) launches and nuclear events. Since then, scientists from astronomers to geophysicists have rushed to get their hands on this mother lode of data.

Among researchers hoping to glean some truth from the declassified data are UFOlogists, long frustrated by the critics' classic retort: "If UFOs are real, why haven't they been detected by our satellites?" Well, some UFO researchers are now saying, they have been. With access to the most sophisticated space data ever generated, say some UFO researchers, they may finally find the Holy Grail of their profession: bona fide, irrefutable, nuts-and-bolts proof of UFOs.

UFO researchers have been searching for such evidence in government vaults for years. In the fifties and sixties, some UFOlogists claim, the military kept alien corpses and a ship under wraps. The search for proof was fueled throughout the seventies by the Freedom of Information Act, which yielded thousands of pages of government documents, but no hard, technical, incontrovertible evidence of UFOs. Finally, in the 1980s, a supposedly explosive memo revealed the existence of a top-secret group, dubbed MJ-12, made up of high-level government officials devoted to the secret reality of UFOs. Only problem is, according to most UFO experts, the memo was a hoax. Of course, data from crude detection systems like gun cameras and radar were available. But they merely confirmed the obvious: that military and government personnel, like many other sectors of the population, saw and reported mysterious lights in the sky.

If they could ever prove their theories, UFOlogists knew, they would have to tap the most sophisticated information-gathering technology available: Department of Defense spy satellites, like the Defense Support Program (DSP) satellites, in geosynchronous orbit above the Earth. In fact, rumor had it, heat, light, and infrared sensors at the heart of the satellites were routinely picking up moving targets clearly not missiles and tagged "Valid IR Source." Some of these targets were given the mysterious code name of "Fast Walker."

Unfortunately for UFOlogists, few secrets in this country's vast military arsenal have been so closely guarded as the operational parameters of DSP satellites. Even their exact number is classified. "That shouldn't surprise anyone," explains Captain John Kennedy, public affairs officer with the USAF Space Command Center at Peterson Air Force Base. "It's an early ICBM launch detection system, and we have to protect our own technology for obvious reasons. If everyone knew what the system's capabilities were, they would try to take steps to get around it." But in recent years, thanks to a loosening of the reins, a few tantalizing tidbits of information have managed to seep under the satellite secrecy dam, allowing UFOlogists a small glimpse of some surprising near-space events.

The first issue for UFOlogists to examine, explains Ron Regehr of Aerojet General in California, the company that builds the DSP sensor systems, is whether the satellites could detect UFOs even if we wanted them to. According to Regehr, who has worked on the satellite sensors for the last 25 years and even wrote its operational software specifications, the answer to that question was revealed in 1990, during Operation Desert Storm. "As we now know," says Regehr, "the satellites picked up every one of the 70 Iraqi Scud launches, and the Scud is a very low-intensity infrared source compared to the average ICBM."

Pursuing the matter further, Regehr turned to an article published in *MIJI Quarterly*, "Now You See It, Now You Don't," which detailed a September, 1976, UFO encounter near Teheran. The incident involved two brilliantly glowing UFOs first seen by ground observers. One object, or light source, an estimated 30 feet in diameter, reportedly went from ground level to an altitude of 40,000 feet, and was visible at a distance of 70 miles. An Imperial Iranian Air Force F-4 jet fighter was sent aloft and managed to aim a Sidewinder AIM-19 air-to-air missile at the target before its electronic systems failed.

"Apart from the visible light factor, there's the indication that the UFO gave off enough infrared energy for the Sidewinder's IR sensor to lock onto it," says Regehr. "You can do a few simple calculations," he adds, "and conclude that the DSP satellites of the day should easily have been able to see the same thing. Of course, I can't say they did, or if they did, whether or not it was recorded in the database."

Part of the problem, according to Regehr, is the sheer mountain of data that the DSP satellites generate. On average, an infrared portrait of the Earth's surface and surrounding space is downloaded every 10 seconds. All of the data is then stored on large 14-inch reels of magnetic tape, "the kind," says Regehr, "that you always see spinning around in science-fiction movies, and which fill up in about 15 minutes." The tapes are eventually erased and reused.

Technicians visually monitor the data stream on a near real-time basis, but only follow up a narrow range of events—those that match up with what the Air Force calls "templates." Based on known rocket fuel burn times and color spectra, the templates are used to identify ballistic missile launches and nuclear explosions. But the system also picks up other infrared events ranging from midair plane collisions to oil-well fires and volcanoes.

"I would say that rarely a week goes by that we don't get some kind of infrared source that is valid, or real, but unknown," admits Edward Tagliaferri, a physicist and consultant to the Aerospace Corporation in El Segundo, California, a nonprofit Air Force satellite-engineering contractor. "But once we determine it isn't a threat, that's basically the end of our job. We aren't paid to look at each and every one."

Tagliaferri and a handful of colleagues are among the few civilian space scientists who have thus far been allowed access to the Department of Defense database. Their research, based on spy satellite data declassified in the fall of 1993, is part of a chapter in *Hazards Due to Comets and Asteroids,* from the University of Arizona Press. "I think the Air Force finally agreed that the data had scientific, as well as political and global, security value," says Tagliaferri.

What Tagliaferri and his collaborators were able to confirm was that between 1975 and 1992, DOD satellites detected 136 upper-atmosphere explosions, a few equivalent in energy to the atomic bombs that destroyed Hiroshima and Nagasaki. Unlike the three- to ten-minute burn periods of an ICBM, these previously unacknowledged "flash events" typically take place in a matter of seconds. They are attributable to meteorites and small asteroids. "Most of what we see are objects that are probably 10 to 50 meters in diameter, about the size of a house, and packing 300 times the kinetic energy of dynamite," Tagliaferri says.

The ramification, however, is that nervous governments might mistake these flash events for nuclear bombs aimed in their direction and trigger a like response. One of the brightest unknown flash events occurred over Indonesia on April 15, 1988, shortly before noon, exploding with the approximate firepower of 5,000 tons of high explosives. A slightly less powerful detonation shook an uninhabited expanse of the Pacific Ocean on October 1, 1990, in the midst of Operation Desert Shield.

"But what if the latter event had exploded a little lower in the atmosphere, and over, say, Baghdad?" Tagliaferri warns. "The consequences could well have been disastrous. Ground observers would have seen a fireball the brightness of the sun and heard a shock wave rattle windows. Given the mindset of the Iraqis, Israelis, and the other combatants in the area at the time, any of them might have concluded that they were under nuclear attack and responded accordingly."

The argument that some UFOs might be capable of triggering a similar false alarm has been made many times in the past by, among others, the Soviets. An article titled "UFOs and Security," which appeared in the June 1989 issue of *Soviet Military Review*, states: "We believe that lack of information on the characteristics and influence of UFOs increases the threat of incorrect identification. Then, mass transit of UFOs along trajectories close to those of combat missiles could be regarded by computers as an attack."

But when asked if some unknowns detected by satellite sensors might represent real UFOs rather than incoming meteorites, Tagliaferri chuckles. "Personally, I don't think so," he says. "But who knows? How can you tell? I'm a scientist, a physicist, and to my mind the evidence of UFOs is just not convincing. On the other hand, I've been wrong before."

UFOlogists, meanwhile, think that proof might be lurking in the stacks of printouts from the DSP system computers. But the only material of this sort likely to see the light of day will probably have to come from inside leaks. And that may have already happened. One UFO researcher, using sources he won't reveal, has turned up evidence of what he believes might be a UFO tracked by satellite. Last year, Joe Stefula, formerly a special agent with the Army's Criminal Investigation Command, made public on several electronic bulletin boards what purports to be a diagram of an infrared event detected by a DSP satellite on May 5, 1984. "I haven't been able to determine that the document's absolutely authentic," says Stefula,"but I have been able to confirm that the DSP printout for that date shows an event at the same time with the same characteristics."

According to Stefula's alleged source, now said to be retired from the military, the official code name for unidentified objects exhibiting ballistic missile characteristics is Fast Walker. "But what makes this particular Fast Walker so peculiar," says Stefula, "is that it comes in from outer space on a curved trajectory, passes within three kilometers of the satellite platform, and then disappears back into space. Whatever it is, it was tracked for nine minutes. That doesn't sound like a meteorite to me."

Regehr agrees: "It was there too long. It was going too slow. It didn't have enough speed for escape velocity." But escape it did.

The May 1984 event allegedly generated a 300-page internal report, only portions of which are classified, though none of it has yet been released. "I don't think they would do a 300-page report on everything they detect," says Stefula, whose efforts to obtain the report have so far been unsuccessful, "so there must have been something significant about this that led them to look into it. My source told me that they basically looked at every possibility and couldn't explain it by natural or man-made means."

Nor was this apparently an isolated event. According to the unnamed source, such Fast Walkers are detected, on the average, "two to three times a month."

Even longtime arch-UFO skeptic Philip J. Klass, contributing avionics editor to *Aviation Week and Space Technology,* admits that the military's DSP satellites could detect physical flying saucers from outer space—but with one very large proviso: "If you assume," says Klass, "that a UFO traveling at, say, 80,000 feet leaves a long, strong plume like a space shuttle launch. But we know that isn't the way UFOs are usually reported."

Part of the problem, according to Klass, who has written a book on military spy satellites titled *Secret Sentries in Space,* is that the DSP system has performed better than spec. "It's too good, or too sensitive, if you prefer," he says. "In fact, it was so good that it was sent back to research and development for fine tuning, in order to eliminate as many false alarms as possible. Obviously, we didn't want a fuel storage tank fire next to a Soviet missile silo to set off a launch alarm," he explains. "Nor did we want the system to track the dozens or hundreds of Russian jet fighters in the air every day."

Klass's best guess is that the mysterious May 1984 Fast Walker event uncovered by Stefula probably represents nothing more than a classified mission flown by our own SR-71 high-altitude Blackbird spy plane. "It's admittedly too long a duration to be a meteor fireball," he concedes, "but the Blackbird typically flies at an altitude of 80,000 to 100,000 feet, which makes its afterburner trail easily visible to the DSP system."

In the same context, says Klass, Fast Walker might be a code name for the recently retired SR-71 itself, or, conceivably, its Soviet counterpart, assuming the Soviets had one at the time. Either way, Klass concludes, "It's no surprise that the Air Force would want to keep much of this information secret."

Apparently, keep most of it secret they will. Despite the success Tagliaferri and a few others had in getting past the military censors, don't anticipate a flood of similar studies, especially one in search of UFO reports. "I don't see the Air Force declassifying a whole lot more of the DSP data to other scientists, not without an incredible amount of cleanup," says Captain Kennedy. "And it's certainly not accessible to requests through the Freedom of Information Act."

Even if some unknowns turn out to be UFOs, the Air Force Space Command isn't going to hand UFOlogists—or anyone else—that information on a silver platter. Meanwhile, the dividing line between what might constitute extraterrestrial technology and our own twentieth century equivalent grows increasingly narrow and blurred with every new device sent into space. Somewhere out there, no doubt, is a sensor system that already knows whether we are being visited by UFOs, but the owners of those systems aren't talking.

✳

Postscript

In October of 1999 I ran into Joe Stefula at a UFO conference in New Jersey. He informed me that the fast walker incident had been mentioned in a fascinating book titled AMERICA'S SPACE SENTINELS: DSP SATELLITES AND NATIONAL SECURITY, written by a political science professor named Jeffrey Richelson, who has had access to classified information for his books on the American intelligence community.

Richelson brings up the fast walker incident that Stacy and I had written about in OMNI and comments on it in the space of two paragraphs. "There were, in fact, two elements of truth to the claims of Stefula and OMNI," he wrote. "There was a May 5, 1984, detection of a space object, and it was an example of a class of sightings designated FAST WALKER. According to Air Force Space Command Regulation 55-55, FAST WALKER denotes detection of a space object, which includes satellites and their debris, in a DSP satellite's field of view. The designation was chosen because the dots associated with DSP observations of spacecraft would be more widely spaced than those associated with aircraft, given the spacecraft's much greater speed."

Despite the 300-page internal report that failed to explain the occurrence, however, Richelson says the May 5th FAST WALKER was explained. "The object that came perilously close to Flight 7 was not a UFO but a signals intelligence spacecraft, probably the VORTEX satellite launched on January 31, 1984, from Cape Canaveral by the publicity-shy group of terrestrials who constituted the NRO [National Reconnaissance Office]. The spacecraft in question had failed to enter its proper geostationary orbit."

While Richelson clearly shows his expertise on intelligence matters, I have serious doubts about his explanation, for several reasons. First, either it was the VORTEX satellite or it wasn't. Why does he say "probably"? Second, why would a 300-page internal report fail to find this explanation? And third, Stefula's source says otherwise. "My source says it's BS," replied Stefula. "He claimed they checked with NRO about other satellites and found none that matched the incident. Somewhere in government is a very thick report detailing the incident but I haven't been able to find it."

CHAPTER 34

The Devil's Design

If there is only one thing I can say for certain about the UFO phenomenon, it's that there is no black and white answer. It's gray. Maybe even Gray. But some people insist that it's one thing and not the other. Extraterrestrial. Terrestrial. Good. Bad. One of the better expositions of the demonic view appears in a book discussed in this "UFO Update" titled "The Devil's Design," which ran in the October 1994 issue of OMNI.

✳

Could some UFOs and their occupants be manifestations of demonic angels hell-bent on destroying our society and faith in God? Absolutely, say two former Air Force men in a self-published book titled *Unmasking the Enemy*. What's going on, explain authors Nelson Pacheco and Tommy Blann, is just the latest chapter in the eternal struggle between good and evil, with the fallen angels coming on as extraterrestrials in order to be accepted, even welcomed, by humans.

"We are dealing with highly intelligent beings," says Pacheco, "and in their effort to subvert us, they will use whatever cover they can." Pacheco, a Roman Catholic, and Blann, a Protestant, did not reach this diabolic conclusion based on their religious beliefs, they maintain, but rather, after decades of studying such phenomena as crop circles, apparitions of the Virgin Mary, and mutilated cattle.

"We have no ulterior motive," notes Pacheco, "not money or fame. We just want to get the truth out. If anything, it's been a risk to our professional reputations."

That reputation is considerable. Pacheco, 49, spent 21 years in the United States Air Force, during which he helped in the targeting of Minuteman ballistic missiles and the tracking of satellites for the

North American Aerospace Defense Command, which keeps watch on enemy craft that pose a threat to the United States and Canada. He was also chairman of the mathematics department at the Air Force Academy before retiring as a lieutenant colonel in 1987. Today, he works for a Department of Defense think tank. Similarly, Blann, now 47 and a second lieutenant in the Civil Air Patrol, served in the Air Force as a radio-intercept analyst for two years, then worked as a chemical technician in the oil and electronics industries.

How did these men, who met each other online while roving a computer information service, come to their demonic theory of UFOs? The first clue, they say, came from the hundreds of credible witnesses who have described these craft as simply "vanishing on the spot." Despite this ghost-like behavior, they add, the so-called craft still sometimes managed to have physical effects, like tracking on radar, for example, or leaving scars on abductees. For Pacheco and Blann these seemingly tangible clues meant UFOs could not be a manifestation of imagination alone.

"So we came to think that the phenomenon must be preternatural," says Pacheco, "which means something not of our world but interacting with it. And that, of course, is very close to the area of traditional religion. It is our belief that what we are seeing conforms very nicely with Orthodox religious teachings on demonic angels."

In fact, say the duo, the evil nature of much UFO phenomena is devilishly obvious. "I don't know how anyone can study UFO abductions and still have doubts about whether what's happening is good or evil," Pacheco adds, citing the aliens' disregard of human free will. "When these beings discuss God, they set themselves up as the true savior of humankind in order to undermine traditional Christianity."

Early comments on Blann and Pacheco's work have been positive but not without reservations. "Their grasp of the data is firm and their position plausible," says philosopher Michael Grosso, "but their reasoning is flawed. Yes, there is a sinister side to UFOs, but this does not imply satanic deception. All kinds of people are critical of, even hostile to, the Christian view of things. Does that prove they are in league with the devil? I don't think so."

CHAPTER 35

Anatomy of an Investigation

In November 1994, OMNI announced a new venture
called "Project Open Book," which the editors described as
"a worldwide quest for close encounters of the documented
kind." It was a ambitious move, part bravado, part
marketing. In essence OMNI would take up where the Air
Force had left off in 1969 with Project Blue Book. But
unlike that failed effort, OMNI's examination of the UFO
phenomenon would be "open to public scrutiny," as its
name implied and as its journalistic roots required. In her
introduction to the new endeavor, editor Pamela Weintraub
explained how OMNI's investigative reporters, yours truly
included, would "wield their craft to go through the data,"
and come up with "a semblance of truth." OMNI was in a
good position to do this, Weintraub explained, "because we
have no axe to grind." Following "OMNI's longstanding
policy of informed skepticism," the Open Book team would
seek the answer to the ultimate question: "Is there any
evidence that proves, to our satisfaction and beyond a
shadow of a doubt, that the alien interpretation of UFOs is
for real?"

Project Open Book turned out to be far too ambitious
for its own good. No magazine could support such a cause.
Not philosophically. Not financially. In any case, I ended up
doing only one such in-depth case investigation for OMNI.
The magazine was in trouble, and if this was an effort on
the part of the publisher—actually his wife, Kathy Keeton,
whose baby OMNI really was—to revive the magazine's
slumping fortunes, it would fall short.

Though my investigation never ran as a casebook,

Weintraub did use a few choice details about the case in her article "Let the Project Begin," announcing Project Open Book: "It was a clear, cold night in Brooklyn, New York, when ham-radio operator Alex Cavallari picked up bizarre, jumping waveforms on his scope. An hour later and some ten miles west in Newark, New Jersey, the same disturbance puzzled former Navy man and ham-radio operator John Gonzalez. Gonzalez's neighbors were disrupted as well: TV reception was interrupted, homes shook as if in an earthquake, and several witnesses reported a flash of light. Gonzalez now claims he could make out a disc-shaped craft inside the light, and contends the craft brushed his ham-radio antenna and knocked down tree branches in his backyard. A strange, ashlike sphere the size of a golf ball was later found in his yard. Rich in evidence, this intriguing incident has already been investigated by police and fire departments and by researchers in a lab. The needed culmination for all this data: a synthesis, in which an explanation might emerge."

Sounds interesting enough, doesn't it? Well, read on.

❋

PART 1: The Incident

Date: March 5,1994
Time: 10:30 P.M.
Place: North Newark, New Jersey
Primary Witness: John Gonzalez, 46.

Category: Close encounter of the second kind, involving multiple witnesses, widespread electromagnetic interference, and alleged physical traces from a low-level UFO.

Statement by Primary Witness: "I've been a ham operator since 1987. On Friday and Saturday nights a bunch of us guys get together and talk on 28.376 MHz. And on Saturday night there is a UFO net on 39.77 MHz. Anyway, between 10:00 and 10:30 P.M. I heard some squealing on 39.77. Then I went down to 10 meters and it was still there—same squeal all over. I heard it on the ham set, on my computer, and on a speaker that was not attached to anything.

"Then something struck my antenna. It sounded like something scraping metal to metal. The clock said exactly 10:30 when it struck and the house started shaking. As I turned around, I saw the compass on my shelf spinning like a top. Then I yelled out to my mother, 'Are you all right?' She said: 'What's going on?' She thought we were in an earthquake. But nothing was falling off the shelves. The house shook for about 6 minutes.

"Also at 10:30 the lights started blinking on and off, constantly. Now my radio clock—if you pull the plug for a second it will go to 12 o'clock—never changed. The computer was on and I shut it off right away because I was afraid it was going to crash. Then I shut the radio off, because it was squealing. But even when I shut it off it kept squealing. A high pitch squeal was coming through all the speakers. So I turned, looked outside, and said, 'Oh, my outside light are on,' but they weren't my lights. And it was too bright. The yard looked like daytime; I said, 'What the hell is going on?' So I opened the [dirty] window and saw my outside lights weren't on. Then I looked up and there it was.

"There was a big bright light above the tree in my neighbor's yard. I watched it a couple of seconds and then went to the bathroom window to get a better look. The light was gone. Now I saw a black object moving south, southwest. All I saw was the tail edge of it, which was rounded in the back. Moving very slowly. No noise. No sound. I went outside right away to see if any of the neighbors saw it and that's when I saw the light come on a second time. The object was about four houses down when it came on. You couldn't see the craft really but you could see the glow of that light from it.

"So I ran in the house right away and called 911. 'We think we had an earthquake here,' I said. I didn't want to look like an idiot with the police telling them it was a UFO. By the time I hung up the phone, the fire department was already coming down the street and the neighbors all started coming out of the woodwork. All together there were two police squad cars, a fire truck, a fire rescue truck, and three or four neighbors out there.

"So I asked them how did you get here so fast, and one cop said we've been having phone calls of UFO sightings all night, since about 9 o'clock. I said, I didn't call for that, I called because of an earthquake. He said there was no earthquake. I said something hit my antenna, something hit my tree. A lot of broken branches were scattered all over the yard, more than a dozen. They were on the roof, too. There was clean, brand-new snow everywhere; it had snowed the night before. The antenna was bent toward the west 2 or 3 degrees off center.

"So they followed me through the alleyway into the back yard, walking around. One cop came into the yard and two firemen, and another guy, I don't know who he was, he had Civil Defense on his jacket, a big CD on the back. This guy put one of his gray bags on the ground and started picking up branches. I said what the heck are you doing. He said 'We take samples.' I know what the radiation insignia looks like, and I saw the yellow insignia on the bags with the red thing on it.

"He was picking up branches, cutting pieces off, putting it in his bags. So I picked up one of those gray bags and it was heavy. I said, 'What the hell is this, lead?' He said, 'Yeah, they're leaded bags in case there's radiation.' I said jokingly maybe that was a UFO. He said we were sighting UFOs all night. At 9 o'clock over Long Island, Pomona, we were tracking three UFOs, three were going to the south and one was to the west. Then I said, 'Oh, that's interesting, I'm a member of MUFON.' I got nothing more out of his mouth.

"The Civil Defense guy left in his own car. The firemen and police said there's nothing to report. Then the guy across the street, a Portuguese man, runs out to the cop and says: 'Hey look, UFOs are coming here, how do you protect us, my wife and my child?' The cops said: 'What can we do? We're cops. We can't do anything.' So I asked him, 'Did you see anything?' He said: 'No, no, no.'

"Afterwards I got back on the radio and said, 'Hey, you guys see anything over this way? Take a look.' Alex Cavalleri in Brooklyn said there are strange lights over here. He said it's got to be south of you. That's when it hit a telephone pole a few streets away. It cut the top of it in half.

"I also called [the utility company] PSE&G, because our lights were flashing on and off. They said we haven't had any problem. Around 11 o'clock Ruben Echevarria said, 'Hey, John, you hear the squealing?' I says, 'Yeah, it started up again.' I looked out the window, but there was nothing there.

"That night we also saw black helicopters. Everybody saw them. One was right over the tree. Alex tells me: 'Go outside and see if they are taking photos, I see flashes.' The helicopters had no insignia on them. They were all black. We also had the Feds in white vans driving up and down the street all night long. The vans had government plates on them."

Background, Primary Witness: John Gonzalez lives in North Newark with his mother. He receives social security disability because of brittle diabetes, a heart problem, and emphysema. He has not worked since 1991, when he was a cabinet-and-furniture maker. Before that he was a truck driver. Gonzalez served in the Navy in 1965 and was discharged from boot camp because of health problems. He has had one previous sighting. On March 19, 1992, he saw four points of light come together in the sky at about 10 P.M. Through his 910 power telescope using a No. 24 lens, it looked like an English bowler hat without a bottom ring. He then pulled out a hand-held spotlight and began shining it toward the craft. "That's the last thing I remember until I got up off the floor at 7:30 the next morning," he says, implying an abduction and pointing to a scar on the left side of his waist, "which was not there before March of 1992." A young woman in neighboring Bloomfield, NJ, also reported a UFO encounter that evening. Gonzalez became a member of MUFON after this incident.

Other witnesses: Several sets of neighbors experienced something on the night of March 5. One was the Susus, John Gonzalez's next door neighbors. When I asked Teresa Susu what she remembered of that night she said, in broken English, "I see a big light. I was scared. [My daughter] Angela was here. We were playing a game. My lights were flashing. I go outside and see firemen."

Later I spoke to Angela Susu. "We just saw some lightning, that's all," she recalled. "We were in the living room, and we just saw the lightning through the window. I think it flashed only once. We were watching TV and it went off for a few hours. The lights went off for a couple of times. Then we went outside, but we didn't see anything outside. Some people out there were saying it was an earthquake. Others were saying it was lightning."

A ham-radio operator in Brooklyn also claims to have seen something over New Jersey that night. Alex Cavalleri lives in Brooklyn, 8 to 10 miles from Newark, on the sixth floor of a building that faces the Verrazano Bridge and has a direct view of New Jersey. At about 8 P.M. that evening, Cavalleri was building an audio pre-amp for his radio. He tried using two different scopes, but neither would stabilize, and his TV "was going crazy." Cavalleri attributed it to local interference. This lasted about 30 to 40 minutes.

Later Cavalleri decided to run his ham radio antenna out the window. "It's a crystal clear, beautiful night," he recalls. "While I'm setting up out the window, I see over the Newark area two or three columns, or flashes, of light. It was exactly over John's house. So I get on the radio, 28.376 MHz. I tune in and there's a lot of commotion. John was on the radio with the other guys before I got in there. I find out what's going on. John's house was shaking. He saw lights. Fire and police and rescue are all there, he tells us.

"Then at about 11 we get interfered with. I'm on the radio and talking and all of a sudden I have this outrageous interference. I really should call it a transmission. I believe it to be a transmission, though I've been getting a lot of flack for that. I believe it was a modulated signal. I don't believe it was any form of man-made interference. While I was on the air, my radio broke into receive while I'm still talking. They are hearing me while I'm receiving this signal. Other than being impossible, the signal itself was extremely peculiar.

"This is hard to explain unless you have heard all the forms of noise that are out there. This was not static. This was not whistles. This was not bells. On our radios you hear a million things, and they sound spacey some of them. Sometimes atmospheric noises sound like a Star Wars video game. So it's common to hear all kinds of crazy noises. But this wasn't noise. It was like a whistle, lowered to the bass range. Between a hum and whistle kind of sound. It was in there with varying amplitude, it would rise and fall in tone. The first time it happened it lasted 20–30 seconds. It happened three times that night until I signed off at about 2 A.M.

"At about 11 P.M. I saw two helicopters flying over me with no lights, no markings, a dark color. I told John they were headed in his direction and would be over there in three minutes. Boom, and they were over his house. Around that same time there were more flashes of light."

Supporting Accounts: John Gonzalez's mother did not see the lights or the object. "I was sitting in my chair reading and I had the TV on," says Mrs. Gonzalez. "I thought it was an explosion. The house shook. My lights kept blinking on and off. The TV went off. I said to John, 'Was that an explosion?' He said, 'I don't know.' I didn't go out till later on, when my neighbors all came out. There were five of them. The police and fire department was there, too."

A few miles away in the center of Newark, a ham-radio operator and auto parts salesman experienced some unusual radio interference at the same time as Gonzalez. "I was on the air at home," recalls Ruben Echevarria, "and all of a sudden I hear a funny noise. We hear all kinds of strange atmospheric noises on the air. But that evening it was a noise that I never heard before, and I've been licensed since 1978. I picked it up on my scanner on my radio. It was a warbling static kind of noise. John told me to look out the window because he thought the thing was coming my way, but I didn't do it. I'm a little skeptical about these things. But this was one strange night. It really was."

Several other ham-radio operators were also involved in the incident, including two in Manhattan. One was Tom Verdell, a Manhattan dentist nearing retirement. He lives on the 23rd floor of a high rise on the west side of the city and can see aircraft landing at Newark airport. "We were just chewing the fat," he recalls, "then John told us these things were happening to him. All of a sudden there was this strange interference on the air. Something I've never really experienced before. I do a little private flying, a bit of two-way communication with other aircraft and tower and what not, and being a ham radio operator for 11 years, I'm used to certain types of interference, but this was really weird. All of a sudden everything just went out. Total silence. It lasted about 5 minutes. But it was different than any silence you ever hear on the air. You couldn't even hear the background noises you usually hear. But my radio was not off. It happened to everybody at the same time. The whole evening was strange."

The other Manhattan ham-radio operator did not experience this interference. "I didn't witness anything personally," says Percy Jones, the bass player for the group Brand X, "but I was talking to a group of other people who were experiencing things. There are a group of us who speak on 10 meters late in the evening on all topics. So when I came on, John in Newark was saying that something had just struck his antenna mast. I think he said he just visually saw the tail end of something disappearing. He was describing all this to the rest of the people who were on that net. Everybody was getting very excited."

PART 2: The MUFON Investigation

"The case is interesting," says George Filer, the New Jersey State Director for MUFON, "because of the confirmed damaged to the oak tree and the numerous ham radio operators listening in at the time of the incident. A similar sighting took place on November 16, 1993, when a 30-foot disc-shaped craft passed to the north of Newark Airport. Our files show 25 UFO sightings in the Newark area since 1950."

Filer and a team of investigators that included two physicians visited John Gonzalez on April 21, 1994. "We took photographs, video taped and interviewed the witnesses," notes Filer. "We inspected John's home and backyard. He has a room at the back of his home packed with his computer, radio gear, scanners and other equipment. We saw one of the remaining branches that had fallen from the tree. The Geiger counter readings on the branches and yard were within normal limits. However, it's normal for radiation to dissipate after a month. Our magnetic field locator that is designed to locate magnetic lines of flux was unable to uncover any abnormal readings in the area. John's rooftop wireless antenna was knocked off center and bent slightly west towards the tree.

"It is apparent from talking with John and his neighbors that on the night of March 5 there were serious electrical current fluctuations in the area. Witnesses agree that the lights went off and on, light bulbs blew out, and appliances such as televisions, radio, ham and computer equipment were affected, or stopped entirely. One neighbor, A.M., indicated her lights went out at about 10:30 P.M. She saw very bright lights outside, but did not see a craft. Then she heard sound like rain. This was probably branches falling on the roof. She thought it was the beginning of a thunderstorm. But the weather report indicates it was clear and cold. Her TV picture was out for 30 minutes. All those interviewed claim that police and fire departments came immediately and most of the witnesses felt the ground shake and thought there might have been an earthquake. We know of cases in Williamstown, New Jersey and Williamsport, Pennsylvania where UFOs caused houses to shake and electrical power to be disrupted."

An engineer from Public State Gas and Electric (PSE&G) told Filer that he thought the trouble in Newark was probably due to an overload rather than a low-voltage condition. Filer also contacted the Lamont-Dougherty Geological Observatory in Palisades, N.Y., and was told by a seismologist that there had been no earthquakes of any kind in the Newark area on that date. He also checked with the Newark Office of Emergency Management, formerly Civil Defense, and was told they had no log entries for that evening. There were no reports of UFOs in the local newspapers.

A chemist at a Massachusetts laboratory analyzed the broken tree branches and told Filer that the beta radiation was slightly above background, but that this could have come from any source and not necessarily a UFO. The lab also analyzed a strange ash-like sphere that Filer's investigative team had found in Gonzalez's backyard. It was about the size of a golf ball, had the consistency of soft chalk, and had an outer shell measuring about one-quarter of an inch thick. The lab told Filer that the ash was an unusual fungus.

"It appears something happened," Filer concludes, "but we have no proof it was a craft. We couldn't get any of the other witnesses to support Gonzalez's story that there was a UFO, though they did support the story that there was a light out there and that effects to their electrical systems occurred. This, in the past, has been an indication of UFOs in the area. There are some conflicting statements. One of the things I've noticed with witnesses is that they have a tendency to pull in data that they think supports their case but actually has nothing to do with it. So all the activity in the area may not be relevant to the case."

A MUFON investigator who wishes to remain anonymous learned from PSE&G that the damage to an electrical pole a few blocks away from the Gonzalez home was caused by a cement truck on March 7 or 8—a few days after the Gonzalez "UFO" incident. This investigator concludes: "Maybe something happened that night, but that's the only thing I've been able to come up with. What I think we have here is a man with so much time on his hands and who wants to believe in

UFOs so much that he's let his imagination run away with him. If he did see a nuts-and-bolts craft, I don't see the evidence for that."

PART 3: The Omni Investigation

After speaking to Gonzalez and his mother and one set of neighbors who were home, the Susus, I checked to see if Gonzalez had indeed called 911 that night. People don't make a habit of calling 911 without a good reason. Besides, I thought that if the police and fire departments did respond to his call, they might be able to shed some light on the matter. I also made a number of other follow-up phone calls.

Police Department: "The call came in at 10:32 P.M.," said Detective Dan Collins of the Newark Police. "The unit arrived at 10:44 and could really find nothing to substantiate an earthquake or anything like that and closed out at 10:46. They contacted PSE&G but could not find anything to substantiate an earthquake or anything like that."

Fire Department: The Fire Department also confirmed that they had answered the call. "An alarm came in at 22:30," said Stanley Kossup, Newark's fire director. "The fire department responded to the location. They sent one company down. It was booked as a 305, a false alarm. There were no unusual events. There weren't any UFOs flying around."

Newark Office of Emergency Management: Gonzalez claimed that Civil Defense had also shown up at his house that night. The problem is that Civil Defense, as such, doesn't exist anymore. Now it's called the Office of Emergency Management (OEM).

"The words 'Civil Defense' are just not used anymore on uniforms or otherwise," says Jim Simons, of the Newark OEM. "Probably the last time any active funding went into anything with the words 'Civil Defense' on it would be the 1950s or early 1960s, around the Cuban missile crisis. The only thing I could think of is a volunteer fireman wearing something like that, but not official fire department people. He must be confusing CD with something else, but I can't imagine what. Some fire jackets might have the letters NFD on it for 'Newark Fire Department.' Our gear says 'OEM' or 'Newark OEM' on it. We don't show anything for that incident and I don't think HazMat responded to it."

Hazardous Materials Office: They did not. "I looked through all the records," said Mike Daley of the Newark HazMat office, "and there is absolutely nothing. There is absolutely no report of it." I have not been able to identify the "CD" person Gonzalez claims was there that night.

National Earthquake Information Center: In looking for a natural explanation for what happened, I first checked to make sure there had been no earthquake that night. According to geophysicist Willis Jacobs there was no seismic activity of any kind in the Newark area on March 5. This left only two possible prosaic explanations for the event: either the incident was weather-related or it was due to a utility company problem. I hoped to find a clue to one or the other from the analysis of the materials found in the Gonzalez yard.

Laboratory Analysis: Matthew Moniz, an analytical chemist in Massachusetts, examined the mysterious, lightweight, golf-ball shaped object MUFON investigators had found in the yard and two oak branches, one of which supposedly had been knocked off the tree by the UFO, while the other was from an unaffected part of the tree.

"The 'golf ball' is a ground fungus," said Moniz, "what's commonly known as a puffball." And the black material on the test branch? "That's another fungus," he replied, "similar to other shell fungus that you find growing on trees. Nothing unusual." But Moniz did initially find a slightly elevated level of radiation for the test branch, although later attempts to verify this proved inconclusive.

"It could have been contamination in the area that I was working in," notes Moniz. "Or the readings may have resulted from short-lived radio nuclides that have half-lives of only days. This may account for the absence of the readings in the following weeks. Short-lived radio nuclides can come from only a few places: nuclear reactors, cyclotrons, particle accelerators as well as some other natural sources such as plasma events like lighting strikes."

One witness thought the flash of light was a lightning strike. Such a strike could also explain the fallen branches, the shaking of his house, and the electrical disturbances he reported. I asked Moniz if he thought a lightning strike could explain the episode. "It very well could have been," he replied." But the witnesses indicated that the weather was 'clear.' "

Weather: Was it? I called David Robinson, the state climatologist for New Jersey, who looked up the weather records for Newark on March 5. "High of 48," he says, "low of 34, no precipitation. That morning they had two inches [of snow] on the ground. On March 6th there was a trace of precipitation. From the look at these records, the day looks pretty tame." He then checked another set of records. "High pressure building over the area on Saturday night will keep skies fair until Sunday morning," he reads, then adds: "Looks like the weather was clear."

"I would reasonably guess that there was not a thunder event, unless I can find in the record one of those squalls that popped into the area that evening. That can happen sometimes, a leftover squall can pop in. It's not out of the question to have isolated lighting in one of those squalls. But they tend to be pretty rare because snow squalls tend not to have a lot of the vertical cloud development you need to get that discharge. So it's kind of unlikely. And it appears in this case there was nothing in the nature of a squall line or anything like that. So I would say that chances are it was not a lightning event. There must be some other explanation. But I won't hazard a guess as to what that might or might not be."

American Radio Relay League: Then there was the matter of all the radio interference reported by the various ham operators that night.

Was there anything to it? "I never heard anything remotely resembling this," says Edward Hare, lab supervisor at the American Radio Relay League, an organization of amateur radio operators, "but stranger things have happened in life." Because the ham-radio operators reported different types of interference that night, Hare believes the phenomena are unrelated.

"But I can imagine some various combinations of things that could cause any one of them," he says. The squealing could be a malfunctioning radio. The "receiving-while-transmitting" interference he calls a "radio defect'" unless "some strong local signal had gotten into the power lines, caused perhaps by a CBer with a powerful mobile amplifier driving by at the time." As far as the "dead radio" interference, perhaps that was caused by a Sudden Ionospheric Disturbance (SID) caused by a solar flare. "A sudden change in the ionosphere can result in the normal HF, or high frequency, propagation virtually disappearing. This can last a few minutes or a few hours. Some SIDs can be fairly local in effect, others can be virtually worldwide." A check of the data for the week preceding March 5th showed stable solar conditions, however.

Utility Company: Finally, I put a call in to PSE&G, hoping they could provide a clue to the mystery. They did have an answer. "We had an underground cable failure and manhole explosion at 10:37 on that date," explained Neil Brown, manager of public information for PSE&G. "The area served by that 26,000 volt circuit just touches the area in question. So customers in that area could have noticed a momentary dimming of lights as a result of that, but not a complete power outage, like the one that affected some customers for one hour and eight minutes. The jolt from the cable failure may have blown off the manhole cover on Bloomfield Avenue. That was close enough [two blocks from the Gonzalez residence] that it could have been felt."

Brown believes the underground cable failure may also have caused the flash of light reported. "At the instant that the cable fails," he explains, "there is a release of energy that could result in a flash, or an arcing, at the same time there is enough force to blow off the manhole cover. It's quite likely people in the vicinity could have noticed that."

PART 4: Conclusion

At first glance, the underground cable failure appears to be a reasonable explanation for the strange events reported in North Newark, New Jersey on March 5th. However, the failure occurred at precisely 10: 37 P.M., according to PSE&G. This is seven minutes *after* John Gonzalez claims to have called 911 to report the "earthquake." His claim is supported by the fact that the Fire department received the alarm at 10:30 and the police got the call at 10:32. Since a cause cannot follow an event it is responsible for, the cable failure is not a likely explanation for what happened in Newark that night.

Of course, the utility company may not be telling all it knows. "Utility companies prefer to deny these kinds of incidents," say Jim Simons of the Newark Office of Emergency Management, "because if they blow up your TV set by putting a power surge through it, they don't want to have to pay for it. They're going to tell you it was a squirrel that nibbled the line and they're not responsible. This is the kind of thing they do."

The only other possible natural explanation is some type of unusual weather phenomena. It's true the weather was "clear" that night. But there is the testimony of the neighbor who thought the flash of light was lightning. And there is the report from the ham radio operator in Brooklyn who says he saw flashes, or columns, of light over New Jersey. Is there such a thing as lightning from a clear sky? There is, though admittedly, it's quite rare.

Such incidents have been reported in the scientific literature. An 1886 issue of *Scientific American* states that on April 27th of that year the captain of the British ship Siddartha saw a thunderstorm in a clear sky while on the northern edge of the Gulf Stream. The sky was clear, the sun was shining brightly, the only thing peculiar was a thin mist about the ship. Suddenly, there appeared a vivid flash of lightning accompanied by violent thunder. The ship's compass reportedly "vibrated" for a full 16 minutes. Similar events have been reported in Detroit on October 4, 1900 and in the Missoula National Forest in Montana on July 2, 1927, according to the *Monthly Weather Review*. Just how lightning can occur without the presence of clouds is not known, however.

So what really happened in North Newark on the night of March 5th? It was not an earthquake. It probably was not due to an underground cable failure. And only the slightest chance exists that it was caused by a lightning strike from a clear sky. John Gonzalez believes a low-flying alien craft was responsible. But no other witnesses have surfaced to support this conclusion, and you would expect many more people to have seen an object of this kind on a Saturday night in such a highly populated area. So doubts arise. And because some portions of the Gonzalez testimony are clearly inaccurate, such as the presence of Civil Defense personnel on the scene, it's possible that Gonzalez may be mistaken about "the object" as well. Nonetheless, I have no firm explanation for what happened that night, and something very clearly did happen.

CHAPTER 36
Alien Implant

Just when I thought the field could not possibly get any wackier, it did. The new focus of interest in the UFO-research community by the early 1990s had become "implants." The aliens allegedly used these devices to keep track of, call, or otherwise annoy, their human victims. And suddenly implants were coming out of the woodwork, if not the flesh. I referred a number of people who thought they had alien implants to UFO investigators and mind control investigators around the country. But this particular implant story stood out from the rest, for one simple reason—it had attracted the interest of a scientist at one of this country's top universities.

MIT's David Pritchard has pursued research in atomic, optical, and molecular physics, and was a pioneer in the study of the mechanical forces of light on atoms, the field of atom optics, and atom traps. Since this article's publication he has been elected to the National Academy of Sciences. I applaud what Pritchard did. If there were more open-minded scientists like him, we might have a clearer idea of what we are dealing with in this field. My article, titled "Alien Implant or—Human Underwear?" appeared in the "Project Open Book" section of the April 1995 issue of OMNI.

✳

For Richard Price, a single traumatic childhood incident has thrown a terrifying shadow over the last four decades of his life. One evening in September 1955, near a cemetery in Troy, New York, Price claims he encountered a couple of humanoids who took him aboard their craft and injected an implant under his skin. Now, a scientist from a world-class university has analyzed that implant and reached a fascinating conclusion.

Price, who was then 8 years old, has never forgotten the episode, especially the moment the aliens implanted something into his—now that the Bobbitt trial has made the word media-acceptable—penis.

"I was tied down to a table in the center of the room," he recalls, "and they had used a machine to scan over my body up to my neck. Then they took this implant from the table and put it at the end of this long needle attached to some type of box and cable. When they inserted the needle into my skin I could see on a monitor in front of me an enlargement where it looked like they were hooking up wires underneath my skin. Then, after they took the needle out and shut everything off, one of them came over to me and, before he helped me put my clothes back on, said: 'Leave it alone, or you'll die.'"

Price reports he was too frightened to tell his parents about the incident. But in 1964 while in high school he did tell a girlfriend and within a week everyone in school was calling him "the spaceman." Finally, after getting into a fight, he was called to see the principal, who referred him to the school psychologist.

Price underwent a battery of psychological tests and was given various medications. But since no one had even heard of UFO abductions back then, he eventually ended up in a state hospital. He was released after three months, but only after "admitting" to the doctors on his case that the incident had never occurred.

More than a dozen years would pass before Price could bear to relate his bizarre tale again, once more trying to convince the outside world it was real. After talking to UFO investigators in 1981, Price was urged to visit a doctor who, amazingly, confirmed the presence of a foreign object in his penis. But since Price felt no discomfort from it, the doctor suggested that nothing needed to be done.

Then in June 1989, while getting dressed, Price noticed the "implant" protruding above the skin, and about two months later it came out. The object was roughly cylindrical, rounded at both ends, and had at least six small appendages. Tiny, measuring about 1 millimeter wide and 4 millimeters deep, it had an amber colored interior and a white shell.

Within two weeks Price had turned over a portion of the "implant" to David Pritchard, a physicist at the Massachusetts Institute of Technology who believes scientists should look seriously at the abduction phenomenon. Pritchard says he agreed to analyze the "implant" for one simple reason: "Proving that life exists elsewhere in the universe would be the biggest scientific discovery of all time." For Pritchard, however, that dream must wait. Indeed, the MIT scientist found the object was made of "the kind of material elements and chemicals—carbon, oxygen, hydrogen, and compounds—one would expect if the object were biological in origin and formed right here on planet Earth."

A dermatopathologist at Massachusetts General Hospital in Boston, moreover, supports Pritchard's conclusion. Thomas Flotte found that the "implant" consists of concentric layers of fibroblasts, a type of cell found in connective tissue, extracellular material like collagen, and some external cotton fibers. The human body apparently produces such calcified tissue in response to injury, either from foreign material like a piece of glass or a wood splinter, or from a trauma of some kind, caused perhaps by a baseball or a table corner.

"This calcification process is common," says Flotte, "though the penis is not a site of trauma all that often." The cotton fibers probably came from Price's underwear; they became incorporated into the body tissue as it hardened.

Pritchard, who with Harvard psychiatrist John Mack organized an abduction conference held at MIT in the summer of 1992, knows of one other penile implant case. Upon examination, that implant, too, turned out to be calcified damaged tissue of terrestrial, and human, origin.

But despite the rather mundane outcome, Pritchard feels that the Price implant case is as good as anyone in the business of analyzing possible extraterrestrial artifacts is likely to get. "I thought this object had an extremely good pedigree because it was associated with a conscious recollection," notes Pritchard, "and Price even has a doctor's report indicating that he had something under his skin 10 years ago."

While Pritchard found no sign that the "implant" was an alien artifact, he states his investigation does not rule out the extremely remote possibility that, as believers might argue, the calcified tissue was actually manufactured by aliens. "It's possible," he explains, "that the aliens are so clever that they can make devices that serve their purposes yet appear to have a prosaic origin as natural products of the human body and fibers from cotton underwear. So this case only rules out the possibility of clumsy aliens. It doesn't rule out the possibility of super-clever aliens."

Other ideas, however, might make more sense. For instance, given the recent connection some scientists have made between the mind and body, it has been suggested that Price may have "induced" the implant much like people who practice visualization exercises have been shown to improve their T-cell counts, boosting the immune system.

But psychologists reject the notion that Price's belief in aliens might somehow have provoked the growth. "To willfully create such a calcification is highly unlikely," says Kentucky psychologist Robert Baker, author of *Hidden Memories,* "almost as unlikely as an alien implant."

Baker also largely dismisses the possibility that Price might be using an alien encounter story to cover up an episode of childhood sexual abuse. "While such things are possible," he says, "it's not usually the case. In fact, over the years we've discovered that people remember very clearly cases of childhood sexual abuse. It's not a question of repression."

More likely, notes Baker, Price's so-called aliens were a hallucination associated with a sleep paralysis episode. The paralysis typically results in very shallow breathing, which reduces the oxygen input to the brain. In some people, such oxygen reduction stimulates the sexual centers. "And then later on if he found anything wrong with his genitals," says Baker, "he would attribute whatever the problem was to what the hallucinated aliens did."

But how did the "implant" get there in the first place? William Cone, a, psychologist in private practice in Newport Beach,

California, thinks he knows the answer. "To my knowledge we have yet to recover an implant that resembles anything alien," he states. "Instead, the chances of somebody finding a little something wrong with his or her body are greater than we think. Statistically, if you look at the population at large, you are going to see a lot of people who have had growths and bumps and pieces of stuff stuck in their body. Out of that large population, some people interested in abductions are going to find things in their body, and, as far as I am concerned, that is probably what happened here."

Meanwhile Price, in an effort to come to grips with the turmoil this and two subsequent alien encounters have caused, is in the process of writing a book about it all with a surprisingly down-to-earth title: *What Affects Your Life.*

CHAPTER 37

UFO Crime Lab

One of the byproducts of living in the Hudson Valley, the scene of so many UFO sightings since the 1980s, was a pastime called UFO skywatching. The activity consists of a bunch of people driving to a good lookout point, or the scene of frequent UFO reports, piling out of the car, and shooting the breeze as all eyes scan the skies waiting for a UFO to show up. Since most people are unfamiliar with the night sky, more often than not they will see something they can't identify in the space of an hour or two. That's no guarantee of an alien spacecraft, however.

So it was that on occasion I would participate in these UFO skywatches with Peter Gersten, the "UFO lawyer" who lived in nearby Peekskill, New York. These would often take place on Thursdays, as most of the UFO reports in the area occurred on that day of the week—a fact that reeks of human involvement, if you ask me. One of those who sometimes joined us for the fun was a tough-as-nails, pale-skinned New York woman named Victoria Lacas. She would always ask pointed questions of women who claimed to have been abducted, like "Did you take your purse with you? Where was your purse?" Outdoors, under a beautiful star-twinkling night sky, she would taunt the unseen, would-be abductors by shouting, "Take me!" (I need not disclose the thoughts of the accompanying males to such an outburst.) The aliens never obliged, of course.

A few years later Victoria Lacas would meet and marry John Alexander, the retired U.S. Army Colonel noted for his expertise on non-lethal weapons. Alexander, who now works for Bob Bigelow's controversial National Institute of Discovery Science in Los Vegas, has long been interested in a wide range of "fringe topics," UFOs included. In fact, a number of researchers suspect he is the DIA's "Colonel Philips" mentioned by former New York Times reporter Howard Blum in his book, OUT THERE.

In any case, shortly after becoming Mrs. Victoria Alexander, she came up with another rather nifty rejoinder to those who believed firmly in abduction accounts: If these abductions are real, and we humans are being victimized, then why isn't anyone treating these abduction locations as crime scenes? Good point. Attempts to set up camcorders in the homes of those who claimed to be regularly abducted have consistently failed. (Either the aliens stay away when the camera is on, or the camera breaks down when an abduction occurs—or could it be that the aliens are abducting no one, after all?) Given what everyone knew was the real interest of the aliens—human sexual reproduction—there should be, Alexander reasoned, some tell-tale ET bodily fluid or particles left behind, either at the scene or on the abductees' clothing. My article on the subject, titled "UFO Crime Lab," appeared in a special Project Open Book section of OMNI, in April 1995.

✳

If UFO abductions are real, there should be real evidence for them. That simple premise has led writer and UFO researcher Victoria Alexander to advocate the use of crime-scene investigative techniques to obtain evidence in UFO abduction cases. "After all," she says, "crimes are supposedly being committed. The aliens are accused of unlawful entries, kidnappings, assaults, and rapes. So I think it's time we start looking at the typical bedroom abduction as a police crime-scene unit would."

Alexander's interest in a forensic approach grew out of her frustration over the lack of physical evidence in abduction cases, the helplessness of the victims, and the apparent willingness of many UFO researchers to simply accept such stories as true. Though the crime lab approach has never been proposed—let alone attempted—in two decades of UFO abduction investigations, Alexander felt it was the next logical step.

"Since the vast majority of abductees claim the aliens are humanoid, not robots," she argues, "there should be biological and chemical traces of their presence. If these are real events, if the aliens are real, if contact is taking place, there has to be real evidence for it—latent fingerprints, fungi, particles, whatever. It's a basic tenet of criminalistics that when any two items come in contact there will be an exchange of microscopic particles."

But the only way to gather such evidence, Alexander realizes, is to recruit the cooperation of "conscious repeaters," those people who claim to be abducted over and over again and remember it the next morning. The first thing they should do is take a urine sample, she says. "Lab tests of urine should show if the body has undergone any stress. And if the abductee wakes up with a bloody nose, they should keep a sample of that, too, for later analysis."

Otherwise, anything the aliens have come in contact with—any part of the abductee's clothes they may have touched, any portion of bedroom floor or carpet they may have walked over—might yield tangible evidence: hair, secretions, prints, or particles from their skin, clothes, or craft.

Alexander is calling on abductees to collect this evidence themselves. "There is not an emergency room in the country that is going to say 'Oh, you've been raped by aliens? Let's run some tests,'" she notes. "No police department is going to believe such a story and go through your place with a fine-tooth comb. Abductees have to do it themselves. And UFO investigators can help. It has to start this way. Then later, maybe, we can attract the help of professionals."

Thomas Van Valkenburgh, bureau chief of the Department of Public Safety's crime lab at the New Mexico State Police headquarters in Santa Fe, finds Alexander's suggestion feasible. "We should be able to use forensic techniques in this situation," he says, "though I have a problem with people doing their own crime scene because they are not trained." He admits, however, that since some police bureaus may turn down requests, people "are probably going to have to do it themselves, at least at first."

The reaction to Alexander's proposal in the UFO community has been generally positive. "I think it's great," says John Carpenter, director of abduction research for the Mutual UFO Network, "if it's done properly. My main concern is who is doing it and how well it's done. Having the abductees do it themselves might stir up new claims of hoaxing and improper procedure. Ideally, it should be done by an outsider."

Temple University historian David Jacobs, author of *Secret Life: Firsthand Accounts of UFO Abductions,* also gives the proposal a thumbs-up. "Any effort to gather evidence is worth doing," he says, though he doubts the aliens have fingerprints based on the reports he has from abductees who have seen their captors' fingers close-up.

Victoria Alexander is now working on a manual describing collection protocols, and she's designing a kit to be used by abductees and investigators. "We have to at least make the attempt," she continues. "Even if it all fails, if the prints are sloppy or don't come out. At least we will be changing the abductees' mind-set about the experience. I want them to stop thinking of themselves as victims and start thinking about trying to find an answer. Doing this has to change their whole experience. This sort of participation should empower them."

Skeptics, not surprisingly, tend to regard such proposals as futile. "In my opinion," says Philip J. Klass, "if abductions were fact and not fantasy, we would have had impressive evidence a long, long time ago."

CHAPTER 38

The Secret Invasion

As the years went by, and abduction reports became downright common, some abductees began mentioning that there were other humans on board the craft along with the aliens. What could possibly be going on here? A possible answer to that question: lots and lots of people are being abducted at once. So when I began probing this question, it all came down to numbers, numbers so large that they no longer made sense. Besides, if so many abductions are taking place, why do we have so few reports (less than a handful, really) from victims' bedmates saying that their partners were missing for some amount of time? Where is this independent testimony? Why is there no "missing bed partner" phenomenon? This feature—"The Secret Invasion: Does it Add Up?"—appeared as part of the "Project Open Book" section of the Winter 1995 issue of OMNI.

$$*$$

Catherine just can't explain it. She has no idea why she felt so compelled to keep on driving that night after leaving the Boston nightclub where she worked as a receptionist. It was after midnight and she had driven past Somerville, where she lives. Nor does she know why she got off the highway about 10 miles to the north, or why she drove around Saugus and momentarily got lost in a wooded area. But after finding her way out, she noted that it was 2:45 in the morning—at least 45 minutes later than it should have been.

Feeling anxious, she raced back home. The next day, on local news, she learned that dozens of people throughout the Northeast had reported a UFO, including a policeman and his wife who had seen an object stop overhead and shine a light on them. Astronomers said the object was a shooting star.

A few weeks later, Catherine decided to contact Harvard psychiatrist John Mack, author of the 1977 Pulitzer Prize-winning biography of T. E. Lawrence and known most recently for his outspoken interest in the UFO abduction phenomenon. In a series of hypnotic regression sessions, Mack helped Catherine unlock a lifetime of apparent abduction memories, beginning at the age of three and culminating in that murky night just weeks before at the age of 22.

Catherine did not enjoy finding out what had happened to her in the woods on the night of March 6, 1991. "I don't want to be there," a very frightened Catherine told Mack while under hypnosis. "I want to drive out."

But she could not. Her car had apparently come to a stop and her body had gone numb. Then suddenly her door had opened. "There is a hand reaching out to get me," Catherine recalled. "It's long and thin and it's only got three fingers." A being with huge, black, almond-shaped eyes then took her from the car, and the two of them were swept up in a beam toward a huge metallic ship.

The alien abductor, the story goes, then took Catherine inside, into a hallway, where four other beings were waiting. When they began pulling at her clothes, she got annoyed. "Stop it," she recalled thinking. "I'm perfectly capable of doing this myself, thank you." Once naked, Catherine was led into an enormous room "the size of an airplane hangar."

She saw rows and rows of tables everywhere. "There are hundreds of humans in here," she told Mack under hypnosis. "And they're all having things done to them." The rows were about five feet apart, she noted, and anywhere from a third to half the tables had humans on them. She estimates there were between 100 and 200 people in that room. But in the mass of bodies and blank faces she remembers one of them specifically—the one on the table to her left. He was a black man with a beard.

Catherine was forced to sit up on her table and the beings then began running their fingers down her spine. The terrifying examination had begun.

The rest of Catherine's traumatic UFO experience appears in John Mack's controversial book, *Abduction: Human Encounters with Aliens,* and is rather typical of such stories. But one detail in her story stands out like a Gulliver in Lilliput—that bit about the hundreds of other humans she saw aboard the alien craft that night. And Catherine is by no means alone among alleged abductees in reporting the presence of large numbers of humans aboard the alien crafts.

What accounts like these suggest is that the phenomenon actually involves mass abductions. It appears, as in Catherine's tale, that large numbers of people are being taken, one by one to central locations that serve as holding facilities for dozens, perhaps hundreds, of others during the same period of time. If the other abductees' stories are true, moreover, sometimes entire groups of people are taken all at once.

Reports of this phenomenon, in fact, confirm some people's worst fears about the alien endeavor. Could we all be pawns in some weird extraterrestrial breeding scheme to repopulate a dying alien world? Or is the entire human race being unwillingly drafted into some hideous alien genetic experiment to produce alien-human hybrids? Whatever the case, one thing seems clear: Quite a large number of us are potential targets.

"The phenomenon is not, as the general public tends to believe, an occasional 'there's one, let's get him' sort of thing on the part of the aliens," explains David Jacobs, a Temple University historian specializing in twentieth-century U.S. history and the author of the book, *Secret Life.* Instead, he asserts, we have a mass abduction program taking place covertly. The notion of a secret invasion inevitably springs to mind.

"What we have here," says Jacobs, "is a continual abduction scenario. Its very much like an assembly line. The aliens get them in. They go into a waiting area where they see other people sitting around. They get shown to a table. There are all sorts of people lying on the tables as various stages of different procedures are being run on them. Then they get them up, get them out and new people arrive. It's a revolving door."

The extraordinary number of people supposedly going through that revolving door should, it seems, help cement the case for the reality of the phenomenon. If multiple participants are involved in an abduction, the logic goes, then the experience cannot be the product of one individual's fantasy or hallucination. In fact, the mass abduction cases seem to offer believers a golden opportunity to cross-check the details of the abduction experience from independent perspectives and develop the proof the critics have always demanded.

These mass abductions certainly appear to take place often enough. Jacobs estimates that abductees see other humans aboard the craft in half, if not most, of the cases. And one out of every four alleged abduction episodes involves multiple participants, according to Thomas Bullard, a folklorist whose 1987 University of Indiana doctoral dissertation exhaustively analyzed about 300 published abduction accounts.

Bullard found that while approximately half of these multiple-participant abduction cases involved just two people—usually family members or friends—the other half involved either three, four, or more people who claimed to have been taken at once. There are even cases in which seven or more people have reportedly been abducted in a single episode. The situation led Bullard to lament wryly that apparently, "there's just no safety in numbers."

One of the earliest mass abduction cases on record actually involved nine people and took place one summer some 40 years ago near Crater Lake, Oregon; it was not, however, reported to a UFO organization until 1989. The participants were a 32-year-old woman known only as Mrs. R., her 15-year-old brother, 10-year-old sister, two daughters and a stepdaughter aged 10-to-13, two younger nephews, and Mrs. R.'s 53-year-old mother.

The witnesses remembered that while looking for a gas station they had come upon what appeared to be a restaurant. Their car engine had sputtered and coasted into a parking area where three or four other cars were parked. The "building" was round and lighted, and the interior was circular. Mrs. R. remembered commenting to her mother that the place was "really unbelievable." The family then sat down at one of the tables and apparently ordered a meal from short, slender people with blond hair who all looked alike and wore identical silver uniforms and boots that sported the same emblem. "When I think about it now," said Mrs. R.'s mother almost two decades later, "I have a funny feeling like maybe we were a surprise to them."

Mrs. R. thinks they ate and paid their bill before leaving. Though the car would not start immediately, it sort of "coasted" onto the highway first and only then got underway. When the family reached the next town, Mrs. R. discovered that they had not spent any money and that no one in town had ever heard of such a restaurant. Though the family returned to search for it, they never found. it.

"I know I was in a UFO," said Mrs. R. almost three decades after the experience, though that realization did not begin to register with her until about 1969, when she started recalling the incident and discussing it with her family.

Perhaps the best documented of all mass abduction cases involves four young men who were canoeing along the Allagash Waterway in the wilderness of northern Maine on August 26, 1976. Under hypnosis, all four experienced missing time and relived a detailed and amazingly similar UFO abduction episode. This case, which was thoroughly investigated by Raymond Fowler, is unique in the annals of UFO research in that it provides four separate, mutually corroborating accounts of the same event.

It went something like this: On the fifth day of their canoe trip, twins Jim and Jack Weiner, Charlie Foltz, and Chuck Rak decided to replenish their now-scarce food supply by doing a little fishing. Before sliding their canoe into the water, they prepared a large bonfire in order to find their way back to camp in the pitch dark wilderness.

They were halfway across a cove when they saw a silent, large, bright sphere of colored light at treetop level about 200 yards away. When Charlie began flashing his flashlight at it, the object began moving toward them. Then, as the sphere—now only about 50 feet above the water—approached, the canoeists decided to head for solid ground and began paddling quickly toward shore. Their paddling became increasingly frantic when the object emitted a beam of light that advanced on their canoe.

The next thing Charlie Foltz and Jim Weiner remembered was standing at the campsite watching the object move away. Chuck Rak remembers staying in the canoe and watching it disappear. Jack Weiner remembers first madly trying to outrun the beam of light, then calmly getting out of the canoe. He finds it odd that they would be in such a hurry one moment and so calm the next. After the object disappeared, the four walked up the beach to find that the huge bonfire they had left just 15 or so minutes before was now all coals. Jim thought the large logs should have burned for two or three hours.

The four men had no memory of what happened during the time it took the bonfire to burn down. And several years would pass before Jim and Jack began to experience a series of strange dreams of alien abductors that would eventually lead them to seek help from UFO investigator Raymond Fowler in May 1988. Over the next two years Fowler hypnotized each of the four men independently and elicited a strangely congruent testimony about being plucked from the water by a beam of light, taken aboard the craft, and forced to undergo medical examinations by aliens.

Each of the four men recalled seeing the other three on board the alien craft. "They were all made to sit on a bench in the nude," says Fowler, "and they watched one after the other being taken off the bench. Some of the examination was done within eyesight of the others and some of it was done after they were taken around the corner from the bench. But when you put it all together like a picture puzzle, you find that everybody is describing the same event from different standpoints."

Fowler went on to produce a 10-volume, 702-page study of this case and subsequently published a book, *The Allagash Abductions,* as well. "All of the Allagash witnesses are of sound mind and reputation," concludes Fowler. "They not only tell essentially the same story, but under hypnosis they relive it with all the trauma and emotions that would be expected of a real physical event. I think the evidence here is undeniable and would stand up in court if we were only dealing with an automobile accident or something like that. But when you are talking about something as bizarre as UFO abductions, people find that very, very hard to believe."

Even harder to believe is a case that appears to involve a mass abduction of hundreds of people in New York City late in the summer or early fall of 1992. The case is currently being investigated by Budd Hopkins, who is probably better known as a UFO researcher than as a modern artist these days.

The story first emerged during one of Hopkins' support group meetings for abductees. One person, Mary, was telling the group about a very vivid dream she had had, though she wasn't sure it was a dream. She recalled being in some sort of huge space filled with what appeared to be "people-movers" and many, many humans all completely naked. The scene somewhat resembled the physical at a selective service exam. And there was a kind of escalator, taking people up to another floor.

At that point, two other abductees in the group, Bill and Joan, became extremely agitated and said, "Oh gee, I've had a dream just like that."

Hopkins immediately cut off the conversation so that he could explore their experiences individually. Later, when Hopkins probed into Joan's dream under hypnosis, she recalled the same large space, a strange chart on the wall, and most incredibly, seeing both Mary and Bill there as well, totally naked. Typically, both looked "out of it" to her.

"Carl Sagan always has the idea that you are going to dash around and steal an alien cocktail napkin or something for evidence as you dash out of the place," notes Hopkins, "as if abductees had all their senses intact. But in this, as in other situations, the abductees were in an altered state."

Joan remembers having a perfunctory conversation with Mary in which they expressed surprise at seeing each other there. Hopkins then asked Joan what Mary looked like naked. Joan said that Mary was very round-shouldered and that she had a big long scar at the bikini line.

Mary, as it happens, is extremely round-shouldered and always wears shoulder pads. And she does have a big long scar; it comes from a bladder operation she had as a child. Joan did not see Bill closely, but Hopkins asked her if he had much chest hair. Joan said no, and, in fact, he doesn't.

Bill's description of the experience under hypnosis was much the same as Joan's. He also saw a chart on the wall, and though his recollection of it is somewhat different, Hopkins is convinced they are describing the same object. Under hypnosis, Mary was less clear about the episode than the other two, but, as Hopkins points out, she generally doesn't have the recall that other people tend to have.

Hopkins has not explored how the three were "abducted" or how they were returned, and he will not describe the strange chart seen by Bill and Joan, nor the "space" the event itself took place in; he prefers to keep such details to himself as a check on the authenticity of future cases.

"It's a very good case," explains Hopkins, "because there is literally no way that they knew about this stuff. None of the three is a friend of the other two in any intimate way. They only know of each other from the support group. So here we are again stuck with one of two possibilities. Either they have cooked this up as a hoax, in which case you have three virtual sociopaths, because there is nothing in it for them. Or it happened."

While it's certainly difficult to believe that vast numbers of humans are being abducted in this way on a regular basis, there is, surprisingly enough, some data to corroborate these harrowing anecdotal reports. Several surveys conducted over the past decade indicate that millions of Americans have experienced something that UFO researchers think suggests the possibility of abduction by alien beings.

In a 1991 Roper survey, the most impressive of the polls, 119 people of the almost 6,000 questioned revealed they had experienced what UFO investigators call an alien abduction. If the numbers are extrapolated to the entire population of the United States, this translates to a staggering five million abductees.

The Roper poll, of course, is problematic. It has been severely criticized on the grounds that the five so-called key indicators of an abduction experience—reporting unusual lights in a room, missing time, flying through the air without knowing why, paralysis in the presence of strange bedroom figures, or puzzling scars on the body—may not in fact mean that an abduction has occurred. Psychologists point out that most of these experiences can also be caused by the little-known but quite common phenomenon of sleep paralysis and the various kinds of hallucinations that accompany it.

But David Jacobs, one of the authors of the poll, begs to differ with his critics. He and Hopkins, Jacobs explains, had thoroughly pretested nine of the eleven abduction-related questions on that poll. And those nine were questions most frequently answered positively by abductees, not non-abductees. (The other two questions tested the reliability of the poll. One of them, for instance, was a fake question which gave the pollsters an idea of how many people had the impulse to answer positively no matter what was asked. The responses from the one percent who responded positively to this question were not included in the final results.)

"When we first got the numbers, the raw statistics," says Jacobs, "the numbers were ridiculously high—7 percent, 8 percent. It was politically unacceptable. So, we decided to look only at the answers to the best five questions—those we considered to be the highest indicators for an abduction—and didn't consider people potential abductees unless they answered four or all five of those questions positively. By doing that, we got the numbers down to a politically acceptable 2 percent. The best we can say is that about one out of every 50 Americans has had experiences consistent with what abductees have had. That indicates that an awful lot of people out there have had abduction experiences. And this, of course, is consistent with what the abductees themselves tell us. They come into a room and they see 50, 75, or 100 other people lying on tables, and they report a constant stream of people. And we figure it's twenty-four hours a day, seven days a week."

But to critics, millions of abduction reports actually prove the opposite—that there are just too many of them for the phenomenon to be real. That's what Robert Durant, a commercial pilot with a long interest in UFOs, thought at first. But when he decided to put his doubts to the test by figuring out how large a work force the aliens would need to carry out the millions of abductions the Roper survey suggested were taking place, he began to think the mass abduction scenario was at least plausible.

"I began very skeptically," notes Durant, "I thought no way could these numbers be correct. But I decided to work through the math to see what I would come up with. I began by assuming that abductions are real physical events carried out systematically by a large work force. If this is the case, then the shop-floor parameters relevant to a shoe factory or medical facility ought to apply equally well to the case of an alien abduction program carried out on a host planet."

To avoid comparisons with other fanciful exercises, like counting the number of dancing angels on the head of a pin, Durant searched the literature for actual data points to plug into his equation. How often does the typical abductee claim to be abducted? Though this varies widely, he found that 10 times was not an unreasonable number. At what age do abductions begin and cease? Typically, they begin around age 5 and end by age 55, he discovered. How long did abductions take to accomplish? The periods of missing time reported by abductees range from minutes to days, but most are on the order of two hours. How many aliens does it take to perform an abduction? It's rare, he learned, for more than six aliens to be involved in any one abduction event.

Based on that data, Durant came up with some hair-raising numbers about the required "alien work force." If five million abductees have experienced 10 abductions over the last 50 years, then an astonishing one million abductions take place per year, or 2,740 per day in the United States alone. If a team of six aliens is required to perform each two-hour abduction, Durant figured that each team could then perform 12 abductions a day. So to perform 2,740 abductions a day, he calculated that the aliens would need 288 teams, or a total of 1,370 aliens.

Even if you double these figures to account for the fact that most abductions take place at night rather than 24 hours a day, the bottom line, Durant discovered, was that "about 500 crews, totaling about 3,000 aliens could do the job." While these figures may appear large, if you compare them with the numbers needed to man naval vessels, says Durant—5,500 for an aircraft carrier and about 350 for a destroyer—the whole thing begins to look, well, plausible. "The way the math worked out kind of knocked me back a bit," he admits. "This is extremely troubling to me because while I'm a total believer in UFOs, I don't buy the physical abduction scenario. And there's no way I'm saying my analysis proves abductions are real, because after all these years, we still don't have a shred of tangible proof."

But Durant's number-crunching exercise was just the beginning. Before long, Dennis Stacy, editor of a monthly UFO publication, the *MUFON UFO Journal,* had picked up the ball. Doing some math of his own, he came to conclude the numbers didn't work. By his reckoning, in fact, the alien work force required was way beyond the limits of possibility.

"If the phenomenon is global in nature, as it appears to be," says Stacy, "then the 1 million abductions a year in the United States grows to 22 million abductions worldwide. You would then need at least 11,000 alien crews, for a total of 66,000 aliens, to carry out the task, and, of course, 11,000 UFOs overhead at any given hour." And if you take into account the need for support crews, reasonable shifts, and such, notes Stacy, the numbers, like the Eveready Rabbit, "keep on growing and growing and growing."

For Stacy, the ridiculously large numbers point to an obvious conclusion. "There must be a terrestrial origin that is psychological in nature, rather than an extraterrestrial origin, to the abduction experience," he says. "The argument that some 200 million people have been abducted aboard physical flying craft in, say, the last decade or so, is simply unsupportable in terms of common sense and logic. What imaginable need of non-terrestrial science would this serve? And think of the logistics such a fantastic undertaking would involve. UFOs would be stacked up over the world's major metropolitan areas, awaiting landing and abduction rights, like so many 747s. The scale of such an invasion would be impossible for any government to plausibly ignore or cover up."

If the numbers don't make sense, then how do we explain the mass abduction memories of people like Mary, Bill, Joan, Jack, Jim, Chuck, and Charlie? William Cone, a clinical psychologist with a private practice in Newport Beach, California, has done a lot of research on abductees and thinks that while some cases of mass abduction are quite impressive, many can be explained as "contamination."

Look, for instance, he says, at the Allagash case—the one involving the four men in the canoe. "It's interesting that all of these guys were heavily interested in UFOs and abductions before ever going to see Fowler. They all knew about abductions, and they walked in to Fowler, who they knew had written other books on the subject. They walked in with a pre-set mind of *We saw something, we have missing time, so we must have been abducted.* And this happens again and again. I find it interesting that 12 years went by when they didn't worry about it, until they read some UFO books.

"The other thing I find incredible," Cone continues, "is that these four guys who have been buddies for all these years go through abduction regression therapy, get all these memories, and manage not to talk about it to their buddies for a year, until they've all been hypnotized. If you were my buddy and that had happened to me, I think I'd tell you. So when they say, we didn't talk to each other, I don't buy that. But I think they really did see something. They really did have an experience. But whether it's an abduction experience, I don't know."

Cone ventures a similar explanation for the mass abduction case of 1992 in New York City, which first appeared in a support group meeting of abductees at Budd Hopkins' home. "There is a great deal of contamination in this field," notes Cone, "especially in support groups. We've known since the days of the nineteenth century French physician Jean Martin Charcot that support groups contaminate memory. It's no secret, but somehow UFO researchers, not being mental health professionals, have never bothered to look at this. They think these people are getting support, but what they are doing is reaffirming their own fantasies. I hear this all the time in hospitals I work at. You put somebody in the support group, and the next day they have their neighbor's story. I think a lot of that is going on."

In fact, an examination of the literature reveals that those reporting shared abduction experiences virtually always know one another beforehand, or contact one another before giving their stories to independent investigators. Because of this, researchers can never really prove there had been no collaboration, either consciously or unconsciously, between the alleged abductees. The ideal case would involve two or more people who did not know each other but who gave collaborating details of the same abduction incident to independent investigators. There is no such case. Of course, if the reports of mass abductions were literally true, there should, in fact, be dozens, hundreds, even thousands of such cases in the files of UFO investigators.

David Jacobs tries to explain why there are none. "The secret aspect of the phenomenon," he says, "is remarkably efficient and extraordinarily effective. The way in which the alien program is instituted militates against having a lot of cases from the same day. And so does the way in which we find out about cases. Most people who have had abduction experiences don't really know what has happened to them. They might know that an odd thing has happened here or there, but linking it to a UFO abduction is not something most of them would probably do. So of all the abductees out there we only hear from about .001 percent of them. But every once in a while we'll have a case where somebody who is an abductee will come up to another person and say, 'I know you. I've seen you before.' And they will trace it back to an abduction event they have shared."

Jacobs does not look to such experiences for verification of the existence of the abduction phenomenon, however, having long ago moved beyond verification in search of answers to such questions as, Who are they?, Where do they come from?, and What do they want with us? "Yes, some people still want to be persuaded," admits Jacobs. "But it's not something that I spend a lot of time on, because for me that's a little bit of wheel spinning. I realize that for others this is extremely important, but I can't be too much bothered with that because it takes a lot of time and effort and it keeps me away from researching what I think are more important aspects of the phenomenon."

For Jacobs, it's the little details in the abduction stories—the kind that have no reason for being there unless they really happened—that tell him this is real. "Just last night," he says, citing one example, "I did a session with a guy who saw maybe 15 other people aboard. He was abducted with his wife and two kids. He remembers being in line with a group of people, and once they went into the waiting area they took their clothes off. He noted in front of him an older guy, heavy set, and bald with just a fringe of hair on his head. He told me in passing that there was a mole on his left shoulder."

A mole on his left shoulder. To Jacobs, that kind of detail just smacks of a real, rather than an imagined event. But such details will never be enough to convince the rest of the world that Catherine, Jack, Jim, Chuck, Mary, Bill, Joan, and millions of other humans have been abducted by aliens. Something more is needed, something more than what any abduction case, or mass abduction case, for that matter, has yet been able to provide: a shred of physical evidence. If there have been millions of abductions, it seems as if by now, we'd have come up with something certifiably alien—a lab tool, a tunic, a skin sample, a heretofore unknown universal law, or yes, even a measly cocktail napkin.

CHAPTER 39

An Unfiltered
Abduction Tale

The year 1995 would mark a turning point for my
career on the UFO beat and for OMNI magazine. As OMNI
began devoting more and more of its editorial space to
UFO stories, my editor wondered if I wanted to write a
monthly column on the subject for the magazine. Not
everyday does a writer get offered a monthly column in a
slick newsstand publication with nearly a million readers,
no matter what the subject. So, of course, I said "yes!" The
column would be called "Eye in the Sky." I got the go-ahead
for four columns in advance. By the time I had finished
the fourth, however, my editor called to say, "Stop. OMNI
will soon stop publishing." The last monthly issue was
dated April 1995. A couple of quarterly issues would
appear later that year and then no more.

It's hard to say exactly what happened. But a series of
turnovers at the top editor position gradually had diluted
the original OMNI vision. The magazine was trying to be
everything to everybody, and this approach was making
nobody happy. Stories also circulated about some poor
business decisions by the publisher that had forced him to
cash in a property, and OMNI was the one to go. The list of
OMNI subscribers was sold to DISCOVER magazine, which
was owned by Disney. Many old OMNI subscribers were
displeased when their subscriptions were fulfilled with
issues of DISCOVER. And understandably so; I could not
imagine two more different "science" publications.

The Big Mouse also wanted to buy the title of the
magazine and turn it into an all science fiction magazine,
but General Media refused. Of the four "Eye in the Sky"

columns I prepared, only one, titled "In Her Own Words: An Abductee's Story," would run in OMNI, the very last print edition of the magazine, dated Winter 1995. Eventually the magazine would make a comeback in digital form.

Cue the theme from the "Twilight Zone"....

*

Meet one Katharina Wilson, an attractive, intelligent, apparently well adjusted, 34-year-old woman. Born in a small college town in the Deep South, Wilson now lives in Portland, Oregon, with her second husband, Erik. She sees herself as "an average American woman," a fitting self-description marred by just one fact: She also claims to be a UFO abductee.

At first glance, Wilson's story sounds rather typical of other abduction lore. She claims to have been abducted and reproductively traumatized since the age of six by small alien creatures with large black eyes. Then, in her late twenties, she decided to come out of the UFO closet and tell all.

What's different about Wilson's account, however, is in the way it comes to us—straight up. She has told her story—all of it, every dirty detail—on her own. It does not come to us secondhand, through a Budd Hopkins or a David Jacobs, to name just two of the most prominent UFO abduction researchers in this country. Instead, the story comes to us pure and wholly unfiltered in a book Wilson has written and published herself.

Why is this so important? Because hearing about alien abductions directly from experiencers reveals aspects of the phenomenon long ignored—or perhaps just swept under the carpet—by most researchers. And in the end, these regularly hidden details may be vital in determining the cause of the UFO abduction phenomenon.

Indeed, as a journalist who's investigated more than my fair share of UFO abductions, I've learned that many aspects of the so-called abduction phenomenon just don't make it into print. Instead, most investigators inevitably process the stories, molding the accounts to fit the theories they favor or the patterns they expect to find. Things that don't fit their preconceived notion of what's really happening "out there" are often deliberately left out of subsequent retellings of the tale.

In the standard abduction scenario, a person may or may not have seen a UFO but is somehow whisked away from his or her home or car by small gray creatures and forced to undergo some sort of medical examination aboard a spaceship. The incident usually turns out to be one of many in the person's past involving a variety of reproductive assaults—semen sampling, artificial insemination, and fetus removal—resulting in the production of human-alien starbabies that the ETs keep.

Generally lacking in the standard scenario, however, is the wide variety of other phenomena that the person often claims to have experienced as well—the psychic perceptions, the premonitions, the bedroom encounters with dead relatives, the ghosts, the time travel, and more. Despite what is often a nearly mind-numbing display of high strangeness, you would be hard pressed to find such descriptions in the published accounts.

In the standard abduction scenario, as brought to us by the "experts," these messy details are summarily expunged. What we are left with is a cleaned-up story, a tale that stays unerringly "on mark," thus fitting the desired "alien" mold.

Of course, to some extent information selection happens, often unconsciously, in every field of human inquiry. But in a proto-discipline like UFOlogy where the basic data is itself a subject of contention, this sort of filtering is particularly damaging.

Now all this has changed, thanks to *The Alien Jigsaw*, Katharina Wilson's courageous effort to buck the wave of censorship and tell all. In this brutally honest, firsthand account, Wilson describes a harrowing lifetime of encounters with what she sincerely believes are aliens. She holds nothing back, and provides numerous surprises along the way. To begin with she tells us of not one, or two, or a dozen abduction episodes, but an astounding 119 of them, occurring in a span of just 26 years. And her experiences involve not just your typical aliens, but also encounters with the dead, time-travel episodes, psychic experiences, and even a vision of an eight-foot-tall floating penguin—everything you can imagine and a whole lot more.

In the middle of one abduction episode, for example, Wilson somehow encounters her present husband as a young man, years before she met him. Later in the episode she is terrified when told by the aliens that it is 1957—three years before she was born. Wilson also credits the aliens with saving her life; she twice had alien premonitions of nearly being killed by lightning, and on August 7, 1989, Wilson put on a pair of rubber-soled shoes just moments before lightning shattered the courtyard wall and nearly killed her.

I don't think Wilson is perpetrating a hoax. If she were, she certainly would have left out the journal entry dated August 4, 1992. "I'm with Senator Gore," Wilson wrote, "and we are in a large room with many people. He is organizing something. Governor Clinton must be here, too—now I'm looking directly at President Bush. He really looks tired—beaten." When Wilson tells Gore that she has never voted Republican, Bush looks at her "with a look of disgust on his face." Later, she realizes that Gore and Clinton are preparing a feast, and she watches as it grows larger and larger.

Following this journal entry, Wilson writes: "Although I did not remember seeing any alien beings associated with this encounter, it felt the same way all of my other visitations felt. It was extremely vivid."

I asked Wilson if she had actually seen Bush, Gore, and Clinton.

"I hope not," she replied with just a touch of humor.

But that's a contradiction, I pointed out. You say your alien encounters are real and that this encounter with political figures was just as real as those you have with the aliens.

"Did I say that?" she said. "Well, I don't think it was Gore because he was very short. I thought that was some form of camouflage." Wilson regards this episode as an alien-inspired vision of the Clinton and Gore win in November 1992.

Wilson also believes one of the beings actually helped her with the book, pointing out before the book went to press that she had transcribed five journal dates incorrectly.

Though some may think Wilson's account ridiculous, it is, in fact, typical of the sort of outré material that abductees consider part and parcel of their alien experiences. It's no wonder that investigators intent on proving the alien root of UFO abductions often leave such material out of their published stories. It clearly weakens their case.

What does Wilson think about her verboten account, so potentially damaging to the alien hypothesis and contrary to UFOlogy's unwritten code?

"Some people suggested that I cut out some of this material," she told me, "but I thought there is a lot more going on, and even though we don't understand it, it doesn't mean that it shouldn't be reported. As far as I know, this has not been done before. The book was really put out there for other experiencers, because I know they are experiencing things that they cannot account for by reading Budd Hopkins' *Intruders* and David Jacobs' *Secret Life*."

Despite her candid attitude, Wilson's ultimate conclusion echoes that of the abduction gurus: "The aliens are probably collecting ova," she opines, landing strictly within the standard-issue abduction scenario and sounding a lot like Budd Hopkins, who was the first to investigate her case back in 1988. In fact, like Hopkins, who has penned the introduction for *The Alien Jigsaw,* Wilson tends to blame aliens for just about all the weirdness. "I know that penguins aren't eight feet tall, and they don't float in midair," she explains. "That was an instance of camouflage and screen memory. And I don't really think dead people are visiting me. I think that's a form of alien manipulation. I do believe that the time travel is real, but I think there have been a few occasions where they manipulated me into thinking that happened."

If you think about it, of course, the surrealistic scenes described by Wilson have the fantastical feel of dreams. Is she, in fact, recalling nocturnal images from the land of dreamy dreams—concocted by a trick of consciousness, cooked in the fires of REM, and transformed in the morning to a cocktail dish of aliens, starbabies, and UFOs?

When I ask Wilson for the temporal context of her encounters, her response is typically straightforward—and telling. "I would have to say that the last thing I remember prior to most of these experiences," she said, "is going to bed."

Isn't that sequence—going to bed, falling asleep, getting "abducted," and waking up—suggestive of the nightly journey we all take to the imagistic outback of the dream?

"That's a fair question," she replies. "But I happen to have dreams all the time and, even if I don't leave my bed, abductions and dreams just do not feel the same."

Whether Wilson is reporting from the land of Nod, the domain of aliens, or some other realm yet unknown, we may never know. But whatever the truth of the matter, it's time to applaud her tell-all book and attitude. Her story is, in fact, far more typical of abduction cases than we have been led to believe. And the only way to learn the truth behind the UFO abduction phenomenon is to let it all hang out.

Wilson's candid tale may have already opened the floodgates. Some researchers new to the field have begun to balk at the prepackaged version of the abduction phenomenon we have been spoon-fed by the experts, and other abductees are beginning to step forward with stories of their own. A 24-year-old businessman from Harrison County, West Virginia, for example, has come forth claiming that he has been abducted by aliens at least 1,500 times.

CHAPTER 40

The Strieber Show

My second "Eye in the Sky" column for OMNI never ran. It was originally slotted for a summer 1995 issue, but by that time the print version of the magazine was on its last legs and discussions about running the story later, online, never bore fruit. I'm glad it didn't. Though it was my idea to do a column on Whitley Strieber, the slant of the story had been dictated by my editor who pictured Strieber as the leader of a UFO cult taking his message to the online masses—just where OMNI itself eventually would end up with its own message, oddly enough. I should have stood up to my editor at the time and objected, but I had just been made a monthly columnist for a national magazine and I chose not to lose that opportunity at the starting gate. Writers aren't perfect; neither are editors.

I have heard Strieber speak on numerous occasions, and have met him several times over the years. Despite his charisma as a speaker, he actually shuns contact with the public. On a one-on-one basis, he is kind, bright, and blunt. Frankly, I can't see this man as a cult leader, though I will not deny that he has hordes of followers, and I have toned down my original column accordingly. His website is currently located at www.unknowncountry.com.

✳

He's back. No, not Freddie—Whitley. Whitley Strieber, the horror novelist who's perhaps the world's most famous UFO abductee. Excuse me, not abductee—"participant." The author of the 1987 best-seller *Communion* remains sensitive about the vocabulary used to describe these experiences. The word "abductee" is disempowering, he explains, and while this may indeed fit what happens to some people—

the humiliation of being repeatedly and helplessly snatched up from their homes and forced to undergo medical examinations and procedures at the hands of small grey creatures with large black eyes—it doesn't reflect Strieber's own experiences. He regards them not as dead-end nightmares with aliens but as the beginning of our understanding of the "visitors," the term he prefers since he's still not sure whether they are aliens, or time travelers, or incursions from another dimension.

Whatever they are, Strieber's back to tell us what he's learned in the past five years. You can read about his latest adventures with the visitors in his new book, *Breakthrough,* or you can check out what he has to say about them online. Like every other famous person and soap opera star—and innumerable John and Jane Does as well—Strieber is now reachable in cyberspace.

What's he doing there, you ask? Well, he's not online to gather evidence. He's already got that, he says. Nor is he there to provide support for troubled experiencers apparently. He's online, he says, "to give readers more direct and faster, more personal replies than I can manage with postal mail," though he promises to answer his snail mail as well. He's just doing the writerly thing, in other words. But that's not the way his online presence is likely to be perceived. It looks more as if the Strieber-and-the-Visitors show has found a new, global venue.

The most interesting element of Strieber's comeback is not so much the newest details of his encounters, or "the positive and viable proof" he claims to now have of the visitors' existence, but the fact that he has placed himself squarely in the center of it all—again. Strieber is setting himself up as the world's authority on the visitors. It's Strieber as Abduction Guru, the "Chosen One," the conduit between us—participants and non-participants alike—and them, the visitors.

A fine mess the visitors have gotten him into. It was, of course, the visitors who, according to Strieber, called him "the chosen one." When asked during an online conference about the title the visitors had conferred on him, he replied: "The 'chosen one' thing troubled me. So many other people have gotten it, too, that I think it's a way of calming down us egotists!" But Strieber doesn't exactly deny the role. When one online questioner asked him flat out if he was "part of spreading that Awareness (of their existence) to the rest of the population?" Strieber didn't say no. "I am doing my best to say what happened to me," he replied, "because I think it might help. I am not part of any organized program that I am aware of."

Strieber does, however, make his central role in human-visitor affairs crystal clear. My new "proof," said Strieber, at the start of one online conference, "involves a contact that the visitors made with an entire town that was directly related to something I had done that precipitated it, and the whole affair is documented."

Where is the documentation, you wonder? Don't get your hopes up. It doesn't involve government officials or scientists, just "newspapers." And the town? Well, Strieber wouldn't say online. All his answers came off as rather vague, but perhaps he just wanted people to buy his book.

His first memoir, *Communion,* the "true story" of his encounters with intelligent non-human beings in his isolated cabin in upstate New York, became so wildly popular that he received a flood of some 140,000 letters from readers and experiencers. When Strieber responded by setting up a newsletter and "Communion" groups around the country, some people accused him of starting a UFO cult. The accusation stung and Strieber shut down his whole operation at the start of the 1990s.

"The years I've spent away from the field," writes Strieber online, "are proof positive that I do not possess a cult, an accusation that was particularly stupid, given my preference for personal isolation." But over the past five years, Strieber actually has given lots of thought to why he had generated so many negative feelings in the press and among the UFO-research community. "I wanted to try to understand why I had attracted this response, so that I could do better next time," he says. "I'm ready to try again because I feel that I have some useful insight into the many different problems that resulted in this overall reaction."

Strieber continues to speak like the "chosen one," however. "The proof came to me in 1989," he wrote in the course of our e-mail interview, "and I concluded at the time that its publication might be a signal to them to engage in much wider contact. I then withdrew from public life, saying that I would not return until I had something genuinely new, because I was not at all sure that I wanted to be responsible for triggering something that might have very negative consequences." But now, five years later, after getting "enough answers" from the visitors, Strieber says, "I am satisfied that the responsible thing is to go on."

If I understand Strieber correctly, what he's saying here is this: My new book gives the visitors the green light to proceed with further human contact. Nice of him to consult us, isn't it?

Whether Strieber wants to be top UFO guru or not, what he's doing, what he's saying, and how he's saying it, are all conspiring to make him one. And as guru's are prone to do, he seems to be forecasting the big breakthrough as well. "I think that a mass sighting might well be in the cards this year," he said during one online conference.

Such pronouncements are, of course, foolish. People have been saying things of this kind for years, and it never ever happens. Maybe this time will be different, but I doubt it. Strieber should know better than to make such statements. What he's doing is setting himself up for the big fall.

Strieber brushes off his on-going battle with the "side show"—the business about being a UFO guru, having a cult, and all—by comparing such matters to mosquitoes. "A man searching the night sky might bat at mosquitoes," he explains, "but he's not there for that purpose." While that's true, sometimes the mosquitoes get the better of you, and you end up going back inside.

CHAPTER 41

Paradigm Shift

In July of 1995 Pamela Weintraub called to tell me that OMNI soon would appear on the internet. She said that this would be the next big thing and suggested I get on and get with it if I didn't want to miss the bus. Actually, I had been on the internet, using email primarily, but my old, underpowered 1990 computer only allowed me access to the web as text, which is roughly the equivalent of watching television with nothing but the sound on. Since I did not want to miss the bus, I went out and bought a new computer and saw what the fuss was all about. This was the future and I was in it. Thank you, Pamela.

Okay, said my editor, now if you want to write for the new OMNI, you have to learn html and turn in your stories coded in advance. (Those were the days before web authoring programs.) It's easy, she said. She was right again. But the planned startup of OMNI online was delayed by a month, then another, until finally about a year had passed.

In the meantime the 50th anniversary of the sighting that started it all, the Kenneth Arnold case of June 24, 1947, was rapidly approaching, and Dennis Stacy was asked to co-edit an anniversary overview of the subject for the book publishing division of the British publication, FORTEAN TIMES. Stacy came to me and asked me to contribute an article. Originally, I suggested that he simply reprint my last OMNI story, "The Secret Invasion," which I considered one of my best. I thought I would just stick a new introduction on it and the entry will be ready for the book.

When I turned in the story with four new opening paragraphs, Stacy and his co-editor, Hilary Evans, liked the new, personal slant so much they asked me to recast the entire story that way. And so I rewrote the entire first half of the story accordingly and came up with a tale of how the abduction experience had come to occupy center stage in the UFO controversy. The story, titled "The Best Kept Secret," appeared in the book, UFOS: 1947–1997, which was edited by Hilary Evans and Dennis Stacy, and published by John Brown Publishing in London in April 1997. I reprint only the first half of the story here and the last few paragraphs, as the second half of the story draws on "The Secret Invasion" (Chapter 38) almost word for word.

✳

Anything can happen in New York. I thought I knew what that meant until I arrived in the Big Apple in 1977, fresh out of journalism school. Within a couple of weeks, I witnessed a shoot-out between a handful of policemen on the sidewalk and someone inside a store on Second Avenue. The scene unfolded in front of me as the city bus I was riding nonchalantly made its regular round of stops down the Avenue. My face was glued to the window as I tried to follow the scene receding quickly behind us. It was then that I realized that, no matter what happens, life goes on.

During those first few weeks in New York I also learned that the apartment I had moved into was just a block away from one of the legends of the early days of UFO research, Ted Bloecher. He had founded Civilian Saucer Intelligence of New York back in 1952 with Isabel Davis, worked for a time at the National Investigations Committee on Aerial Phenomena, produced the *Report on the UFO Wave of 1947,* and had begun compiling the "Humanoid Catalog" with David Webb. Bloecher and I quickly became friends, and he soon introduced me to a New York artist who had become interested in UFOs.

His name was Budd Hopkins. Hopkins' apartment and studio

became the meeting ground for a handful of investigators, UFO witnesses, and other interested parties, such as myself. On a monthly basis, if I recall correctly, we would meet at Hopkins' place, drink white wine, eat cheese and crackers, and discuss UFOs. Actually, what we discussed the most was the abduction phenomenon. That was Hopkins' abiding interest. He was convinced that the aliens were able to block the memories of those they abducted and that these hidden events could then usually be revealed through hypnosis. Hand in hand with that conviction came Hopkins' belief that just about anyone could be an abductee. You didn't need to have a conscious memory of being abducted. You didn't even need to recall a UFO sighting. All you needed was a nagging feeling that something may have happened at some point in your past.

Actually, you didn't even need that much. Curiosity about UFOs was enough to mark you a potential abductee in Hopkins' eyes. He thought that my own interest in the UFO phenomenon might be motivated by a forgotten but real abduction experience. He offered to have me hypnotized to ferret out my abduction episode, but I refused. Sure, I'd seen a strange orange object in the sky as a nine-year-old growing up in Newport News, Virginia, but "unidentified" is all it was. I had no "missing time" episode. (If I did, it was missing.) No, I could barely bring myself to believe that abductions were real. To think that someone was an abductee on the basis of one's interest in UFOs seemed patently ridiculous.

I was not the only one to think so. Peter Gersten, a criminal lawyer in the Bronx who had been attending the gatherings and who would later file a landmark Freedom of Information Act lawsuit for the U.S. government's UFO documents, thought that Hopkins had a one track mind and was on the wrong track at that. Disagreements erupted and soon the once-congenial meetings of that core late-1970s group were no more. Bloecher became increasingly uncomfortable with the subject and soon dropped out of the field altogether. Having landed my "dream job" as a staff writer at *Newsweek* and being disappointed by the experience, I decided to move to the serene setting of a farmhouse near Charlottesville, Virginia, to continue my writing.

A year later Hopkins came out with his first book, *Missing Time,* and forever changed our concept of the UFO phenomenon. When the 1961 abduction episode of Betty and Barney Hill became public in the second half of the 1960s, it seemed like a unique case. By the late 1970s, with the Travis Walton, Pascagoula, and other cases having made national headlines, it became obvious that the Hills were not the only ones to have experienced a "UFO abduction." Then came the early 1980s with Hopkins sending chills down our spines with the suggestion that many people who had been abducted were probably not aware of what had happened to them. And so Hopkins began his crusade to let them—and the rest of the world—know exactly what had happened to them.

I was back in the New York metropolitan area by the second half of the 1980s, at a time when the public seemed seized with alien fever. Huge triangle-shaped objects were being seen over the Hudson Valley, where I was living, and a well-known horror novelist, Whitley Strieber, confessed to his own bizarre UFO abduction experiences in upstate New York in the best-seller called *Communion.* By that time Hopkins had figured out what the aliens were doing with the humans they were abducting. His second book, *Intruders,* detailed the cases he drew upon to support his conclusion that the human species was the subject of a genetic experiment conducted by alien beings. It was the summer of 1987 and for a while I got caught up in alien frenzy. On some very hot days I found myself almost believing that the aliens were here.

Though Hopkins and I were still friends, I was no longer welcome at regular gatherings, which were now largely comprised of abductees. The once informal get-togethers had become support group meetings with Hopkins acting as counselor. He took a lot of flak for this. But he had no choice but to take on that role, he argued, as therapists and other social scientists were reluctant to deal with the problems facing abductees. Hopkins was now even hypnotizing his own subjects. Given the number of abductees who had come forward since *Missing Time,* it had become too time-consuming and costly to find psychologists to conduct all the regression sessions that needed to be done. While I understood the constraints under which Hopkins was operating, I felt that he was doing irrevocable harm to his case by putting his own subjects under hypnosis. Who was to say that the subjects were not telling Hopkins exactly what he wanted to hear?

Then, as the 1990s unfurled, the most unsettling revelation to date about the abduction phenomenon was unveiled. The aliens seemed to operate on a scale that was previously unimaginable. Unimaginable to everyone, perhaps, but Hopkins.

We're talking mass abductions. But cases with dozens, maybe hundreds, or thousands of people involved should provide a critical mass of independent testimony to prove the reality of the phenomenon. And if such mass abduction reports were true, of course, then UFO abduction researchers should have dozens, if not hundreds of abduction reports on the same day. But they do not.

David Jacobs attempts to explain away this "hole" in the data by calling the aliens' secret program "remarkably efficient and extraordinarily effective." Besides, the way researchers find out about abductions just makes this secrecy doubly hard to break. Remember, the basic tenant of abduction research—first conceived of by Hopkins back in the late 1970s—is that most people who have had abduction experiences don't really know what has happened to them. Jacobs is convinced that researchers only hear about a tiny fraction of the cases, maybe about .001 percent. People might know that an odd thing has happened here or there, but linking it to a UFO abduction is not something most of them ordinarily do—not until Hopkins came along, anyway.

The anecdotal case material does not support the secret invasion scenario. I don't see any concrete evidence that the entire human race is being unwillingly drafted into some hideous alien genetic experiment to produce alien-human hybrids. Hopkins and I are still friends, I think, despite my skepticism, but our contact is now essentially one of journalist and subject.

From my current vantage point, living in a small rural town about an hour's drive north of New York City, I can still see the glow given off by the vast galaxy of lights that is Manhattan. But what I don't see is a fleet of hovering UFOs, each one patiently awaiting their turn to abduct block by city block of citizens. Somewhere along the way, the numbers have outstripped reality—or vice versa. Life goes on.

CHAPTER 42

Dick and Jane Meet ET

When OMNI finally went online in 1997 one of the "Eye in the Sky" columns that I had written for the print magazine finally appeared. It's a review of a not-altogether kosher children's book about UFO abductions. I thought it set a dangerous precedent, and I said so. After all, this column was supposed to represent my voice and reflect my opinions. The story, titled "Dick and Jane Meet ET," ran in the Project Open Book section of OMNI online sometime in 1997. The lack of a precise date serves to alert the unwary of what can happen with the posting of online stories. All web stories should be dated.

※

What should we tell the children about *them?* For believers in the reality of extraterrestrial visitations, that's the highly provocative question raised by the publication of an illustrated children's book about alien abduction. *Ceto's New Friends,* written by abductee Leah Haley, illustrated by Lisa Dusenberry, and published by Greenleaf Publications (which is operated by Leah's husband, Marc Davenport), appears to be the first of its kind.

It's not a bad idea—on the surface, anyway. Abduction researchers have run into an increasing number of cases involving very young children. Being both an abductee and a mother, Haley has obviously tuned into this trend and written a book to ease the fears that young children may have about extraterrestrials.

At first glance, the book seems harmless. It's a Dick-and-Jane-makes-a-new-friend story, only their names here are Annie and Seth. And the new friend is a little gray humanoid with big black eyes called Ceto.

The story begins with Ceto coming to Earth, seeing Annie and

Seth playing, and asking to be their friend. Then, after playing ball and marbles together, the three hold hands and a beam of light sweeps them aboard Ceto's silver spaceship. The ET teaches the Earth kids to float in the air and "speak with their eyes." Annie and Seth play with the spaceship's bright-colored control buttons and watch colored lines wiggle across the screen.

When Annie and Seth begin to tire, Ceto takes them back to Earth. In the end, they exchange gifts—a terrestrial marble for an extraterrestrial purple rock—and say their farewells before Ceto takes off in his spaceship. Cute.

But the story has tapped into a long-smoldering debate in the UFO community. The issue is this: Are the ETs friendly like Ceto, or are they in fact cruel, self-centered, emotionless creatures whose interactions with humans verge on evil?

Abduction researcher Budd Hopkins, who is anything but enamored with the alien "grays," feels the book is extremely dangerous. "Leah should know better," he says. "Teaching children that ETs are friendly is like teaching them to take candy from strangers." His anger rises so rapidly when talking about the grays that he has trouble finding words—other than expletives—to express his feelings. But one gets the impression that in *his* eyes, at least, the aliens and, say, Hannibal Lecter are cut from the same cloth.

Even so, Hopkins' reaction is positively mild-mannered compared to the visceral outrage the book has elicited from others—like Robert Girard, who runs Arcturus Books, Inc., a mail-order UFO book business, out of Port St. Lucie, Florida. "My jaw dropped so far down when I saw this that my belly button hurt for a week," he says. "It may be the most unfortunate development in UFOlogy in many years."

If the aliens turn out to be real—and real nasty—Girard may have a point. The book's "apparent intention," writes Girard, "is to introduce toddlers to alien abductions early (say, age 3 or so), before they find out the hard way—later in life—via trauma, ruined lives, etc., and to make the introduction a *friendly* one, in which the toddlers apply their innate trust in all things and all beings to the very monsters who are going to stick long needles into their bellies, ram huge contraptions up their behinds, empty their brains, make them pregnant and then rip out the fetuses, cut them, scrape them, inflict unspeakable pain on them and tell them (if anything at all) 'it is necessary that we do this.' Of course, none of those things happen to the two tykes in the book—and that's what strikes me as the ultimate Big Lie that one could ever inflict upon a totally impressionable mind: the idea that the grays are our friends."

On the other side of the UFOlogical fence are those, like Sacramento behavioral scientist Richard Boylan, who tend to view alien encounters as essentially positive. Boylan recommends the book highly because of its usefulness in getting children to talk about their ET experiences. He compares it to books that have been developed for children in alcoholic families or for children who have been abused. "I think it creates a window of opportunity for a parent and child to sit down and talk about what happened to the child," says Boylan.

"What we know from child psychology," he continues, "is that it's better to give children the chance to talk through their experiences. And many children are reluctant to talk through their contact experiences. They are afraid that adults, their parents, won't believe them, or the kids may not have the verbal category to talk about the experience, since extraterrestrial contact is not commonly part of our culture's vocabulary yet." And even if the tenor of the child's experience happens to differ from the one the book portrays, Boylan feels "there is enough triggering in the story to allow a child to say, 'Well, gee, I had that meeting, too.'"

Of course, all this assumes the aliens are real. Being an evenhanded sort of fellow, I'd say it's possible they are not, in which case this book is a fantasy and it should be perfectly okay to portray the aliens as nice—except for one thing. How is a child to differentiate an alien, real or imagined, from an ill-intentioned human stranger—a kidnapper, a pedophile, a child pornographer? If you're three or four, that might be a tough proposition.

And that's my strongest objection to the book: A third of the way into the story, Ceto asks Annie and Seth: "Would you like to go for a ride in my spaceship?" And what do the children in the book do? They go. No resistance. No question. They just go.

You don't teach little tykes that it's okay to go for a ride with a stranger, regardless of who that stranger happens to be—human or alien. For a children's book, it's a fatal mistake.

Haley, a 46-year-old mother of two college-age daughters, should know better, not least because the real-life episode that Haley claims this book is loosely based upon happened quite differently. It supposedly occurred in Alabama when Haley was three and her little brother was one. But in *that* episode, when the alien asked if they wanted to go for a ride in his spaceship, she replied: "My mother would get mad at me." Good girl, Leah. (It didn't help, of course. The cunning little alien managed to brush off her concerns, and off they went.)

CHAPTER 43

Against All Odds

One of my duties as a contributing editor to the online version of the new OMNI was to write pieces for the Antimatter section. These covered a wide variety of slightly-off-the-edge topics, including the occasional UFO story, of course. The following story mixes UFOs with politics and shows the two subjects are like oil and water— they just don't mix. Some people have even tried to run for political office on the UFO ticket. It failed when Gabriel Green ran for President in 1960. And it failed for Frances Emma Barwood, a Phoenix, Arizona, councilwoman who lost the 1998 election to the office of Arizona secretary of state, after calling for an investigation into the March 1997 UFO sightings flap in Arizona. The subject is still associated with lunacy—that's something people like in their movies but not in government. The story, appropriately titled "Against All Odds," ran as an Antimatter in OMNI online in 1997.

*

Some politicians will say almost anything to win an election. But the story Lynne Plaskett told before the last elections was decidedly alien to politics as usual.

Two months before voters went to the polls to decide whether Plaskett, 46, should be reelected to the Volusia County Council in Florida, the hard-working councilwoman appeared on the Maury Povich Show. Before an audience of millions, she announced that one night back in 1975, a small disc-shaped object with tiny windows flew into her house and scanned her from head to toe, curing her of cancer. "When I woke up the next morning, I knew I was going to be all right," she told the talk show host. Then, four months later, Plaskett learned that the lymphoma doctors thought would kill her was in remission.

On November 5th, a cancer-free Plaskett lost her council seat to former Port Orange Mayor Jim Ward: 15,074 to 17,416. But her ET claim, insists Plaskett, had nothing to do with the loss.

"Absolutely not," she says. "I lost because I took a strong stand on environmental issues that affected people's pocketbooks. We also have a 50-year history of driving on our beaches around here and I took a strong stand against that. And the reason I know my story had nothing to do with losing the election is this: When you're on the council and someone disagrees with you, they write you, they call you, they tell you. During the campaign, I never received one negative phone call or piece of mail about this."

Plaskett, a city planner by profession, is now consulting—and writing a book on her experience. She's calling it: *Against All Odds.*

CHAPTER 44

Extraterrestrial Trash

For those convinced that squadrons of aliens routinely swoop down on the Earth, the SETI program comes off as ridiculously conservative and cautious. Frankly, they think it wastes peoples' money. They have a point. But UFO fanatics show just as much bias as the scientists they criticize, in their belief that there is only one real or possible route to ET contact. The scientists put their money on radio contact. The believers conclude it's happening now as physical contact. But other options exist. This story about the possibility of alien artifacts being found right here on Earth was titled "Extraterrestrial Trash" and appeared in the Antimatter section of OMNI online in 1997.

*

Scientists who believe in the possibility of extraterrestrial life tend to think that the SETI (Search for Extraterrestrial Intelligence) system of using radio telescopes to scan the heavens for repeated, non-natural signals is our best bet of finding them. But A.V. Arkhipov of the Institute of Radio Astronomy in the Ukraine takes a decidedly contrarian view in an article published in a recent issue of *The Observatory,* a respected journal of astronomy published in England since 1877.

Arkhipov suggests that it might be possible to discover evidence of extraterrestrial intelligence right here on Earth. He argues that space activity tends to pollute a solar system and that artifacts resulting from such activity would tend to leak into the interstellar medium. "If there are alien artifacts between the stars," he writes, "some of them are likely to fall to Earth at some times." Arkhipov estimates that some 4,000 such artifacts, each weighing about 100 grams, could have fallen here to Earth since the planet was formed 4.5 billion years ago. Astronomer Tom Van Flandern, author of the book *Dark Matter, Missing Planets and New Comets,* is intrigued by Arkhipov's suggestion but finds his calculation of probabilities somewhat lacking. "His estimate of the frequency of chance artifact falls on Earth is very optimistic," he says. "To mention just one problem with it, 100-gram objects cannot survive passage through the Earth's atmosphere. In fact, evidence suggests that nothing smaller than 10,000,000 grams ordinarily survives the passage unless it starts inside a larger body that melts away like a heat shield.

"Nonetheless," continues Van Flandern, "I agree that we should be vigilant about recognizing ET artifacts in the event we might encounter one. After all, any advanced civilizations that may exist in the galaxy ought to be capable of sending robotic probes seeking out habitable planets such as Earth. So it might not be necessary to make the pessimistic assumption that all artifacts could arrive only by chance."

CHAPTER 45

On Horse Mutilation Mysteries

Because UFOs remain a mystery, many people tend to associate just about everything else that is unexplained with UFOs. Such reasoning is simply and utterly wrong. But that is how Bigfoot sightings, crop circles, horse mutilations, and all sorts of other subjects become ufologized, to coin a term. The Danes, however, seem to have a bit more sense than most in this regard. My story, titled "The Monic Affair," appeared in the Antimatter section of OMNI online in 1997.

※

Denmark was thrown into a panic in 1996 over reports of animal mutilations. It began on July 25 when Monic, a $25,000 Arabian breeding mare, was found dead with a small hole in its skull between the ear and eye. The veterinarian who performed the autopsy was mystified: he found no bullet and could not trace the wound to any conventional weapon. Worse yet, one month earlier, two other horses had been found dead with unidentifiable wounds 3 to 6 inches deep.

The Monic mystery recalls that of "Snippy," the Appaloosa mare found dead in southern Colorado in September of 1967. The horse had been stripped to the shoulders and a subsequent investigation discovered that all the internal organs in her chest had been surgically removed. Since UFOs and other weird moving lights allegedly had been seen in the area, it didn't take long for some UFO buffs to link Snippy's death to extraterrestrials, and thus the story spread around the world.

However, despite ample opportunities to do so, the Danes made no such connection to UFOs in the "Monic Affair." At first the rumors suggested that the horse had been shot by an arrow, which had been retrieved by an archer. But regular hunting arrows do not leave such small holes. Later, Monic's death became linked to a wave of horse mutilations across the German border. It seems that since 1992, 89 horses had been killed and 229 others had been injured in a crime epidemic the German police called *Pferderippern* or "horse rippers." When reports rose of injured horses in Denmark, Danish police appealed for calm and warned of smear campaigns against the Germans. "As it is," said a police spokesman, "we don't really know that the holes are man-made."

A lack of evidence finally led Danish police to give up trying to link the "Monic affair" to the German mutilations and the case remains unsolved. But the fact that UFOs never were pinned with the blame in this case intrigues Bill Ellis, an associate professor at Pennsylvania State University in Hazleton and president of the International Society for Contemporary Legend Research. "The UFO scenario has been one of the dominant scenarios in the United States since Snippy the horse was supposedly done in by extraterrestrials back in the 1960s," he says. "It's easier for us to refer a mysterious event to an existing theory explaining mysteries than to invent an even more mysterious new scenario. That's why the Danish event was interesting: you could see the media and police grappling with the evidence and looking for scenarios rather than recycling old ones."

But Ellis can only guess at who was responsible for Monic's death: "From what the press says, it seems likely that someone, either for a nasty prank or for a grudge kept out of the papers, murdered the horse with a bolt-pistol (normally used to kill horses in slaughterhouses). But without on-site investigation, I don't want to make any call. As a folklorist, I'm much more interested in how people construct satisfying narratives from initially mystifying details. It's a serious analog to the 1-minute detective stories' people used to play and maybe still do:

"Man found hanged from the ceiling in a room with no furniture, and no way for the man to have reached the rope. No other physical signs of anything on the floor, but the detective notices that the man's bare feet are burned. 'Suicide.' How come?"

CHAPTER 46

Military Abductions

Unless you are quick to dismiss the abduction phenomenon as due to night terrors and related hypnopompic images, you have a neat little mystery on your hands. The most surprising thing about the following explanation, which claims that military personnel are playing a key role in UFO abductions, is the response I received from the Joint Chiefs of Staff when I asked them point blank if they were involved in the so-called "UFO abductions." Here we have one instance where a standard reply seems positively incriminating. My story, titled "Military Abduction" appeared in the Antimatter section of OMNI online in late 1997 or early 1998. Helmut Lammer, whose theory airs here, would later write a book on the subject called MILABS: MILITARY MIND CONTROL AND ALIEN ABDUCTION, published in 1999 by Illuminet Press.

✳

It gets more outrageous all the time. The latest wrinkle in the UFO abduction phenomenon has abductees claiming they've been kidnapped by military and intelligence personnel, who take them to hospitals and work side-by-side with the aliens.

Now, Helmut Lammer, a space scientist at the Space Research Institute in Graz, Austria, has decided to examine the claims and set up Project MILAB, short for MILitary ABductions. Lammer, in particular, looked into the notion, widely held in conspiracy circles, that UFO abductees might be victims of government mind control.

Could UFO abductions be "cover stories" induced by hypno-programming military psychiatrists? Could military personnel be using rubber alien masks and other special effects during these military abductions, as one abductee has reported?

Lammer thinks not. In his recently released preliminary report, he suggests what he calls a "more plausible" explanation. If you've ever wondered why military and intelligence agencies don't seem to have much of an interest in the UFO abduction phenomenon, he has the answer: They actually do.

Lammer believes that a secret military/intelligence task force is involved in monitoring and kidnapping alleged UFO abductees. "They are monitoring the houses of their victims, kidnapping and possibly implanting them with military devices sometimes shortly after a UFO abduction experience," he writes. "It appears to me that they are searching for possible alien implants, too. Their gynecological interest in female abductees could be explained, if they are searching for alleged alien/hybrid embryos, since most of the abducted females had missing embryo/fetus experiences."

When we asked the Office of the Chairman of the Joint Chiefs of Staff at the Pentagon for a comment, their spokesperson was initially amused. But after seeing Lammer's report, no one appeared to be laughing. "The formal Joint Staff response," says Major David Thurston of the Joint Staff Public Affairs Office, "is 'no comment.'"

CHAPTER 47
Sagan's Scintillating Evidence

Like me, Carl Sagan was apparently obsessed with UFOs and aliens as a teenager living in New Jersey, according to the recent biography by Keay Davidson, titled CARL SAGAN: A LIFE. As a junior in college in 1954, Sagan still believed UFOs might be extraterrestrial vehicles. But after reading two books—FADS AND FALLACIES IN THE NAME OF SCIENCE by Martin Gardner and EXTRAORDINARY POPULAR DELUSIONS AND THE MADNESS OF CROWDS by Charles Mackay—it dawned on Sagan that UFOs probably had a psychological and sociological explanation.

By 1966 Sagan had developed "an amiably skeptical stance on UFOs," according to Davidson, but he continued to "hang around this subject." Sagan served on the Air Force UFO advisory panel, known as the O'Brien Committee, that evaluated Blue Book and advised the Air Force to commission an independent, full-scale study of the phenomenon. In his later years Sagan took on an increasingly negative stance toward UFOs, but he still believed in the existence of extraterrestrial life and, in fact, became one of the chief promoters of the SETI program. I think, as the following story suggests, that he may even have suspected that contact had been made. This story, titled "Sagan's Scintillating Evidence," was posted in the Antimatter section of the OMNI website in 1997.

✳

Despite years of effort, astronomers scanning the skies with radio telescopes for signals from ET have found no solid evidence. Nonetheless, the little-known truth is that these searches—known, collectively, as the Search for Extraterrestrial Intelligence, or SETI—have yielded numerous tantalizing hits astronomers are unable to explain. The trouble is that in each and every case these mystery signals could not be detected a second time. And since once-is-not-enough in the world of science, we haven't seen leading astronomers or NASA scientists on the evening news, shouting: "We're not alone!"

But in a rather surprising recent paper, the late Carl Sagan and co-authors Jim M. Cordes and T. Joseph Lazio, all from Department of Astronomy and Space Sciences at Cornell University, state that this lack of confirmation cannot be taken as evidence that the signals are not real. Apparently, recent research into how signals propagate through space suggests that these bleeps—these candidate signals—could have been "weak extraterrestrial signals momentarily amplified by the interstellar medium," according to their paper, entitled "Now You See Them, Now you Don't," published in *Mercury*, "The Journal of the Astronomical Society of the Pacific."

This "amplification" would occur because of a phenomenon known as *scintillation*. "Natural processes, like scintillation," explains Cordes, "which comes from irregularities in the interstellar gas (analogous to optical twinkling of stars from atmospheric irregularities), can cause the strength of ETI signals to vary enormously."

But scintillation is both the good guy and the bad guy in this story. "If there are extraterrestrial signals," write Sagan and company, "it is likely that they will be discovered because of scintillation." On the other hand, scintillation has probably also hampered the re-observations: "Within a few minutes of the initial observation, the amplification sources sink back into the noise," they state.

Cordes notes that scintillation would not affect the search for ETI signals from nearby stars, only those farther away—such as the 11 unexplained candidate signals from the META search conducted by Paul Horowitz and his students at Harvard over a five-year period.

These, conclude the Cornell astronomers, were either produced by terrestrial sources that mimicked what one would expect from an extraterrestrial signal, or they were real alien signals temporarily amplified by scintillation.

CHAPTER 48

UFO Home Videos

One of my "Eye in the Sky" columns that never had a chance to run in the print edition of OMNI focused on the work of Jeffrey Sainio, who analyzes UFO videos for the Mutual UFO Network. The story sat in the OMNI story vault until I suggested to my editor that we do a story on a fascinating analysis of a UFO video performed by Bruce Maccabee, the other ace UFO photo analyst, that showed an unidentified flying object undergoing humanly impossible acceleration. Pamela Weintraub liked the idea and suggested we combine it with my earlier column on the subject and run the whole thing as a feature. The result, titled "UFO Home Videos: Seduced by Venus and Other ETs," ran on the OMNI website in 1997. Note that the beginning of each section recapitulates the major theme of the story, providing continuity, as each section ran on a separate web page. Perhaps the reader would forget what he or she was reading while waiting for the page to load?

✳

UFO fever hit Vista, California, just north of San Diego, a while back. Perhaps most interesting, though, the rash of sightings was highlighted by a UFO apparently seen and caught on videotape. Embedded on silicon is the image of a glowing yellow ball, dimming and brightening as it slowly and quietly crossed the sky. After about six minutes the UFO stopped and dropped a series of five or six glowing balls. Then suddenly the balls blinked out and disappeared. While many other witness came forth with similar descriptions of this object on this and other nights, it was the videotape that everyone—media and UFOlogists alike—all turned to for "proof."

For the field of UFOlogy, often caught short in the arena of proof, the home video explosion promised great things: With the ability to reliably and permanently capture the entire sequence of a mysterious event for later analysis, UFOlogists were confidently proclaiming that video cameras would provide the long sought for evidence of the reality of UFOs.

Part of that dream has become reality: As the price of camcorders has dropped, a potentially critical data-gathering instrument has made its way into the hands of more and more front-line UFO observers—the general public. And as the number of video cameras in everyday use has increased, so have the number of UFO home videos. Jeffrey Sainio, who began analyzing photos and videos for the Mutual UFO Network a few years ago, notes that videos now account for about 80 percent of the submissions.

With the tens of millions of camcorders now in use in the United States, it seems reasonable to expect that, if there were strange craft in our skies, we ought to have some good home videos of them by now. Do we? Well, if we did, you wouldn't have to read this column for an answer. There would be no need for a Project Open Book. With the evidence of UFO overflights and landings and alien abductions captured on videotape, the world would certainly have experienced that much touted major paradigm shift by now. And talk about a New World Order. The news of alien visitation would fill every newspaper, magazine, and television broadcast.

Flaming Toilet Paper

Despite the burgeoning use of camcorders, evidence of alien vessels and visitation has not been documented, in startling verisimilitude, on tape. In fact, I know of no video ever submitted to any UFO organization or news outlet that really provides even a whiff of evidence for the existence of extraterrestrial craft. Nonetheless, the hundreds of UFO home videos that have been produced and submitted to the media and UFOlogists for analysis do provide some concrete "proof" of what many UFOs are.

What they are primarily, are IFOs, or identified flying objects. "Right off the bat," notes Sainio, "you can eliminate about 60 percent of the videos as yet another good shot of the planet Venus. Or you look at others and say, how could people not recognize an airplane? By the time you're done with that, 85 to 90 percent of them are easily recognizable."

The San Diego area UFO video was a little tougher for Sainio to decipher, but it too ultimately was identifiable. "That turned out to be a case of third party fraud," he explains. "Some local teenage boys were inflating garment bags with candles and these things would go drifting off. But they had also tied toilet paper to the bags in such a way that when the candles burned down, the paper ignited and fell off, producing a fairly spectacular display. It even fooled me for awhile."

Sainio has looked at more UFO videos than he cares to remember. Of these, about 50 he calls "memorable," but less than a handful of them still puzzle him. Four tapes, he says, show evidence of anomalous acceleration. The best of these, taken in March of 1993, shows something accelerating at about 500g. That's enough to crush any living thing, human or otherwise, to a pulp. When a manned space vehicle leaves the Earth's atmosphere, the gravity pull of 6 g is considered the maximum tolerable for the human body. But even these curious videos do not show a clearly anomalous object shape, or provide any clues to just what the objects are. "Until I can make out 'Pleiadian Star Command' on the side of it," says Sainio, "or the 'Vietnamese Air Force,' I really can't say where they come from."

Nor have any videos yet shown an abduction episode or credible humanoid entity, though there have been submissions of alleged ETs videos. "I got one just yesterday," says Sainio. "It was taken at a country music concert, and the person was panning around with his camcorder and sure enough at one point there appears to be a human shape out there. But from what I can tell, it is a human. And from the stance he's in, I suspect he was urinating."

Video Future

The video evidence for UFOs has been disappointing, especially since videos might provide strong evidence for any legitimate alien ship.

Even Philip J. Klass, the field's number one skeptic, will admit to that. One huge selling point for Klass is that videos are so much more difficult to hoax than still photos. The usual tricks of photography, like double exposures and negative sandwiches, can't be done on video, though given enough skill, money, luck, and patience just about anything else can be done on video these days. Still, video has a kind of built-in honesty meter. The creation of a fake image must be accompanied by a fake soundtrack. Cries of "Hold that fishing pole steady" would be a dead give-away.

That's not to say that videos are the perfect form of evidence. The picture quality, or resolution, and color of video is inferior to still photographs, but videos do provide a record of an object's motion and speed. Perhaps the best thing about videos is that they are essentially free, meaning that people will shoot nearly anything—and they do. And unlike still photography, videos lack the "shame factor." You don't have to hand your film over to some clerk who is going to smirk at you and say, "Gee, what's this? Have you had aliens visiting you?"

Home videos are actually good enough to serve in scientific investigations. In fact, a precedent has already been set for using amateur videos in scientific analysis. When a meteor streaked over West Virginia on the night of Oct. 9, 1992, and 40 seconds later crashed into a parked car in Peekskill, New York, 14 videotapes were taken of the object's trajectory. Using these tapes, scientists calculated the meteor's path, its ablation characteristics, orbit, etc., and published their findings in the Feb. 17, 1994, issue of the prestigious scientific journal, *Nature.*

Actually, one notable UFO episode has already been caught on tape by more than a dozen videographers. During the total solar eclipse of July 11, 1991, at least 18 videos were taken of a small, bright, silvery object which hung motionless in the sky over Mexico City and nearby Puebla. Mexican TV journalist Jaime Maussan called it "the most important collection of videotapes ever assembled in history." But UFO investigator and journalist Antonio Huneeus discovered otherwise. "It was the Queen of the IFOs," says Huneeus. "Venus was precisely at that spot in the sky where the video cameras had taped the so-called UFO during the eclipse."

Videography Primer

Even if someone were lucky enough to spot a true UFO, getting a good video is no easy feat. A lot more information could be extracted from UFO videos, notes Sainio, if people would follow a few simple rules. First, use "SP," the slowest tape speed. Second, get reference points—like trees, telephone poles, buildings, and other aircraft, if possible—in the same shot as the UFO. Third, describe what you see as you are taping, as well as the time, wind, temperature, etc. It would also be extremely helpful, says Sainio, if people provided complete documentation with their video tapes, in other words, the camera type, direction in which it was pointed, etc.

But Sainio is not hopeful that such instruction will bear fruit. "The problem is that people who are interested are rare and sightings are rare, and the cross section of the two is even rarer," he says. "And that's another thing you learn. If you run across a bunch of people who are going out to find a UFO, they will. They will videotape a Cadillac headlight, or an airplane flying over, but they will come back with a UFO. I really shouldn't knock them, they're trying. But it wastes a whole lot of time."

That, in the end, is what it all comes down to. So far, the video evidence for UFOs has been a waste of time. If there were indeed strange craft in our skies, we ought to have some good, clear home videos of them by now. That we don't suggests that there are no strange craft in our skies. But that conclusion, of course, is tentative.

I won't say, as some skeptics might, that such things are impossible. Anything is possible. And I would love to see the evidence of a real extraterrestrial craft on video. Once analyzed and certified by experts, a good video of a sharply defined, obviously manufactured, strangely-shaped object doing things that no human-made craft can do would go a long way toward convincing me and many others of the existence of "flying saucers." And certainly such a video would qualify as better proof for the existence of alien visitation than anything yet mustered.

The Shadow Knows

Few UFOs caught on videotape remain unidentified after analysis. But there are some exceptions, and during the last few years Bruce Maccabee, a Navy physicist by day and UFO photo analyst by night, has examined a handful of examples that he believes prove UFOs are capable of flight characteristics—acceleration in particular—far beyond the capabilities of any terrestrial technology.

Among the most remarkable of these videos is one shot by the notorious Ed Walters of Gulf Breeze, Florida. Walters' numerous sightings and photographs over the past decade have been the subject of several books and considerable controversy. As a result, the UFO video that Walters managed to take on July 21, 1995, will not convince any of his critics. But Maccabee has produced an analysis sure to thrill UFO buffs.

The full story of this video actually begins on July 13, 1995, when Walters saw a strange object flash through the sky. Hoping the object would return, he set up his videocamera with its telephoto lens on a tripod in his office and kept up his daily surveillance-by-video until the effort finally paid off. Walters was working at his desk on the morning of the 21st, when he noticed a flash in the sky. So he turned on the camcorder and shortly afterward the object returned.

Its brief reappearance and Walter's description of it are recorded on the videotape: Looking like an inverted layer cake, the UFO appears suddenly at the left of the screen and moves over the Santa Rosa Sound and a line of trees 7,600 feet away on the opposite shore. The object darts rapidly toward center of the screen, reverses direction, and quickly exits left.

When Maccabee received a copy of Walter's video, he was

delighted to see that the UFO sequence appeared to show the object's shadow—a roundish, rapidly moving area that slightly darkens the tree line as the object moves back and forth across the screen. "The shadow meant that we could locate the UFO in three dimensions," says Maccabee.

After Jeff Saino computer-enhanced the images, Maccabee used an astronomy program to calculate whether the shadow "belonged" to the passing object. He determined that it did. Maccabee found "strong evidence that the darkened area on the trees is, in fact, the shadow of the UFO." This enabled him to also calculate the size of the object. It measured about 27 feet by 13.5 feet, give or take a foot or two.

Maccabee was then able to determine that the UFO had been traveling at about 500 mph, then decelerated to zero, producing about 150 "g's," reversed direction, and departed at about 550 mph. That's probably enough force, notes Maccabee, to "turn a person into soup." It's this acceleration, rather than mere speed, that poses a challenge to physics as we know it. "Speed is not the thing," he adds, "it's how fast it takes you to get up to speed that counts."

The sudden acceleration displayed by this and other UFOs captured on videotape has led Maccabee to believe that this extraordinary flight characteristic may help explain why so many eyewitnesses report UFOs suddenly disappearing. "Maybe the objects are not actually disappearing," notes Maccabee. "Maybe it's simply the inability of the eye to follow them at a high rate of acceleration."

But did Walters capture a genuine UFO on his video? Many don't believe so. Rex Salisberry is one of them. "I doubt that it's real," says Salisberry, who thoroughly investigated the Walters story for the Mutual UFO Network. "Some of his previous photos did not hold up under our technical scrutiny, and to me, that casts doubt on his other evidence, too."

Maccabee did consider the possibility of a hoax, but after much thought, finally dismissed the idea. "Even a Hollywood special effects person," he states, "would have to be a major genius, use lots of high powered technology, and spend lots of time to get it right."

CHAPTER 49

A Government Insider's Account of Alien Contact

As a contributing editor to OMNI online during its brief existence (about a year and a half), I also conducted live online chat interviews every other week with people promoting their new book or theory on UFOs or some aspect of the paranormal. The program was called "High Strangeness" and appeared as part of OMNI's "Prime Time Live" schedule of chat shows. At the time, the technology to conduct these online chat interviews was terribly primitive and difficult to use. Often subjects simply could not log-on. Or the connection would fail. Or their answers vanished into the ether. Or all of the above. The delayed timing of questions and answers also took some getting used to. Since most subjects failed to "grok" the technology, the resulting interviews were often worthless.

Even on those occasions when the technology was relatively transparent, however, other problems loomed. Although I often viewed with skepticism much of the material presented on these shows, I could not come right out and ask the pointed question, for fear that the subject would simply log off and leave me alone in front of viewers, who varied in number from a couple to perhaps as much as a thousand. Occasionally these peripheral participants (only identified online as "Guests" by the chat software program) were allowed to post their questions, and this would sometimes add to the confusion. But on a few nights we were blessed with good connections and the person I was interviewing was both interesting and computer savvy. This is one of those successful interviews, which took place on the last day of 1997, edited for print. The original version of this and other High Strangeness interviews is posted at www.omnimag.com.

✳

Welcome to High Strangeness! My name is Patrick Huyghe and our guest tonight is former USAF Staff Sergeant Dan Sherman, author of the new book *Above Black: Project Preserve Destiny, Insider Account of Alien Contact and Government Cover-Up.* Dan Sherman has a story you won't believe—or maybe you will.

Sherman claims to have spent almost three years working for the National Security Agency as an "intuitive communicator" in contact with the aliens. In *Above Black* he tells of his training, the things he learned from his alien contacts, and the events that led him to seek a discharge from the USAF at all costs. Sherman believes that the project he worked on, called Preserve Destiny, is only one of the US government's many alien-related projects.

Sherman served a total of more than 12 years in the USAF. He was recognized for heroism and has been decorated with the AF Commendation Medal and the AF Achievement Medal. He also received the AF Outstanding Unit Award and was honored for service in the Persian Gulf.

Now to begin….

When did the event take place that you are talking about?

Dan Sherman: I'm not sure what you mean by "event," but I was indoctrinated into the program in early 1992. By the way, I was a Technical Sergeant.

Okay. Thanks for the correction. What is Project Preserve Destiny (PPD)?

Sherman: Well, that is a long explanation. A short version, as was told to me…it is a program designed to cultivate humans who have the ability to "intuitively" communicate with an alien race to provide a worldwide communication link in the future where there will presumably be no electromagnetic means of communication.

At the NSA you were told that your mom had been visited by aliens in 1960 and that you were given an "interesting ability," which is called Intuitive Communication. What is IC exactly?

Sherman: Intuitively communicating is the term utilized by my superiors that was ascribed to my abilities. It is an ability, through the mental manipulation of one's mind, to communicate. The actual communication I liken to looking at a tapestry (and feeling/seeing all the colors and textures…). It is a VERY rich means of communicating.

IC sounds like a cross between "remote viewing" and channeling. Is it?

Sherman: My take on channeling is that one actually takes on the traits of the one being channeled. That had nothing to do with IC'ing. Remote viewing seems to be much more vague. My communications were very much based in reality. There was nothing left to doubt.

Exactly how were they supposed to "cultivate" these people?

Guest: What group at NSA where you presumably working in/for?

Hold on, guests. Give Dan a chance to answer one question at the time.

Sherman: First question is too long to answer here. The program began in 1960...they started abducting to test for compatibility for the particular procedure...and goes on from there. (It's all detailed in the book obviously.) The actual NSA unit I was assigned to is classified. I printed a copy of my orders in the book and it even says "DATA MASKED." The unit is part of the "Black" project and therefore I cannot talk about that aspect of my experience.

Can you tell us the general subject matter of the black cover project that hid PPD?

Sherman: This is the reason I have been able to talk about the "grey" aspect of my experience with impunity...because I have not revealed anything of the black projects I worked on. Believe me, they are very sensitive projects that ARE vital to national security. I'm not out to betray my nation, only to reveal info that has nothing to do with national security and is only a power play within inner circles of the "grey" government.

How can aliens NOT be a matter of national security if they are abducting people right and left?

Sherman: Well, if there was a security issue directly related to the security of our nation regarding PPD, I was not made aware of it. Perhaps there are security issues surrounding other alien projects that I am not aware of...but not with PPD.

Guest: Sgt. Sherman, did Roswell actually occur? Or was there no mention made during your time with Project Preserve Destiny?

Sherman: During my initial meeting, when I was told about PPD, the Captain made a reference to 1947 and PPD was a result of our contact with an alien race during that year. It didn't mean anything to me at the time, because Roswell was not as well known as it is today.

You were told to take some pills before most of your IC sessions. What do you think these pills were? How do you know your experiences were real? Could the pills have been designed to make you THINK you were communicating with aliens?

Sherman: One of my conversations with my second alien contact made me think the pills were some kind of oxygen enhancer, like anti-oxidants perhaps. He referred to us (humans) as "water-humans" (my interpretation), which led me to believe that perhaps my bodily oxygen level was crucial to the IC ability. The communications were real, I just know. It was an extremely lucid event each and every time.

But how do you know you were actually communicating with aliens?

Sherman: When you are called by your mother, how do you know it is actually HER? I was not absolutely, 100 percent sure it was an alien, but the fabric and content of the communication was unlike any other form of communication I have ever experienced.

Guest: These aliens that you communicated with, in what star system are they located? How did our government know to enhance your oxygen levels? And why are these aliens participating?

Sherman: I am unaware of where they have come from. Everytime I tried to talk about such things my alien contacts were vague and even when we discussed principles of time, I was completely lost as to what they were saying. They do use "time" for their propulsion. One thing that was interesting...he said they can't go through time, but they can go "around" time. All those types of conversations were quite interesting for me, even though I didn't understand half of what was being said.

As you say so yourself in your book, you initially found what your

NSA boss told you rather unbelievable. Don't you think they might have been pulling something on you?

Sherman: I thought they were pulling something over on me initially. But you don't experience what I experienced (interacting with a computer screen without being attached to it in any way, for one) without becoming a believer in your Intuitive Communications abilities.

What did most of your alien communications consist of?

Sherman: Initially, my comms were strings of numbers then gradually they became more image based...military launches (foreign and domestic), military movements...etc. Toward the end they started comming to me abduction scenarios, which directly led to my seeking a discharge.

What made you think that some numbers had to do with alien abductions?

Sherman: Numbers were initially. Abduction info came later. I started to receive info such as Potentiality for Recall with a number assigned to it. Other categories were Residual Pain Levels...with a number assigned to it. What would you decipher these types of comms as?

Guest: Did you catalogue these numbers and their meanings?

He was not allowed to write anything down.

Sherman: I could probably have gotten away with writing this stuff down, but, mind you, I never figured I'd ever speak of this so it never entered my mind to document anything. It was a part of my life and was nothing special after a while.

What made you decide to quit the program and the military? And how did you manage to get out since they initially refused to let you out?

Sherman: There wasn't just one thing that led me to seek a discharge…it was a culmination of things and one final event that cemented my resolve. Unfortunately, the way I did it forces me to not talk about it. Seeking a discharge under false pretenses is punishable …if that were the case in this case, of course. I know this is cryptic, but there are certain things my lawyer has advised me not to speak of.

What was the "final event" you speak of here?

Sherman: The "final event" is too involved to be done justice here…It had to do with some e-mail correspondence I had with my commander.

Did you not fear prosecution? Have you had any "official feedback" since you published your book?

Sherman: I most definitely feared prosecution. What I feared most was not my talking about the grey project but my revealing it and at the same time not revealing something they would get me on regarding the "black" projects I worked with. It was a very narrow road I traveled in writing about my experiences.

Any feedback from officials?

Sherman: No official feedback. Because I have had none, I will be releasing the book to be sold through stores now. You should be able to request it through any bookstore. It'll take longer but you can get it through stores now. My website (www.aboveblack.com) will tell you the other ways.

Guest: Sir, although your belief may be genuine, place yourself in our shoes. You story sounds like so many others, remiss any tangible clues to trace your understanding. It sounds too much like you are turning your grey government black world into green backs in your pocket.

Sherman: Believe me, if I wanted to make lots of money I would have come up with a lot more believable story than this to appeal to a wider audience. This is the whole truth and nothing but. I'm not sure if you're aware of the financials in these matters but I could make more money selling Amway. :)

Being a published author myself, guest, I can tell you that Dan speaks the truth about making a fortune from writing books! What have you done—other than writing the book—since you left the military?

Sherman: I have been in the Senior Citizen insurance market since my departure. My goal in releasing the book (financially) was to attempt to make enough income to go through school and finish my degree in Computer Science. No mansions and fast cars here.

Well, we've run out of time. Thank you very much for being with us tonight, Dan Sherman. Good luck with your book. For High Strangeness, this is Patrick Huyghe. Goodnight!

CHAPTER 50

Those Top Secret NSA Documents

In complete contrast to the prior story, we have this one, the last article I wrote for OMNI magazine online. It never ran. Publisher Bob Guccione suddenly pulled the plug on the venture in March of 1998 and the web site (www.omnimag.com) was quickly tidied up for eternal viewing, but frozen at that moment in time.

Too bad, it was a great story. It came about after a conversation I had with Philip Klass at the 1997 Fortean Times UnConvention in England. I was there promoting the British edition of my book THE FIELD GUIDE TO EXTRATERRRESTRIALS, and he was there being himself, the old stick-in-the-mud of UFOlogy. The article marked a real breakthrough for Klass as it constitutes the first of my stories where he finally got top-billing. Klass and I get along quite well, by the way. He remains as much a UFO fanatic as I ever was, if not more so.

I came across a draft of this story as I scoured my files looking for articles for this book. When I read it, I realized that the story never broke in the popular press. So after polishing it up a bit, I send it to FORTEAN TIMES, which proceeded to "sit" on the story for two months. Finally, unable to get a reply from the editor, I emailed the story to Scott Martin, whom I had met at a UFO conference in San Antonio, Texas a couple of months earlier.

Martin worked at a new web site called SPACE.COM, founded by Lou Dobbs, who surprised everyone by leaving his post as anchor of CNN's top-rated "Moneyline" program for this internet venture. Martin was responsible for the site's UFO section, called "Area 51" at the time, among others. Originally, the Area 51 section was on equal par with other sections on the site such as Space and Astronomy. Then they hired former NASA astronaut Sally Ride to be president of the site, adding the respectability and NASA connections that Dobbs sought for his new venture. Trouble was, Ride is anti-UFOs, but Dobbs, who is apparently very interested in the subject, insisted the disreputable topic remain. And for good reason—it happened to be the most popular section of the site. So a compromise was struck: the UFO section stayed, but would now be grouped along with books, movies, and television under an umbrella section called "Space Imagined."

In any case, less than five minutes after I had sent Martin my story about the wily Mr. Klass, he replied, saying that SPACE.COM wanted the story. A few hours later, at precisely 02:43 pm EST on the 13th of January 2000, the story was posted on the web under the title "Klass Counts Coup." I was stunned. The web had reduced the minimum three-month lead time I was used to in dealing with monthly periodicals, to a matter of hours. Nothing better illustrates the changing face of journalism the web has fostered. And, yes, I was very happy to see my work appear in a "respectable" mass-media venue once again.

*

The UFO controversy is full of strange stories, but this may be the strangest yet. Few people are aware that a few years ago, Philip Klass, the lone-gun UFO skeptic despised by UFO believers as "the enemy," managed to do something that the most devoted UFO believers had attempted for years without success—getting the supersecret National Security Agency (NSA) to release portions of its long withheld UFO documents. The surprise move by Klass could have backfired, but instead has turned into a remarkable coup.

For the past two decades, the Holy Grail of those who believe the government is staging a massive cover-up of UFO evidence has been the 156 UFO-related documents that the NSA has refused to release in any shape or form since 1979. Even the court battle to get those documents released under the Freedom of Information Act (FOIA) in the early 1980s served only to stoke the fires of conspiracy. When UFO researchers managed to get a hold of the 21-page affidavit that NSA had presented to the court to justify its actions, the affidavit came back heavily blacked-out and censored. But it made a good prop for the TV cameras and seemed like pretty tangible proof to back-up the claim of some believers that the government was indeed hiding what it knew about UFOs.

Enter the unflappable Philip Klass. In October of 1996 he wrote a letter to the director of the NSA, Lt. Gen. Kenneth Minihan, in effect tugging at the top-secret curtain that hides the NSA's UFO documents from public view. Klass, as contributing editor for *Aviation Week and Space Technology,* had interviewed him two years previously on the subject of electronic warfare, when Minihan was director of the Defense Intelligence Agency, and just two weeks before sending out the letter, Klass had heard Minihan, now director of the NSA, give a talk at a conference of the Association of Old Crows.

In his letter Klass explained to Minihan that his hobby for the last 30 years had been to debunk claims that UFOs are alien spacecraft visiting Earth and that the government was engaged in a massive UFO cover-up. After this and other preliminary remarks, Klass sprung his request on Minihan. Now that the face of world politics had so changed, might the NSA reconsider declassifying at least some of its UFO-related documents, asked Klass? Releasing this material, most of which are COMINT, or communications intelligence, reports dating from 1958 to 1979, would help "expose the absurdity of claims that these documents prove a government UFO cover-up," Klass wrote.

A couple of months rolled by and then in January of 1997 the mailman arrived at Klass's door with "a gigantic package from

NSA." And there they were, the never-publicly-seen 156 NSA documents, as well as a heavily declassified version of the 21-page NSA court affidavit. What the documents and affidavit reveal, says Klass, is that NSA's earlier refusal to release the documents was aimed squarely at keeping secret the agency's eavesdropping on Soviet air defense radar sites. In fact, the 156 NSA UFO documents are still heavily censored to hide the identity and locations of the Soviet radar sites whose communications the NSA was able to intercept.

But the "UFO content" of the documents is now available for everyone to examine, though all places and dates remain censored. Perhaps the most startling of the 156 documents is one that indicates the Soviets launched a number of interceptor aircraft to "attack" a UFO. But the results of the attempted intercept with the slow moving UFO are unknown as the next eight lines of the document are blacked out. Business as usual? Well, yes and no. The analyst did note that the UFO was "probably a balloon." In fact, most of the 156 NSA UFO documents report UFOs that are "probably balloons," according to comments in the documents themselves.

What's all this about balloons? Klass explains: "When NSA intercepted messages from Soviet radars which reported tracking an 'Unidentifiable object' some NSA analysts translated that into 'Unidentified Flying Object,'" he wrote in his *Skeptics UFO Newsletter* (404 "N" St. SW, Washington, DC. 20024), which originally broke the news of the declassified NSA UFO documents. "Because the Soviets used balloons carrying radar reflectors to periodically check the performance of their air defense radars and the alertness of their radar operators, a NSA translator analyst would add 'Probably a balloon' where it seemed appropriate." But after UFO organizations began making FOIA requests in the late 1970s, Klass believes that someone must have told the NSA translator/analysts to stop using the term "UFO" for the balloon-borne targets. Apparently NSA hasn't used the term since.

What the NSA documents show, according to Klass, is not a grand conspiracy to hide the fact that UFOs are alien spacecraft, but that the Soviets had "deployed height-finder-type radars capable of tracking targets up to altitudes of nearly 80,000 ft." Yes, Klass admits, there are about a dozen "true" UFO reports in the bunch. These contain summaries of visual UFO sightings and apparently come from Soviet facilities other than radar installations whose communications the NSA had managed to intercept.

Here is a typical example, with the "X's" denoting censored material: "[XXXX] REPORT SIGHTING OF UNIDENTIFIED FLYING OBJECT. AN UNIDENTIFIED FLYING OBJECT WAS SIGHTED BY [XXXX] BETWEEN THE [XXXX] OF [XXXX] AND [XXXX]. THE OBJECT WAS DESCRIBED AS HAVING A SEMI-CIRCLE SHAPE AND LOOKED LIKE AN ARC IN THE SKY. THIS OBJECT WAS ALSO NOTED AS BEING WHITE AND VERY LARGE. IT WAS SEEN FOR A PERIOD OF ABOUT TEN MINUTES AND IT SEEMED TO JUST HANG IN THE SKY FOR A FEW MINUTES BEFORE MOVING ON IN A WESTERLY DIRECTION. [XXXX]"

The report is, at best, interesting. But there is certainly nothing here to suggest an alien spacecraft, and now that this and other similar NSA UFO documents are out in the open, no evidence of a government cover-up either.

Peter Gersten, the attorney who filed the original UFO FOIA suit against NSA, seemed non-plused by the release. "There is nothing in the NSA documents that either confirm or deny the reality of an extraterrestrial presence," says Gersten. "The documents relate exclusively to NSA operations." And Stan Friedman, the nuclear physicist and UFO investigator who often used the blacked-out NSA court documents in his public talks, is still not happy with the situation. "There is no question that the NSA is still withholding UFO information preceding 1980," he notes on his website.

But there is no question that Phil Klass has scored big here. He has shown that the believers' "smoking gun" lacked fire of any kind. It barely even packed a squirt.

CHAPTER 51

A New Day for UFO Research?

It wasn't the proverbial flying saucer landing on the White House lawn. But it was one of the most noteworthy sightings in years, if for no other reason than the fact that the story got considerable play in the media. And part of the reason for that is the National Institute for Discovery Science's decision to send out some former FBI agents to investigate the case. The remarkable sighting would later become the subject of an excellent hour-long TV documentary entitled "UFOs over Illinois" on the Discovery Channel.

My story was based on an in-person interview with Colm Kelleher, while I was in Las Vegas in February of 2000. It appeared under the title "A New Day for UFO Research" on SPACE.COM at 12:43pm on March 15, 2000. Note that my original title was followed by a question mark at the end.

*

The Air Force did it, albeit reluctantly, for about two decades. A few private UFO organizations tried it, too—and promptly lost their shirts. Now the National Institute for Discovery Science (NIDS) is doing it—fielding a rapid response team to investigate promising UFO reports. The question is: will they succeed where others have failed?

NIDS was founded in 1995 by Las Vegas real-estate tycoon Robert Bigelow to investigate UFO sightings, animal mutilations, and other anomalous phenomena. Through its first four years of operation, during which Bigelow hired a staff of scientists to run the institute, NIDS was largely silent about its work and cagey in its public statements. Few people were even aware of its existence and those who were, primarily UFOlogists, regarded the fledging institute in the desert with suspicion.

All that has now changed.

"About a year ago we decided it was time to start reaching out so that people could come to us with reports," notes biochemist Colm Kelleher, who runs the day-to-day research operations of the institute. Four months ago the institute actually began mass mailing a NIDS brochure and sticker promoting its 24-hour hotline (702-798-1700) and web address (www.nidsci.org) to police departments and radio and television stations.

"These are the people who get called about UFO sightings, but they are not trained to investigate these things and are not even interested most of the time," Kelleher said. "We were hoping to persuade these people to call us and we would do the rest."

The plan worked. NIDS has been getting about 100 calls a month, but until the morning of January 5 when a call came in from a police officer in Illinois just east of St. Louis, no hotline UFO report had been deemed worthy of an all-out NIDS investigation.

This one was. Craig Stevens of the Milstadt Police Department called NIDS about two hours after his UFO sighting at 4:28 that morning. Stevens had been monitoring radio traffic when he heard that the Highland police department had a report of a large object flying in the air.

So he drove to the north end of town where he observed a very large object shaped like a fat arrowhead flying slowly at an altitude of 500 to 1000 ft. Police officers in Shiloh and Dupo also witnessed the object, as did a police officer in Lebanon.

The low-flying, triangular object was described as being between 200-600 feet long and 40-60 feet thick with bright white lights angled downward at the corners and a red light near the center.

After numerous follow-up phone calls, NIDS decided to deploy their two full-time investigators, former FBI agents, to Illinois. Why FBI? "We like guys with a lot of forensic background," says Kelleher, "because in the mutilation area and in the tiny percent of cases where alleged landings occur, you really need people who can secure the scene and handle the evidence properly so that we can stand behind it."

The NIDS investigators arrived in Illinois two days after the initial sighting, spending almost four days interviewing eyewitnesses, taking photographs and seeking a possible explanation from a local Boeing facility, nearby Scott Air Force Base, and the FAA.

NIDS immediately put the transcripts of the interviews on their web site in the hope of unearthing other witnesses who might have seen the object. Such openness in their investigation stands in stark contrast to similar efforts by the Air Force decades ago.

But their efforts to find a prosaic explanation for the sightings failed. The FAA had not seen anything on radar. Scott Air Force Base officials said they didn't know anything about the object and there were no stealth B-2s in the area at the time.

NIDS even considered the possibility that the UFO might have been a secret blimp that resembled a small experimental model built and patented 30 years earlier by a New Jersey company called Aereon, but that design, according to Aereon's CEO, never went past the proof of principle stage.

NIDS' eight eyewitness reports suggest that the object came down from Lake Michigan just north of Chicago at 10:00 p.m. on January 4 and headed southwest, appearing 6 hours later in Highland, before finally disappearing outside Dupo just before 7 a.m.

"That's about 9 hours in the air," notes Kelleher. "That's a long time. On the other hand, according to at least one police officer, the object would literally jump across the sky in a matter of seconds. The other weird thing is, if it's trying to be stealthy, what's it doing so low with these unbelievably bright, blinding lights?"

Physicist Bruce Maccabee, like many UFO believers, gave NIDS a thumbs up for "their quick response and excellent work in interviewing witnesses on the scene. I also congratulate them for publishing their results on their web site."

Not so for UFO skeptic Phil Klass. "By curious coincidence," he writes in the March issue of his *Skeptics UFO Newsletter,* "a very bright planet Venus was just rising in the southeast on Jan. 5 at the time of the Illinois UFO sightings."

Klass accuses NIDS of not even considering the possibility that the UFO might have been Venus. "Although I have not personally met [the NIDS investigators]," Klass told me in an email interview, "I suspect they are quite competent to investigate 'cattle mutilations,' but believe they are ill-trained to investigate UFO reports."

But according to NIDS astrophysicist Eric Davis, they did consider, then rejected, stars or planets as possible explanations for this case. In fact, Davis told Michael Lindemann of *CNI News* that Venus was below the horizon when the UFO was first sighted near Highland at approximately 4 a.m. Venus actually did not rise until 4:25 that morning and would have been difficult to see initially because of the surrounding trees, rolling hills, and structures in the area.

"But we still can't rule out the military," concludes Kelleher. And there, rather typically for a UFO sighting, the matter rests.

Whether NIDS will ultimately succeed where the Air Force and so many others have failed over the past 40 years is another question entirely. "We have an ability to go to the wall, if necessary, on the analysis front," explains Kelleher. "We have the resources to pull out all the stops, our science advisory board has the ability to open doors, and Bigelow is in this long term. He's been into this ever since his family members had a sighting when he was a kid. He's been putting money into this for quite a while. Plus we have a full time staff not doing anything else. We are not a volunteer group doing it on our own time or funds. I think NIDS has a lot of potential."

Stay tuned.

✳

Postscript:

In the spring of 2001 NIDS released a paper summarizing the 127 reports they had received in the prior 14 months on the triangular craft phenomenon. The report notes that the craft description and performance characteristics are generally not consistent with any acknowledged aircraft being currently deployed by the United States military. The craft are huge or large, are brightly lit, sometimes with multi-colored lights, and they fly silently at low or very low altitude, sometimes hovering or flying very slowly (less than 100 MPH). The report concludes that the extremely low altitudes of these triangular aircraft, seen by dozens of eyewitnesses in dozens of locations in the United States, "probably constitutes a public safety hazard and should be investigated by appropriate authorities."

In a subsequent report, dealing with just ninety-four triangular craft UFOs seen between 1990 and the present, NIDS looked for possible patterns to these sightings by plotting each one on a map of the United States. One map shows the proximity of these triangular UFO sightings to 17 U.S. Air Force bases under the Air Mobility Command (AMC) or an affiliate. "It appears that the sightings are predominately within corridors between bases," notes the NIDS report. A second map adds the 16 bases belonging to the Air Force Materiel Command (AFMC) to the picture. Again, the report notes, "the sightings are predominately within corridors between the plotted bases. In the Eastern United States, Wright-Patterson AFB, HQ AFMC, seems to be a focal point, with Scott AFB, HQ AMC, running a close second. It is interesting that the January 5, 2000 sightings by five police officers in Illinois were in such extremely close proximity to Scott AFB."

Curiously both maps reveal a large corridor in the mid-western United States with no reported sightings—and an absence of AMC or AFMC bases. "The totality of the evidence leads us to hypothesize that the flight paths are suggestive of the deployment of military aircraft hitherto unacknowledged," the NIDS report concludes. This conclusion is of particular interest in light of the following story.

CHAPTER 52

Taking the Cause to Court

What were those triangular-shaped objects? NIDS wasn't the only organization on the case. So was Citizens Against UFO Secrecy, headed by attorney Peter Gersten. He had been pressuring the US government on the subject for some time and now the case was in court.

This story, which ran on SPACE.COM as "Taking the UFO Case to Court" at 6:43 pm ET on 20 March 2000, was one of a half dozen UFO stories I would write for the website in 2000.

✳

"The search was a sham," says Peter A. Gersten, the Arizona attorney who founded and directs Citizens Against UFO Secrecy (CAUS). Gersten has just learned what "keywords and identifiers" the Department of Defense used in its search for information on the huge, black triangular-shaped object that thousands of people have reported seeing around the country for the past couple of decades, most notably in Illinois in January of this year, in Phoenix in March of 1997, and in the Hudson Valley area of New York in February of 1982.

Last year's DOD search, performed on the heels of a Freedom of Information Act lawsuit filed by Gersten on behalf of CAUS, had produced no records on this rather too obvious object, despite the fact that Gersten had provided them with 33 affidavits from eyewitnesses around the country, including sketches and a photo.

But when the DOD tried to have the case dismissed last month in Phoenix, U. S. District Court judge Stephen M. McNamee ordered the DOD to first provide CAUS with the specifics of the government's search. That's where today's "keywords and identifiers" come in. "It's obvious the Department of Defense treated the suit like an ordinary request for UFO information," says Gersten.

In their search for information from Joint Chiefs of Staff (JCS) and the Defense Advanced Research Projects Agency (DARPA), the DOD used a whole grab bag of terms, including "UFO, unidentified flying object, spacecraft, alien craft, flying saucer, v-shaped, delta, boomerang, triangular, triangle, football field, big, large, float, hover, soundless," and such general words as "house, appear, underneath, underside, bottom, red, centered, multiple, trailing" to describe the object.

"If they had to use all these words to come up with a match, I'm not surprised they didn't come up with anything," says Gersten. "On the other hand, if just one word could trigger a record, how could they not come up with something? Besides, I never mentioned the words 'alien craft,' and I specifically told them not to use the word 'UFO.' They never focused in on this object.

"But the fact is that DOD *must* have information on something so obviously within their responsibility of intelligence and security," says Gersten incredulously. "It's absolutely inconceivable that the DOD would have no information about a soundless, hovering, low level, football field sized triangular object—no matter what its origin or identity. How can the Defense Department not collect this information? We are not talking about something that crashed 53 years ago in Roswell, we are talking about something being seen in this country today."

Gersten will ask Judge McNamee to deny the Department of Defense's Motion for Summary Judgment in the case. "Their search obviously wasn't done in good faith," he says. Most curious of all was the Form 472 item signed by DOD declassification specialist Betty M. Goode, who apparently first checked the "Records Found" box, then blacked it out and checked the "No Records" box instead.

"I'm not saying it wasn't an honest mistake," says Gersten, "but it's surprising that she didn't just destroy the 'incorrectly' marked form and fill out a new one. Why have an ambiguity? Is someone trying to tell us something? Some people think that within the Department of Defense there are good guys who are for disclosure and bad guys who aren't and sometimes they give us little messages. Could this be one of them?"

After the hearing last month, Gersten received a congratulatory email from Will Miller, retired commander of the U.S. Naval Reserve: "I am certain that the documentation you seek exists [...] At the same time, I firmly believe that many senior government officials, such as the director of DIA with whom I recently met on this subject, are 'protected and isolated' from knowledge of this subject and from data gathered by their own Department of Defense intelligence organizations. The military leadership has both interest in and concern about the UFO phenomenon. If there are any 'keepers of the keys' they reside in DOD middle management and civilian DOD contractors (BDM, SAIC, Boeing, Lockheed-Martin, etc. and the comptrollers who monitor the flow of money to certain classified and Special Access Programs [SAPs]). Unfortunately in many cases the DOD folks charged with looking for information may themselves not know where to look."

Gersten is thoroughly puzzled by the DOD's treatment of this case. "I thought the DOD would have come forward and said, 'Yes, we have information, we have 62 documents—they're protected by national security.' No judge, nobody would ever question that. The agency has complete discretion to determine national security. But they didn't do that. Why?"

This case is just the latest in Gersten's bulging briefcase of UFO-related lawsuits. It was during his 25 years as a criminal attorney in New York City that Gersten's interest in UFOs led him to represent a private UFO group called Ground Saucer Watch in 1978 in its FOIA suit against the CIA.

The case produced spectacular results, leading to the release of nearly a thousand pages of UFO documents from the CIA, DIA, Air Force, Navy, Army, and other government agencies. The documents confirmed a widespread suspicion on the part of UFO buffs that despite official denials, the CIA and other government agencies did indeed have a long, often secret, interest in UFOs.

Four years later Gersten was standing before the US Court of Appeals in Washington DC arguing on the behalf of CAUS for the release of 156 UFO documents being withheld by the National Security Agency. But when the agency produced a 21-page top secret affidavit explaining its reasons for withholding the documents, the judged dismissed the suit. The heavily blacked out affidavit did nothing to squelch the suspicions of UFO buffs, however.

Then Gersten was hired by Texas UFO witnesses Betty Cash and Vicki Landrum following their encounter in December of 1981 with a mystery object that supposedly caused radiation-related injuries. But the attempt to place the blame on the government crumbled when efforts to track down the gaggle of helicopters the witnesses claimed had followed the object on its departure failed.

Most of Gersten's UFO-related lawsuits eventually hit a dead end–sometimes literally. Like the suit against the Army for the autopsy reports on the alien bodies from the Roswell crash which Col. Philip Corso, as chief of the Army's Foreign Technology Division, claimed to have seen in 1961, according to his book *The Day After Roswell*. Corso died last year in the midst of the suit. "The Army didn't say Corso was lying," notes Gersten, "they just said they didn't have any documents."

Surprisingly Gersten is rather pessimistic about ever seeing any official disclosure on the UFOs. "It would be like opening a can of worms," he says. "They couldn't control it. The media would be all over the story. People would want to know why the government lied to us in the past. The hysteria would dwarf that of the OJ trial and the impeachment hearings.

"There would be an insatiable desire for information: *What about Mars? What about the Moon? I got abducted last night, aren't you going to protect us? Oh, there's the object again!* It would jam everything up, just like the 1953 CIA Robertson Panel said would happen. So the bottom line is that there will never be an official disclosure. It's a practical impossibility. It will never happen. "

But that won't keep Gersten from trying.

✳

Postscript:

At the end of March 2000, a federal judge in Phoenix granted the government's request to dismiss the lawsuit brought by CAUS for information about the mysterious triangular-shaped objects observed by witnesses across the country over the past two decades.

In his decision, Chief U.S. District Court Judge Stephen M. McNamee ruled that the Department of Defense had conducted a reasonable search even though it did not find any information. "This case is not one over the existence or non-existence of UFO's," wrote Judge McNamee "but whether the government has conducted a reasonable search regarding information on specific aerial modes of transportation."

Gersten subsequently filed an FOIA request for the DOD documents on the their fruitless search, and by September Gersten was headed back to court. The newly released documents showed just how lightly the DOD had treated the matter.

The documents included responses from Defense Advanced Research Projects Agency (DARPA) employees who were directed to conduct a search for information on the triangular aerial object. Though the DOD component has over 200 employees, only 9 responded, 6 of whom viewed the CAUS request as a joke. For example, one DARPA employee responded that she carpools to work each day on such a craft, while another asked if the request was "a joke."

"What concerns me most" stated Gersten, "is Tricia Rohrkemper's response when one of the DARPA employee's asked to see the photo and sketches I had included in the CAUS request. She emailed the employee that 'this is not the response I wanted.' Not unexpectedly the employee emailed back that he had no information about the craft.

"And what happened to the other 190 employees who didn't respond at all?" asked Gersten. "Did they simply throw the request in the shredder? DOD regulations require employees to conduct a reasonable search. The DOD submitted affidavits to the court stating that no records were found. Now we know why. You can't find records if no search is attempted. There is no question that the DOD misled the court."

Gersten believes that if these documents had been included in either the original or supplemental DOD affidavits, Judge McNamee would not have concluded that the DOD conducted a "reasonable search" and would not have dismissed the lawsuit. So on Oct. 23, Gersten filed a "Motion for Relief from Judgment" in the CAUS lawsuit against the Department of Defense. When asked about the case, Assistant U.S. Attorney Richard Patrick said he believed the DARPA responses reflected "interoffice chatter" and nothing of any significance.

In November 2000, CAUS filed its appeal in the U.S. Court of Appeals in San Francisco. Gersten, who is now defending the rights of Native Americans for the Navajo County Public Defenders Office, expects the appeal to be heard sometime in November of 2001. Though Judge McNamee has yet to rule on the CAUS motion, Gersten has asked the Appellate Court to take judicial notice of these newly released documents.

You can follow the continuing legal action at www.caus.org.

CHAPTER 53

Are UFOs an Air Safety Hazard?

If UFOs represent spacecraft from outer space manned by extraterrestrials, they certainly don't pose any obvious threat to the human species. For UFO buffs that's a bit of a problem. If UFOs did pose a direct risk to national security and the populace, getting the phenomenon recognized as real would not be a problem. But that hasn't exactly been the case. Of course, you have to disregard some troubling violent UFO episodes in South America and the David Jacobs and Budd Hopkins interpretation of abductions as a threat to the human species. Still, there is some reliable evidence that they do pose a risk—however small, however unintentional. The following story, entitled "Report: Are UFOs an Air Safety Hazard?" appeared on SPACE.COM on Dec. 1, 2000.

By year's end many changes had taken place at SPACE.COM. UFOs had been relegated to the "Phenomena" subsection under "Science Fiction," and Sally Ride was gone. With the internet undergoing a thorough shake-up and shake-down, the site began focusing only on "hard news." In April of 2001 Lou Dobbs decided to return to "Moneyline." By then it had become clear that UFO news no longer had a home at SPACE.COM.

✳

While en route to Boston the pilots of a TWA flight noticed a circular group of twinkling lights slightly below their altitude. Whatever it was, they quickly realized, the "thing" was "huge," "moving in a hurry," and "about to cross in front of, or about to collide with us." To avoid a disaster, the captain "slammed on some power, hauled the nose up, and prayed we'd go over the top of the thing." They did.

This hair-raising incident, which occurred on December 22, 1977, and others like it, also raises a good question: Do UFOs pose a hazard to aviation safety in America today? Yes, they can, is the answer according to a recently published study entitled "Aviation Safety in America—A Previously Neglected Factor," which refers to UFOs as Unidentified Aerial Phenomena (UAP).

The author, Richard Haines, is a senior aerospace scientist and a member of the International Society for Air Safety Investigators, which assists the NTSB in accident investigations. The study was supported by a grant from the International Space Science Organization and is the first technical report on the subject of air safety and unidentified aerial phenomena produced by a newly formed organization called NARCAP.

Says Haines, "If government authorities are concerned about low probability events such as winds hear, bird strikes, and lightning strikes—which don't occur very often but when they do they can be disastrous—then they should also be concerned about UAP. The FAA has set up training requirements if pilots encounter wind shear, even though wind shear might occur once in every one and a half careers, which means you might go through your whole career and never encounter wind shear. Nonetheless authorities are taking it very seriously.

"I argue that the kinds of events I'm talking about occur with at least that level of frequency, or more, and can produce significant changes in the readout of cockpit instruments which can effect navigation and guidance and flight control particularly with glass cockpits and fly-by-wire."

In searching through his personal database of 3,400 pilot sightings from the past 50 years, Haines found more than a 100 documented close encounters between an unidentified object and a US commercial, private, or military airplane that raised air safety issues.

Most involved near-miss and other high-speed maneuvers by the UAP near the aircraft, such as that experienced by the TWA crew in 1977. A handful of these cases have actually involved passenger injury following abrupt avoidance maneuvers by the pilot.

In about a quarter of the cases Haines examined, proximity to the unexplained object affected the aircraft's instruments or displays. These involved electromagnetic effects to the aircraft's navigation, guidance, or flight control systems.

In a March 12, 1977, case, for example, a United Airlines flight from San Francisco experienced an uncommanded heading change to the left. When the puzzled crew looked to the left they saw an perfectly round, extremely bright white light as big or bigger than a DC-10 at about their own altitude. Noticing that their three compasses "were all reading different headings," the flight officer uncoupled the autopilot as the object kept pace with them for about 4 or 5 minutes before finally picking up speed and disappearing.

The pilot never filed an official report on the incident. In fact, fear of ridicule or worse prevents most pilots from reporting such encounters; some have even been told not to report their sighting publicly. Haines calls this "the law of diminishing reports," and estimates that "for every pilot who is brave enough to come forward with a case of something he can't identify, there are probably 30 to 40 who don't."

Haines notes that those who are brave enough to report such encounters almost always use terms other than "UFO," "UAP" or "flying saucer" to describe their encounters, making it almost impossible to track down these incidents in government databases of the NTSB and FAA.

Instead, Haines believes that pilots often use such generic terms as "traffic" to report these unknowns. "If that's the case," he says, "the numbers of such encounters swells to the thousands."

Haines' study raises questions that should make any frequent flyer sit up and take notice. What if the pilot makes the wrong control input at the wrong time, or otherwise overreacts, during an extremely close encounter with a UAP? What if the pilot is relying on his instruments while anomalous electromagnetic effects are causing them to malfunction? Could close encounter flight performances create cockpit distractions that inhibit the crew from flying the airplane in a safe manner? Despite raising the alarm, Haines emphasizes that "an immediate physical threat to aviation safety due to collision *does not exist.*" Why? Not thanks to the pilots' evasive maneuvers but because of the reported high degree of maneuverability shown by the UAP in such encounters. What do aviation experts think of this new report on UFOs and air safety?

"If his goal is to convince people that they need to look at it, that's fine," says Andy Turnbull, co-author of "Aviation Accident Analysis," a 1999 NASA-sponsored analysis of U.S. aviation accidents. "Our report is based on the NTSB. If he wants the NTSB to change their accident database, he has to show sufficient proof that the UAP is a significant factor in aviation safety. And he states at the beginning of his report that UAP are not a significant threat to air safety."

"But " says Haines, "they *can* pose a hazard to aviation safety and should be dealt with appropriately and without bias, whatever UAP are."

Haines recommends several concrete steps to deal with the situation. Aviation officials should take the phenomena seriously and issue clear procedures for reporting them without fearing ridicule, reprimand, or other career impairment and in a manner that will support scientific research.

He also believes that airlines should implement instructional courses that teach pilots about optimal control procedures to carry out when flying near UAP and also what data to try to collect about them, if possible.

Finally, he recommends that a central clearinghouse be identified or established to collect, analyze, and report UAP sightings for the continuing benefit of aviation safety as well as scientific curiosity. "I believe," says Haines, "that we should not wait for a midair collision to occur before we take this subject seriously and do something about it."

NARCAP: New Player In Town

The National Aviation Reporting Center on Anomalous Phenomena was organized to improve U.S. aviation safety related to various kinds of unidentified aerial phenomena. Based in Boulder Creek, California, this non-profit scientific organization aims to "provide pilots and air traffic controllers with a special telephone number, confidential reporting web site, and other means to use to report their sightings." Their web site is located at www.narcap.org.

Ted Rowe is NARCAP's executive director. Richard Haines is chief scientist. Technical advisors include a retired DC-10 captain and a retired air traffic controller, as well as a physicist, a metallurgist and a meteorologist.

It was Haines' idea to establish this national-level reporting and analysis center. When he mentioned the idea to his colleagues, it met a groundswell of support. "Air safety is the first and primary concern of our organization," says Haines. "The second is to collect scientifically reliable data on these anomalous phenomena."

But NARCAP takes no position or the source or nature of such phenomena. "One of the objectives of NARCAP," Haines says, "is to encourage the government to change its reporting procedures in a responsible way that doesn't lead to panic but that does encourage pilots to report whatever they see honestly and completely. It doesn't matter what they call it."

CHAPTER 54

The Best UFO Case Ever?

In 1998 a British magazine called THE X FACTOR asked me to write a 10,000 word UFO story with sidebars for a new publication that would feature one major UFO case per issue. I found the notion interesting and chose to write about the Socorro incident from a list of topics the editor offered me. I picked Socorro for a simple reason: I had recently become aware of the work of a researcher who claimed to have the solution for this major incident in UFO history, and I relished the opportunity to look into it to see if the proposed solution held up. I began by reading all the major accounts that had been written on this incident and then interviewed a number of participants, including the original witness himself, who still had the same phone number listed in the original report on the incident almost 35 years ago!

But the publisher of the soliciting magazine decided not to proceed as planned. Instead, the decision was made to split the story in two: one greatly shortened piece dealing with the Socorro incident itself; and the other featuring a long sidebar I had written about other sightings by policemen. Both would eventually appear in THE X FACTOR itself. The turnabout disappointed me, of course, as I had put lots of work into the Socorro update, only to see it trimmed down to a standard little magazine article. So I did my own edit of the original 10,000-word story, trimming only some of the tangential material, like the sidebar on the sightings by other policemen. A version of this story ran in THE ANOMALIST:8, Spring 2000, a small print journal that I edit and publish with Dennis

Stacy. The web address is www.anomalist.com.

＊

Introduction

Like no other UFO story before it, the Socorro incident managed to convince a whole generation of people that UFOs were not merely mystery objects flying around our skies, but that they were probably piloted by denizens from another world. The Socorro case was by no means the first claim of an apparent encounter with extraterrestrials. Such stories had circulated for at least a half century. But until policeman Lonnie Zamora's sighting made the news in 1964, all other accounts of meetings with the space people came from witnesses of dubious credibility and reputation. And their stories were laughable.

Zamora's story was different. He was a *policeman,* a highly credible witness. So with this case, the widespread feeling—even among UFO believers—that there was something absurd, if not ludicrous, about humanoids, simply crumbled. From this point on, the diminutive pilots associated with the landings of mysterious objects called UFOs were irrevocably tied into the phenomenon.

The Event

On the afternoon of April 24, 1964, the sky over Socorro, New Mexico, was clear and sunny with just a few scattered clouds. The wind was blowing hard, however, and the law itself was hard after a speeder in a black Chevrolet. Lonnie Zamora, a police officer in Socorro, was driving police car No. 2, a white 1964 Pontiac, and chasing the offender at 5:45 that Friday afternoon when suddenly he heard a roar and saw a flame in the sky. Thinking that a dynamite shack in the area might have blown up, Zamora wisely decided to abandon the chase and headed instead toward the mystery flame.

Wearing green sunglasses over a pair of prescription glasses, Zamora watched the flame descend slowly as he continued driving. The flame had a blue and orange color and was shaped like a funnel.

It was twice as wide at the bottom than on the top and four times as high as it was wide. Zamora could not see the very bottom of the flame, however, as it continued down behind a hill.

The noise Zamora heard was a distinct roar, not a blast or a jet sound. As he drove with his windows rolled down on the rough gravel road leading up to the dynamite shack, the noise from the flame changed from a high frequency to a low frequency over a period of about 10 seconds.

During this time Zamora had considerable trouble driving up the steep, rough hill. The wheels of his car kept skidding on the loose gravel and rock, and he twice had to back up and try again. By the third attempt, he no longer noticed the flame or the noise, but he did finally make it up the 60-foot-long hill.

Once at the top, Zamora traveled westward slowly on the gravel road but noted nothing for about 15-to-20 seconds. Looking around for the dynamite shack, whose exact location he could not recall, he suddenly noticed a shiny object to the south about 800 feet away. He stopped the car immediately and observed the scene for a few seconds.

At first the shiny object up ahead looked to Zamora like a car turned upside down. Seeing two people in white overalls close to the object, he suspected that it had been turned over by some kids. The "car" looked white against the moss background and the two figures appeared normal to Zamora, who assumed they were either small adults or large kids. They were about one third the size of the object, or about four to four-and-a-half feet tall. One of them then turned in Zamora's direction and seemed startled.

Hoping to be of assistance, Zamora started driving toward them quickly. On his way, he radioed the sheriff's office that he had found a possible accident and would be out of his car, checking out the situation in the arroyo, a dry shallow gully. While still talking on the radio, he stopped his car about a 100 feet from the "overturned car." As he started to open his door, Zamora dropped his mike, which he picked up and replaced in the slot before getting out of the car. As this happened, Zamora heard two or three loud "thumps," a second or less apart. It was as if someone had opened and slammed closed a car door.

Even before he turned to the scene, Zamora heard the roar again, which became louder as it rose from a low to a high tone. At the same time, he saw the flame under the object, which he finally realized was not a car at all. The object was rising straight up slowly, emitting from the middle of its underside a light blue flame, the bottom of which was orange in color. The flame seemed to be kicking up dust in the immediate area but there was no smoke.

Zamora got a good clear look at the object as it ascended. It was egg shaped and aluminum colored. It had no doors, windows, or other features except some markings in red. These insignia-like markings measured about two and one half feet wide in the middle of the object. When the object was about three feet off the ground, Zamora noticed that it seemed to have "legs" on the bottom that were slanted outward toward the ground.

As the roar increased, Zamora thought the object might blow up, so he turned away and, in a panic, ran back toward his car. At one point, as he looked back at the object, he bumped his leg on the back fender of his car, fell to the ground, and lost his glasses. He immediately got up, however, and kept running toward the edge of the hill. As he glanced back he noticed that the object had risen completely out of the gully and was now in the air at the same level as his police car.

He was so scared of the roar that he intended to continue running down the hill, but when he got there the roar stopped and he heard a sharp whine that lasted maybe a second. Zamora then ducked just over the hill, turned toward the ground, and covered his face with his arms. In the silence that followed, however, he decided to look up and when he did, saw the object going away in a southeasterly direction. It traveled in a straight line, about 10-to-15 feet above the ground, clearing the eight-foot-tall dynamite shack by about three feet.

Zamora then ran back to his car, keeping an eye on the object as it rose up and headed off across country silently and without a flame. He picked up his eyeglasses, but left his sunglasses on the ground, and got into the car. He immediately radioed Ned Lopez, the police radio operator, and told him to "look out the window, to see if you could see an object." What is it, asked Lopez? "It looks like a balloon," replied Zamora, who could still see the object as he spoke to Lopez. It seemed to lift up slowly and to "get small" in the distance very quickly. After just clearing Box Canyon or Six Mile Canyon Mountain, it just disappeared.

Zamora then gave directions to Lopez and Sergeant M. Samuel Chavez, a New Mexico State Trooper, on how to find him. As he waited, he got out his pen and drew a sketch of the insignia he had seen on the object. What he drew was a half circle over an arrow that pointed up from a straight-line base. (There is some suspicion that Zamora's drawing was later "changed" by the U.S. Army investigator and that Zamora originally described the insignia as "an inverted 'V' with three parallel lines underneath.") Zamora then went down to where the object had been and saw the brush burning in several places. At that time he heard Sgt. Chavez calling him on the police radio in his car and asking for his location. So Zamora returned to his vehicle and told Chavez to look straight ahead—he was standing right there.

That Same Day in New York

At 10 o'clock in the morning of April 24, 1964—about 10 hours before the Socorro event—Gary Wilcox, a farmer living in Tioga City, New York, saw a craft that very much resembles the one seen in Socorro, as well as two similar figures who were dressed almost identically. Wilcox described seeing a shiny object in the woods. As he approached it, he saw a 20 foot long, egg-shaped object hovering about two feet above the ground. When Wilcox began to examine the object, he was confronted by two beings, each about four feet tall and wearing silvery white outfits that covered their heads. The stocky figures were carrying trays of soil.

One of the beings approached Wilcox and began talking to him in English. They spoke for two hours about such subjects as air pollution, space probes, agricultural methods, and the fact that the beings claimed to be from Mars. The Martians told Wilcox not to tell anyone about his experience, then entered their ship, which emitted an idling sound as it took off.

Wilcox realized how absurd his story was and thought someone was playing a prank on him. He then called his mother to tell her what had happened, and eventually the story got out. In the days that followed, various people came to interview Wilcox, including the sheriff, two federal agents, UFO investigators, and newspaper reporters. They all found Wilcox an extremely reticent subject; certainly no one would accuse him of being a publicity seeker. Wilcox did not hear about the Socorro event until a week later when his father showed him a newspaper clipping about it.

The Investigation

Minutes after the encounter, the investigation of the Socorro incident began. Through both coincidence and circumstance, it would be one of the most heavily investigated UFO incidents in history.

Sergeant Chavez of the New Mexico State Police pulled up in his car just moments after Lonnie Zamora had seen the object disappear in the distance. Chavez took one look at Zamora who was pale and sweating, and said: "You look like you've seen the devil." Zamora replied: "Maybe I have." When Zamora briefed the trooper on what had happened, Chavez was skeptical. Later he surreptitiously looked into Zamora's car to search for tools that might have been used to produce the landing marks they would discover. He found nothing to incriminate Zamora, however.

When Zamora and Chavez first walked down the arroyo where Zamora had seen the object, they found burn marks here and there. Smoke appeared to be coming from one burnt bush, but there were no flames or coals. Chavez noted that the burned bush was in the center of four wedge shaped imprints. Chavez then broke a limb from the bush but it was cold to the touch. The four impressions on the ground had apparently been made by the legs of whatever it was that had landed there.

Minutes later, State Policeman Ted V. Jordan, Undersheriff James

Luckie, and cattle inspector Robert White, who had overheard the police radio traffic, all arrived and examined the site. Jordan took photographs. At 7 PM Chavez and Zamora left for the State Police office. When they arrived, Zamora spoke to FBI agent J. Arthur Byrnes, Jr., who happened to be in the office on other business and had heard about the incident over police radio.

Byrnes immediately contacted the executive officer at White Sands Proving Grounds, who in turn contacted Army Captain Richard T. Holder, the senior military officer in the immediate area. Holder arrived at the station 20 minutes later, and both he and Byrnes interviewed Zamora. Later they visited the site along with several Socorro police officers. Then, after returning to the police station, Holder called in some military police, who roped off the site that very evening and, using flashlights, took measurements and collected samples. At one o'clock in the morning Holder completed his report on the incident. Still later that morning Holder would receive a call from a colonel in the war room of the Joint Chiefs of Staff at the Pentagon who wanted to be briefed on the incident over the scrambler.

The Air Force then began its investigation. Major Hector Quintanilla, who had been the director of Project Blue Book for just a year when the Socorro case occurred, admitted that "all hell broke loose" when the story hit the newspapers on April 25th. Reporters began calling Quintanilla early at home, so he left for his office immediately to direct the investigation. When he got there the telephones were "ringing, ringing, ringing," he recalls; he had a dozen calls waiting for him. But he answered none of them. The first thing he wanted to do was reach Major William Connor, the UFO investigating officer at Kirtland Air Force Base in Albuquerque, New Mexico, 55 miles from Socorro. Though Conner was inexperienced, Sgt. David Moody, who was Quintanilla's chief analyst, just happened to be on temporary duty at Kirtland.

It took hours to get the Air Force investigation under way. A Geiger counter had to be found and the base photographer had to be located. Moody and Conner finally managed to check the site for radioactivity two days after the event, but the results were negative. They were also unable to locate any radar track of the object's passage. In addition, Moody and Conner obtained copies of Holder's preliminary investigation as well as the photographs that Undersheriff Jordan had taken.

Soil samples taken from the scene on the evening of April 24 were analyzed by the Air Force Materials Laboratory. A spectrographic analysis completed on the 19th of May revealed no foreign materials in the soil sample. No chemicals were found in the charred or burned soil that would indicate the presence of a propellant. Nor did the lab find any significant differences in composition between the control and site samples. The lab concluded that there had been no foreign residue at the site.

The news media pressed the Air Force Information Office for a response but, noted Quintanillla, "there was nothing from which we could draw a definite conclusion or a decent evaluation." Quintanilla had no idea what Zamora saw, but he was determined to find out what it was. He decided to send Blue Book's scientific consultant, Northwestern University astronomer J. Allen Hynek, to Kirtland to help with the investigation.

Meanwhile, on Sunday April 26th, Jim and Coral Lorenzen of the Aerial Phenomena Research Organization in Tucson had arrived to conduct their own investigation. They found that the impressions made by the legs of the object measured 8 by 12 feet in area. The impressions were wedge-shaped and 3-to-4 inches deep. They also reported four circular depressions, about four-and-one-half inches in diameter and approximately three inches deep; they assumed these were made by the ladder the figures must have used to get in and out of the craft. Four other prints with a little crescent shape in the middle were found where the two figures stood; these were thought to be their footprints.

Tuesday April 28th saw the arrival of Ray Stanford, representing the National Investigations Committee on Aerial Phenomena, a private but high profile UFO group based in Washington, D.C. Stanford, a psychic who had seen UFOs many times himself, also interviewed

Zamora, visited the site, and collected what appeared to be metallic scrapings from a rock in one of the depressions in the soil where the object had landed. A subsequent analysis by scientists at the Goddard Space Flight Center in Greenbelt, Maryland revealed that the material was simply silica—just sand. But Stanford insists that the scientist doing the analysis initially told him that the scrapings were a zinc-iron alloy unlike any known on Earth and indicated that the Socorro object could have been an extraterrestrial craft.

Many people investigated the Socorro incident, but probably no one did a more thorough job of it than Ray Stanford, whose *Socorro Saucer in a Pentagon Pantry* was the one and only book published on the Socorro incident. Despite its thoroughness, however, Stanford's investigation is heavily colored by a near-paranoid attitude, which was widespread at the time, about Air Force UFO secrecy. Stanford was convinced that the authorities had tried to cover-up their involvement in the Socorro case and conceal the evidence and its implications. Indeed, FBI agent Arthur Byrnes requested that his name not be mentioned as a participant in the Socorro investigation. Byrnes had also asked Zamora not to mention having seen the two figures associated with the object. And Army Captain Holder suggested to Zamora that he not mention the symbol he saw on the side of the craft to anyone except official investigators.

Later, Stanford learned through James McDonald, a senior atmospheric physicist at the University of Arizona, that a radiological chemist with the Public Health Service in Las Vegas had analyzed materials gathered at Socorro, including some vitrified sand that had been collected at the landing site. But it seems that Air Force personnel took all the chemist's notes and materials and told her not to talk about it any more. The Air Force had also taken (and never returned) the photographs of the landing site that State Patrolman Ted Jordan had taken minutes after the object's departure; the reason the film was never returned to Jordan? The film was ruined, apparently irradiated.

By the time astronomer Hynek arrived in Socorro for the Air Force, there was little he could do to add to the investigative efforts that had already been carried out. Zamora re-enacted the entire episode for Hynek, who also wandered far from the actual scene of the incident in search of similar "landing marks" in the area but found none. "The marks themselves were only two or three inches deep, sandy, clayed and hard-packed, and they appeared to be scooped out, as though a heavy mechanical device had slid rather gently into position." Hynek personally observed some of the greasewood bushes that had been charred in the immediate vicinity of the incident.

Hynek decided to focus his attention on the character and relationships of the people involved, and Zamora in particular. He hoped to invalidate Zamora's testimony somehow, but that effort failed. "It is my opinion," Hynek concluded, "that a *real, physical* event occurred on the outskirts of Socorro that afternoon...."

Quintanilla meanwhile did his own checking. He called the Holloman Air Force Base Balloon Control Center in New Mexico to check on balloon activity in the area at the time of the incident. He and his secretary, Marilyn Beumer Stancombe, called all the weather stations and Air Force bases in New Mexico for the release of weather balloons. They also looked into the possibility of helicopter activity, as well as government and private aircraft flights in the state that may have provided an explanation for the Zamora sighting.

But everything came up negative. There had been no unidentified helicopter, balloon, or aircraft in the area, and the radar installations at Holloman and Albuquerque had observed no unusual blips, though the radar site closest to Socorro, the Holloman Moving Target Indicator Radar, had been shut down that day at 4 in the afternoon. Desperate, Quintanilla even called the reconnaissance division at the Pentagon and the Immigration Service. Finally, at wit's end, he decided to check with the White House Command Post. But that also proved to be a dead end—a general informed Quintanilla that the only activity they had in the area was some flights of the U-2, America's premier high-altitude spy plane at the time.

After days of checking one thing or another, Quintanilla finally received Hynek's report on Socorro. But it added "practically nothing" to the report that Connor and Moody had submitted. In fact, Quintanilla was furious at Hynek for adding "more flame to the fire" at his press conferences on the matter. "I was determined to solve the case come hell or high water," Quintanilla noted. But Quintanilla, like Hynek, was convinced that an actual physical craft had been present. The question was: was it extraterrestrial or man-made?

Quintanilla suspected that the solution to the case lay in a hanger at Holloman Air Force Base. After pulling some strings at the Pentagon, Quintanilla flew out to Holloman himself to interview the Base Commander at length. During his four day visit Quintanilla spoke to everyone and searched the base from one end to another. He even spent another day with the down-range controllers at White Sands Missile Range. But in the end he left Holloman dejected and convinced that the answer to the Socorro mystery did not lie at Holloman after all.

On his way back to Wright-Patterson Air Force Base in Ohio, Quintanilla came upon another potential solution to the Socorro mystery. Could Zamora have seen a prototype of the lunar landing module being tested in the field? As soon as he got back, he requested briefings on the subject, as research on the lunar lander for the Apollo moon program was being conducted right there at Wright-Patterson. He spent a lot of time pursuing this angle, and for good reason. It was an excellent guess.

In late 1962 NASA had selected Grumman to build this crucial piece of hardware for America's race to the Moon. The contract was signed on January 14, 1963, and Grumman spent the first three months establishing a practical external shape for the vehicle. Much attention was focused on guessing what the surface of the Moon would be like and how to design for a safe landing. The designers realized that they did not need an aerodynamic streamlined vehicle, as would be needed in the Earth atmosphere. Since the craft was to operate solely in the vacuum of space, it could be as ungainly looking as was necessary. Like the Socorro craft, it would be a two-man vehicle.

NASA decided that the lander's propulsion systems would be

tested at White Sands. They also expected to flight-test the lunar module in New Mexico, according to a NASA history of the program. But over the years, the design of the lunar lander changed considerably and in the end Grumman came up with a huge, spidery-legged bug quite unlike what Zamora saw in New Mexico in 1964.

In his quest, Quintanilla even wrote to all the companies involved with field testing the lunar lander, but all their answers came back negative. No lunar lander was operational in April of 1964.

In the end, Quintanilla, forced to pronounce judgment on the case, labeled it "Unidentified." He did this although he felt that many essential elements of the case were missing, "intangible elements that were impossible to check." Writing in a journal called *Studies in Intelligence* in 1966, Quintanilla did not for a minute doubt Zamora's reliability: "He is a serious police officer, a pillar of his church, and a man well versed in recognizing airborne vehicles in his area. He is puzzled by what he saw, and frankly, so are we. This is the best-documented case on record, and still we have been unable, in spite of thorough investigation, to find the vehicle or other stimulus that scared Zamora to the point of panic."

Corroborating Witnesses

Determined as it was to explain away the case, the Air Force never tried very hard to find other witnesses to the Socorro event. But others apparently did see Zamora's object, including two men from Dubuque, Iowa, whose testimony, however, later proved dubious. On the evening of the incident, the police radio dispatcher received three reports from locals who claimed to have seen a blue flame of light in the area, but he failed to enter their names in the log. An Albuquerque TV station reportedly received a call just before 5:30 from a caller who claimed to have seen an egg-shaped UFO traveling south toward Socorro. But again the caller's name was not recorded. Two women on the south side of Socorro claimed to have heard the roaring sound associated with the object, but they never saw the object itself.

Two days after the incident, Opel Grinder, the manager of the

Whitting Brothers Service Station, came forward with a fascinating, though unsubstantiated, story. Grinder said that a group of tourists— a man, his wife and three boys—had stopped at the station late that afternoon and remarked that "aircraft fly low to the ground around here." When Grinder said there were many helicopters in the area, the tourist commented: "It was a funny looking helicopter, if that's what it was." The object had flown over their car, apparently heading right for the gully where Zamora had encountered the object. The man even commented that he had seen a police car—probably Zamora's—heading up the hill. But the man never came forward to identify himself once Zamora's sighting made the news.

Years later, still other witnesses came forward. Robert Dusenberry, who had worked for the Socorro Electric Corporation, claimed to have seen the object's departure along with two other men while they were driving by the "landing site" on that day. And several hours after the incident a master sergeant at the nearby Stallion Range Station of the White Sands Missile Range spotted a blue glow in the sky. As the glow intensified, the engine of his car died and its electrical system failed. But after the glow faded, he was able to start his car again. The glow had appeared in the southwest, just the direction the object was headed toward when Zamora had lost sight of it.

The Sole Cry of Hoax
Only one person in Socorro actually thought that Zamora had fabricated the whole story and that dubious honor belongs to Felix Phillips. Phillips lived close the landing site and was at home with his wife at the time of the incident. They lived so close, in fact—just a thousand feet away—that Phillips believed he should have heard the loud roar that Zamora had reported, especially since Zamora claimed to have heard it from 4,000 feet away over the sound of his own speeding police car. Although Phillips had several windows of their home open that afternoon, neither he nor his wife had heard any such sound.

Phillips was the only person to regard Zamora a hoaxer, but Hynek found the charge unacceptable.

In all the years, no other suggestion of a hoax would ever emerge. "It's shameful to pick on anyone as honest as Lonnie Zamora," says investigator Ray Stanford today. "This man is as honest as the day is long."

Theories and Explanations

Everyone believed that Zamora had seen *something*. But what was it? Despite the Air Force's own conclusion, the skeptics, like Donald Menzel, an astronomer at Harvard University and the leading UFO debunker of the time, thought someone had pulled a prank on Zamora. Menzel's elaborate scenario involved high school kids using a balloon and various chemicals to "get back" at Zamora for one reason or another. Years later, however, Menzel had changed his mind: perhaps, he thought, Zamora had seen a "dust devil."

Initially, Philip Klass, a writer for *Aviation Week and Space Technology,* thought that Zamora had seen a plasma phenomenon related to the nearby high-voltage transmission lines. But he too changed his mind years later, and came to believe that Zamora had conspired with the mayor, who owned the property on which the incident took place, to make up the UFO story and attract tourists. If they did, it failed.

Most people in Socorro thought the object Zamora had seen was probably a secret experimental device. UFO investigator Jacques Vallee thought so, too. It was the insignia Zamora had seen on the object that made him suspicious.

The Insignia: What Could It Be?

Perhaps the most intriguing facet of Zamora's sighting is the insignia he clearly remembers seeing on the mysterious egg-shaped object. It's quite rare for UFO reports to contain descriptions of any kind of markings at all on the craft. Indeed, such markings are a particular feature of *man-made* aircraft. An insignia of this kind is normally placed on an aircraft for one purpose—identification. In theory, if we could match the markings that Zamora saw on the UFO with a known insignia, we should be able to determine the nature of the craft.

Zamora's description of the markings reminded J. Allen Hynek of a typical cattle brand, but obviously what Zamora had seen was no cow. Jacques Vallee, who was working closely with Hynek at Northwestern University back in 1964, thought the insignia looked very much like the logo of *Astropower,* a subsidiary of the Douglas Aircraft Corporation. He had found the logo in an ad in a special computer issue of the *Proceedings of the Institute of Radio Engineers* dated January 1961. The insignia made Vallee suspicious. He had never heard of a genuine report of a saucer with an insignia painted on the side. This led him to wonder if the Socorro craft could be a military prototype of some kind. Like Quintanilla, Vallee also suspected it might be a lunar lander prototype.

Up, Up, and Away!

At least one person is convinced that what Zamora saw was a hot-air balloon instead. Larry Robinson thinks he knows what Lonnie Zamora saw that day. Sometime between 1965 and February of 1967, Robinson, now an engineer at Indiana University, remembers seeing a magazine article about a multi-state series of hot-air balloon flights. A map with the story showed the balloon landing points. One anecdote told of an amusing adventure along the way: "The balloon had an encounter with a lawman who they thought was going to shoot it out with them," recalls Robinson. "The balloon freaked him out. They later found out he thought he was seeing a spaceship." Unfortunately, Robinson has not been able to locate this article.

Then in March 1967 Robinson bought the *Look* magazine special issue on flying saucers and, for the first time, read the account of the Socorro sighting. The name Socorro was familiar to him because he had recently seen it on the map published with the magazine article.

In June of 1968 Robinson saw for the first time the markings that Zamora had seen on the craft and immediately recalled an ad he had seen in another magazine back in 1963 or 1964 that showed a balloon belonging to, or sponsored by, the International Paper

Corporation. Their logo was a circle with an arrow made of the letters "I" and "P" pointing up. But he discounted a balloon explanation for the Socorro sighting because he did not know at the time that balloons could be so noisy.

Then one day in the summer of 1976 Robinson heard his dog bark and a loud roar outdoors. When he went out into his yard, he saw a round object about 200 feet up. It was a manned hot-air balloon owned by a local winery. The balloon roared again and he saw a flame come from the burner that provided lift. When Robinson reread the Socorro account in February of 1996, everything fell into place.

"All of the observed effects tally nicely with what the balloon does," concludes Robinson, who notes that these hot-air sport balloons were only a couple of years old in 1964. "When the balloon landed, the pilots shut down the burner pilot for safety. They probably had the flat triangular platform used before 1966. As it landed, it left three marks. The crew then set up a stand or held the mouth ring to hold the envelope mouth open. In doing so they probably made the fourth mark and the footprints. They then relit the burner (i.e. the thumps Zamora heard) and refilled the envelope. The burner blasts sideways during refilling until the envelope lifts. This process probably set fire to the brush. With a possibly deranged cop hiding behind things, maybe ready to shoot it out with them, they beat a hasty retreat into the sky."

Robinson believes the markings Zamora saw on the object was the International Paper Corporation's logo and that the object was one of their balloons. But a check with International Paper's headquarters in Rye, New York, failed to bear out his hypothesis. The International Paper logo that does indeed look like what Zamora saw was not used by the company until 1968, four years *after* the Socorro incident. And it was not *red,* as Zamora described.

"I think I know what happened," replies Robinson. "In balloon racing, the emblems on balloons must be readable from a distance to identify the balloon. The previous logo for International Paper would not suffice at all to identify a balloon to the officials. So the new logo may have had it's start here. Or someone else had a similar logo."

Or could the balloon have been a secret military project? An article by Peter Stekel on balloon pioneer Don Piccard notes: "During his years at Raven [Industries], between 1962 and 1964, Piccard devoted his energy to marketing the Vulcoon, one-man thermal balloons. Stressing his lack of security clearance at the time, Piccard says he worked strictly on sport balloons and had no contact with any of Raven's military contracts.... Reflecting back to those days at Raven, Piccard thinks the company's sport balloon division was a cover-up for the military applications of ballooning. 'The sport balloon program, which was not believed in by the Raven Industry management, was strictly getting this crazy guy who liked to fly in balloons and make cover. So, when one of these other balloons went down, it would just look like a sport balloonist.' When the Navy terminated its contract with Raven, the sport balloon program died, too. That was in December of 1964."

A Design with "Legs"

It is possible to deduce some information about the Socorro craft from the depressions it left behind in the desert ravine. The object left behind four "landing pad" marks in an asymmetric arrangement. Three of the four marks were a couple of inches deep in the center with a mound of dirt two inches high pushed up away from center of each equilateral pad mark; the fourth mark was only one inch deep and ill defined. It has been estimated that you would need the gentle settling of at least a ton to produce each of the pad marks left in that type of desert soil. The vehicle itself, then, could have weighed anywhere from 4 to 10 tons.

Most peculiar, however, is the arrangement of the four "landing pad" marks on the ground. The marks suggest a quadrilateral figure with the distance between pad marks ranging from 9 feet 7-and-a-half inches, to 13 feet 2-and-a-half inches. Significantly, when lines are drawn from opposite pad marks, they cross in the center at 90 degree angles. A careful engineering analysis by William T. Powers in 1968 showed that the various measurements are internally consistent.

Furthermore, Powers showed that if the center of gravity of the object was directly over the center burn mark, then equal weight would be supported at each midpoint of the lines drawn between the four landing pads—assuming the linkage among the "legs" was flexible.

"We must conclude," wrote Powers in *Flying Saucer Review,* "that everything argues in favour of the hypothesis that a vehicle landed near Socorro, on four pads." Powers was surprised to find that the landing pads seemed to have been placed "to serve the convenience of those using the vehicle (the footprints, and presumably the door, are located next to the mark that appears most 'misplaced') rather than according to a compulsive attachment to symmetry...." And, it does so, Powers noted with considerable astonishment, "without sacrificing any requirements for good engineering."

Insight into Lonnie Zamora

At the time of the incident, Lonnie Zamora was 31 years old, a stocky, bespeckled, 10-year-plus veteran of the Socorro, New Mexico, police force. No one has ever doubted that he did indeed see something on that fateful day of April 24, 1964. And everyone has always had the highest praise for Zamora. To his supervisor, Police Chief Polo Pineda, Zamora was "a good guy," an expression that covers a lot of ground among police officers. Lincoln La Paz, who was director of the Institute of Meteoritics at the University of New Mexico in Albuquerque at the time, had known Patrolman Zamora for 15 years. To La Paz, Zamora was an honest and reliable man. Sergeant Sam Chavez, of the State Police, had the highest regard for Zamora's reliability and unquestioned integrity. He knew Zamora as a sober man who was dedicated to his work. And, supposedly, as if drinks had anything to do with it, the *last* drink Zamora had prior to the incident was two or three beers more than a month earlier.

Lonnie Zamora's true name is Dionicio Zamora. He was born in Magdalena, New Mexico on Sept. 7, 1933. At the age of 17, he joined the New Mexico National Guard and served for 24 years. Though he never saw combat, he did help suppress some prison riots in the

1980s. Zamora joined the Socorro Police department as a part-time officer in 1951 and became full time at the age of 21.

It seems that one of the most significant UFO incidents of all time would change a man forever. Had this incident changed Zamora? I decided to find out. Locating Zamora was easy enough. He still lived in the same town. His phone number was the same as it was more than a quarter century ago. And at the age of 66 he was still a working man. But he was very reluctant to talk to me.

At first he attempted to dissuade me. "I don't even remember it now," he said. "I don't do interviews anymore." But he was too kind and gentle a man to insist, and answered my questions anyway, however briefly. Zamora came across as utterly sincere, though clearly he is still as bewildered by the incident today as he was then, 35 years earlier.

I began the brief interview with a question about the length of the encounter. The literature claims that less than two minutes elapsed between the time Zamora first saw the flame and the object's subsequent disappearance in the distance. But this seemed to me like an impossibly brief period of time to encompass the event, including his three attempts to get his police car up the hill. So I asked him if he remembered how long his sighting had lasted: "Yes, I remember. Oh, I'd say it was about six or seven minutes."

When you realized that the object was not an overturned car, what did you then think it was?

"I don't know. I didn't think nothing. I just ran. I didn't....I didn't....I was so scared, I didn't think."

What was it that scared you about it?

"The noise. The appearance of the object."

What are your current thoughts about what happened back then, 35 years ago?

"I don't know. I don't think about it very much. I don't go there. I don't talk about that no more. But people are still calling me up about it."

Did this incident have a big effect on your life?

"It didn't affect my life at all. It's just something that happened, and I just went on from there."

How long were you with the police department?

"Fifteen years total. But just for two years after the incident and then I quit. I got transferred to landfill, you know, filling in land. I'm still doing it today."

Has the town of Socorro changed since the incident?

"No, not at all. It's still a little town, nothing much."

What do you think it was that you saw that day in 1964?

"I still don't know. It was nothing from here though. It's something from some other place, I guess. I don't think it was a secret project or nothing like that."

But the two figures you saw standing by the object, they looked pretty normal didn't they?

"I didn't see no figures. I just thought I did from way back up the road there. I didn't actually see them. I thought I saw some coveralls there, but actually I didn't see them." [Two hours after the incident, when Zamora was first questioned about his sighting by FBI agent Byrnes, Zamora was told that it would be better if he didn't mention seeing the two small figures in white, because no one would believe him. More than three decades later, Zamora still had a hard time admitting to strangers that he had indeed seen these figures. Or had he?]

Did you ever figure out what those markings were on the object?

"No, I haven't figured it out. Nobody has, I guess."

One person has recently tried to explain your sighting, saying that there was a hot-air balloon race at the time, and what you saw was one of the balloons making a brief stop. What do you think of this idea?

"People have said all sorts of things. At that time, everybody knew what it was. Everybody had an explanation. They said it was a 'pogo' [a vertical takeoff and landing aircraft], it was a hot air balloon, that it was a vortex, you know, one of those funnels that come down. They've said a lot of things, but I know what I saw. And it wasn't any of those things."

Have you seen anything else like it since?

"No."

Do you believe in extraterrestrial life?

"I don't know. Maybe. I saw something, but I don't know what it was."

What does your wife think about all this?

"She thinks I'm crazy." [Laughs.]

All wives say that about their husbands, though.

"That's true." [Laughs.]

Conclusion

The Socorro incident stands as one of the most remarkable UFO cases of all time. Extensively investigated and thoroughly analyzed by some of the best minds of the time, the case is, notably, Blue Book's *only unexplained case involving a landed craft and its occupants.*

Several factors elevate this case above most UFO sightings. The primary witness was a policeman and a highly trustworthy individual. A number of secondary witnesses also claim to have observed one aspect or another of the event, which occurred notably at close range in broad daylight. But perhaps most important, the event left behind physical evidence—holes in the ground and charred bushes—that was highly suggestive of the presence of a physical object at the claimed landing spot. Another factor that casts this case in such a favorable light is what happened immediately after the sighting itself. No sooner had the object disappeared from sight did the first in a long series of investigations begin.

In sum, who could doubt that a real object was involved? But what was it? A number of people were convinced that it was a secret military weapon or a NASA device that had made a brief emergency landing. But despite going through the highest channels, Blue Book director Quintanilla was never able to confirm such a possibility. And certainly, even if the secret had been kept from him, we should expect to know what it was by now, more than a quarter of a century later. But nothing like it has ever emerged from the black vaults of the Pentagon.

Could it simply have been a hot-air balloon making a momentary pit stop, as Indiana engineer Larry Robinson suggests? *Possibly.* After all, as Robinson correctly points out, Zamora himself had said it looked "like a balloon." But there are several factors that strongly mitigate against such an explanation. Zamora saw no basket, gondola, or platform under the balloon, no ropes either, and the flames that he saw came from the *bottom* of the object, not the middle, and they fired *downward.* Moreover, Zamora clearly panicked at the sight of this object; in his 13 years as a police officer he had never seen anything like it. Robinson insists the modern hot-air balloon was only two years old at the time of the sighting. People were just not familiar with the roar and flame of these balloons at the time. But if it was a balloon, how could it leave landing marks in the desert as if it were a 4-to-10-ton craft? Robinson thinks the impact of a balloon with a metal platform would have been sufficient to create these indentations. After all, he reminds us, the figures left footprints, too. "Were they overweight?" he asks.

But one would think that such a mundane explanation would have been thoroughly investigated at the time. Had there been just the slightest chance that it was a balloon, Blue Book would certainly have jumped on it as their explanation. After all, Quintanilla was desperate for a solution. How could he—and everyone else—have missed something so simple? On the other hand, if Robinson is correct, who would think to ask a company that makes cardboard boxes if they had a balloon in the area? While the balloon explanation is not impossible, it is highly unlikely. But perhaps not as unlikely as an extraterrestrial craft.

Could it have been a craft from another word? The number of UFO sightings doubled in the month of April 1964, and this sighting seemed to be a prologue to the start of the 1960s UFO "flap." But if it was an extraterrestrial vehicle, why then did it appear to be so "human" a craft? Loud roaring noises and bright flames are the exception rather than the rule in UFO reports. No, if it was from another world, it must have been from our own—from our future, perhaps. It's unclear, however, why a time machine would have to make so much noise and spit out such a huge flame.

The truth is we just don't know what Zamora saw that day in a Socorro ravine. Perhaps one day someone will find an answer. But more than 35 years later, that day clearly has yet not come.

✳

Postscript

One day in the Spring of 2000 I got a call from a very excited Jim Moseley of SAUCER SMEAR fame, who had just spoken with Charles Moore, a scientist who worked on Project Mogul, a 1940s Top Secret Army Air Force balloon project whose aim it was to detect signs of Soviet nuclear explosions. (The Air Force claims a Mogul balloon was responsible for the "Roswell Crash.") After his chat with Moore, Moseley seemed to think that the Socorro sighting might have an explanation in a test of the Lunar Surveyor spacecraft.

But Moore himself was actually quite doubtful of the possibility: "Although Jim Moseley seemed exhilarated by our conversation, there is no conclusive new evidence," Moore wrote to Karl Pflock, who is Jim's deputy on SAUCER SMEAR and the author of ROSWELL: INCONVENIENT FACTS AND THE WILL TO BELIEVE. "Jim McAndrew located the range schedule for April 24, 1964, which includes an entry for the testing of the Lunar Surveyor using a helicopter on that day. Duke Gildenberg pursued this by talking to some of the Land-Air and perhaps the Ryan people and learned that these tests were aimed at checking out the Surveyor's geological-identification abilities operating over the northern end of WSMR [White Sands Missile Range] doing touch-and-go spot landings. It is Duke's guess that the test crew got off the missile range and made an unauthorized landing south of Socorro, whereupon, after all the furor, no one would admit as to what happened. Other than the range schedule and the probably questionable memories of Duke's informants, there is no new information."

Moore was no Johnny-come-lately to the Socorro affair; in 1966–1967 he had done some investigation of the incident at the request of physicist James MacDonald, who pursued the UFO subject intensely in the late sixties. "I did examine the site closely," says Moore, "looking for fused rock. I screened the soil at the mid point between the pad-impression markers with no finding of any heated fragments. I did find some charred mesquite stems near ground level but nothing else that was significant."

Moore finds little to suggest that the Socorro sighting was of an extraterrestrial craft. "Since the sighting clearly did occur," he says, "I suspect that the most likely explanation involves operations related to the White Sands Missile Range."

Pflock, who has a keen interest in the Socorro case, suggested I contact Tom Tulien, of the Sign Historical Group Oral History Project. Tulien had done an interview with Ed Yost, the father of modern ballooning, and had asked Yost if the work he had done in the early 1960s could have been responsible for the Socorro sighting.

Tulien provided this summary: "Modern hot air ballooning began in 1960 when Ed Yost...developed a fuel and heating system using common household propane. This combined with strong, new lightweight fabrics led quickly to the resurgence of hot air balloons. He holds a number of world records. Ed was one of the original General Mills aerologists and went on with others to start Raven Industries in the fifties and eventually his own company. Yost did work for a client he calls the "Potomac Sand and Gravel Company" who were particularly interested in sport balloons for, well, for their own reasons. Yost demonstrates the devices he helped develop and manufacture for the leaflet drops, which began in the fifties over Soviet controlled Eastern Europe and continue to this day, having been utilized during the Gulf war. He stated that they would launch as many as 1000 balloons a day each carrying four pounds of leaflets. Mr. Yost did not have any UFO sightings but was aware of the sightings others had experienced and was particularly impressed by a sighting he had heard about of objects circling a balloon ascent at White Sands, which was observed through theodolites. He did not think that the Socorro incident was a result of his work."

For what it's worth Pflock doesn't buy the idea that what happened had anything to do with the Surveyor program or anything else going on at White Sands, and I don't either. "To my mind," says Pflock, "the only thing 'earthly' that makes any sense is something to do with that hot-air balloon project. But IF the wind were out of the SW as reported by Hynek, that would be out, too. Problem is, there is no wind data available, and other than Hynek's mention, there's nothing in the official records or contemporary reports about wind conditions that day.

"Zamora definitely saw something, and credible sightings around the state within hours and days involving UFOs closely resembling what he said he saw provide some 'backup.' But...."

Unfortunately, "buts" are all we are left with on this case.

Afterword

On such slim evidence does the reality of the UFO phenomenon rest. Perhaps it is all human foolishness. But I think not. As a journalist who has written about this subject for more than 20 years, I am often asked: What do you believe? Unfortunately, my answer pleases neither skeptics nor believers. I know that all but a small percentage of UFO reports can be explained as misidentifications; that statement cannot be repeated often enough. But the perplexing residue of cases should compel anyone who has devoted some time to studying the phenomenon, to continue seeking an answer or answers. Even the Air Force acknowledged the existence of these truly unexplained cases after its 20-odd years of investigating the phenomenon. And so, too, do the skeptics. But while skeptics assert that solutions to this small percentage of cases could be found if only more information about these cases were available, I refuse to throw out these remaining unidentifieds on such a flimsy assumption. We have a real phenomenon out there that defies explanation and to dismiss it out-of-hand in this fashion will not make it go away.

Pity the press, which has tried, though perhaps not hard enough, to cover this controversial topic. Despite appearances, however, I believe the press is not in bed with the government on UFOs. The mainstream press doesn't do UFOs, because the subject is not sexy enough, like Hollywood, or important enough, like politics. Official consensus—government, science, etc.—deems the subject a waste of time. "Only puny secrets need protection," wrote Marshall McLuhan. "Big discoveries are protected by public incredulity."

I do agree that the government is being secretive in its knowledge of UFOs, but I think the secrecy is meant to downplay its own lack of knowledge. If there was any real government concern and secrecy over UFOs, the Air Force would not refer people who spot UFOs to MUFON or the National UFO Reporting Center, both private UFO organizations. If they really knew these UFOs were visitors from outer space, would this be a logical reaction? To think that the government or a clandestine select few individuals within it, or on its periphery, could control the media, Hollywood, and more, is simple foolishness. To think, as some do, that Hollywood alien movies are all part of a controlled education process regarding ET reality shows a lack of understanding about the science fiction genre. Ideas, regardless of their truth, can profoundly influence culture. We are talking memes, not aliens, unless you want to regard memes as being somehow alien.

Yet, quite obviously, some people in government—such as the CIA—do have an intense interest in the subject. This seems not to be a mandated, or missions-and-functions, interest, however, but a personal interest that is, perhaps, officially sanctioned. There are also individuals within the government and on the outside who persist in gumming up the works. But their disinformation gamesmanship probably serves as cover of some sort for something that has nothing whatsoever to do with the phenomenon itself. To them, UFOs are mere pawns in a modern power game.

Nonetheless a popular notion prevails that the press simply should go out there and investigate UFOs and uncover the truth, "60 Minutes" style. This belief stems from a misunderstanding about what the press really does. For the most part the press *reports*. It has little time or money for *investigation*. The investigations that do take place usually have a narrow focus. Their subject matter consists of, you might say, easy targets. When it comes to UFO sightings, the press cannot scramble jets and chase after these objects. I do wish the press would cover the topic more honestly, however: subject witnesses to less ridicule, and question the often dubious explanations of the debunkers.

Though I don't like to make generalizations of this kind, I think that the press is making a mistake in denying, for the most part, the existence of the UFO phenomenon. The phenomenon exists, whatever it may turn out to be. Of course, the press is being egged on in this direction by the Committee for the Scientific Investigation of Claims of the Paranormal, which conducts no scientific investigations, by the way. The group largely operates as a haven for debunkers. Though it prides itself on being a candle in the dark world of superstitions, CSI-

COP merely serves as the leading American organ of deviation sniffing. This is not science.

On the other hand, the study of UFO reports has been dragged into the "science wars" by some sociologists and other cultural studies scholars who like to deny the cherished scientific notion of "objective reality." While I reject the use of UFOs as a symbol of the subjective nature of reality, I do agree with one sociologist's recent observation that the stigma attached to UFOs overrides rational analysis. I find it startling, for example, that both the law enforcement community and mainstream science seem to have no interest at all in alleged UFO abductions. Imagine if the aliens were Mexicans or Iraquis, as Robert Anton Wilson has pointed out.

Most of the ideas that I've dealt with on the UFO beat have been other people's. I have simply collated and digested their work, for the most part, and delivered it up to the reader. Until recently I have been somewhat reserved in expressing my own thoughts on the subject, or on what I've experienced. But for what it's worth, not only do I now admit to having seen a UFO, I have also personally experienced what the skeptics believe is responsible for UFO abductions—sleep paralysis. In its simplest form, sleep paralysis is the inability to move or open one's eyes for several minutes, either as one falls asleep or before waking. The prevalence of the phenomenon varies from about two percent of the population to as much as 40 percent. According to the latest study, led by Maurice Ohayon of the Philippe Pinel Research Center in Montreal, Canada, about 30 percent of those who suffer from the syndrome report experiencing hallucinations during the episodes.

While in my teens, I occasionally would experience sleep paralysis episodes. As I drifted off to sleep, I suddenly would realize that I could not move my arms or legs, or open my eyes. Why I would even struggle to move in my sleep puzzles me, but I still felt conscious. Sometimes, I felt a weight on my chest and had trouble breathing. Naturally, I would interpret this "weight" as a presence of some kind but I never did see anyone or anything. Most often the experience involved the stomach churning feeling of falling through dark empty space. I would struggle and sometimes scream silently. Finally, I would awaken in a cold sweat. But I never saw any gray beings with wrap-around eyes. I never saw any beings of any kind. No flying saucers, inside or out. I never was abducted.

And that is the biggest problem with the sleep paralysis explanation of UFO abductions. Those who report abduction events insist that they saw and interacted with one or more "aliens," rather than this amorphous "other" that I experienced. Their experience is qualitatively different from mine, and suggests to me that something entirely different is going on. Besides, in the first decades of the UFO abduction phenomenon, most abductions took place outdoors, not indoors. Victims were not in bed or asleep. They were "driving automobiles, fishing, hunting, making rounds as police officer, and driving a tractor," as Budd Hopkins correctly notes. In addition, studies have shown that the incidence of sleep paralysis is higher in males than females, yet most of those who report abduction experiences are female. The notion that abductions can simply be explained as sleep paralysis and night terrors seems a little too pat for me.

I think Budd Hopkins is right on target in calling the sleep-disorder explanations of abductions "junk science." What I find particularly curious is the fact that some believers in the reality of aliens and crashed saucers actually buy into the sleep paralysis explanation of abductions. This is curious, because abductions are part of a continuum of phenomena. These half-believers are drawing an arbitrary line in the sand, labeling everything on one side of the line as real alien, everything on the other side as sleep disorder, hoaxing, etc. If only life were that simple.

UFOs and abductions qualify as experiences on a continuum; they exist not entirely separate from one another. In the first decade or so after the Kenneth Arnold sighting in 1947, people would mostly report seeing objects—apparently solid craft. In the decade or two that followed, more and more people began reporting "occupants" or "beings" seen in, or in the vicinity of, these craft. By the sixties and into the seventies, people were reporting being abducted by these beings into these craft. Then, by the eighties, we have reports of "bedroom" abductions, often without a craft being seen at all. So on one end of the continuum, you have the craft alone; on the other end you have the beings alone. Where on this continuum of experiences do you draw the line between reality and imagination?

For this reason, if for no other, I find it difficult to dismiss all these "occupant" or "beings" that have been reported in conjunction with UFOs. While I can't bring myself to believe that all the different so-called "aliens" being reported are visiting us—and have been doing so for the past 50 years—I do not view these "alien" reports as merely the product of people's overactive imaginations, either. I think that for the most part witnesses honestly describe what they experience. Hoaxes do occur, and some people may be trying to fatten their bank accounts. But generally, this easy answer evades the crux of the matter. Something underlies these experiences; something triggers them.

The literal interpretation tells us "they" really are aliens—just as the witnesses describe them. But what's more likely, if they are aliens, is that "they" are draped in our expectations. Then again, what is it that makes us *assume* an extraterrestrial origin in the first place? (Probably science fiction and Hollywood.) Perhaps "they" are something else entirely. The extraterrestrial hypothesis is really too simple; it's an extrapolation based on human technology and human desires. If UFOs are indeed produced by something exotic—something alien—it's likely to be something we have neither the concepts nor the vocabulary to describe.

After more than 35 years of following the phenomenon and its subculture, and writing about it professionally for more than 20 of those years, I still have no answers to all the questions it poses. I wish I did.

One last story. It's the kind of story that keeps me from simply shrugging my shoulders and walking away from the UFO beat. It's Harry Trumbore's story actually. Harry is now a newspaper reporter, but in the past he has drawn some truly superb illustrations for my series of unorthodox "field guides." His story takes place in Ireland in the early 1980s, long before I met him. Harry was at the bar in Shannon Airport waiting for a flight back to New York when he struck up a conversation with the man next to him.

He was a big guy, Harry recalls, muscular and a little overweight, with a dark beard and brown hair. He wore a suit and, most notably, a big white cowboy hat. The man was coming back from a pilgrimage to Lourdes with his wife and mother. It turns out that this devout Catholic was a farmer in Kansas, and quite a prosperous one, apparently, as he described his acreage as stretching from one horizon to the other. When Harry said something about Kansas being flat, the man described how it's actually like being in a little ship at sea when he's out there riding his combine, often on his own at night when things have to get done.

Must be hard, Harry said.

"No," the man said. The combine and the cab atop it was state-of-the-art: comfortable, air-conditioned, full stereo, loaded in other words. The wheat or corn or whatever it was—Harry doesn't remember—would be cut down, processed, and wrapped up automatically right behind him. With the stars shining in the darkness, music playing in the cab, and the lights from the barn and the farmhouse fading out in the distance, all he had to do was follow the field lines to the next horizon. No, he told Harry, he loved being out there at night.

The man then took a long pause, staring down at his drink the whole time. "Until they come," he said finally.

"What do you mean?" said Harry, flustered. "Who's 'they'?"

"When the lights come down," he said. "One minute they're not there and the next minute you look out the side window and there they are, keeping pace with you. Then as fast as you can blink, they'd circle around and be on the other side."

"UFOs?" Harry asked. But the man wouldn't say what they were, just what they were not: helicopters, aircraft, headlights, reflections, etc. And he said all this without pretense, as if everything was fine in his life except for this one thing that bothered him. He clearly didn't like it—or them, whoever they were.

"So what do you do?" asked Harry.

"I do what I have to do; I just do my job," he replied. "Eventually, they just shoot up in the air and disappear. It's really unnerving."

That's the story, and mine also. Like the Kansas farmer with the big white cowboy hat, I just do my job, too.

Acknowledgments

My thanks to the following editors and their publications at the time for permission to reprint the stories in this volume: Pamela Weintraub at *Omni,* Scott DeGarmo at *Science Digest,* Sandy MacDonald at *New Age,* Glenn Collins at *The New York Times Magazine,* Martin Singer at *Saga UFO Report,* Craig Glenday at *The X Factor,* Scott Martin at *Space.com,* Richard Hall at the *MUFON UFO Journal,* Larry Martz at *Newsweek Focus,* as well as Dennis Stacy and Hilary Evans, editors of *UFO 1947–1997: Fifty Years of Flying Saucers.* And to Larry W. Bryant, of course.

Index

www.ingramcontent.com/pod-product-compliance
Lightning Source LLC
Chambersburg PA
CBHW062157270326
41930CB00009B/1560